THE LIMITS
OF LAW

NOMOS

XV

N O M O S

NOMOS XV

Yearbook of the American Society for Political and Legal Philosophy

THE LIMITS
OF LAW

Edited by

J. ROLAND PENNOCK *Swarthmore College*

and

JOHN W. CHAPMAN *University of Pittsburgh*

L

LIEBER-ATHERTON
New York 1974

The Limits of Law: Nomos XV
edited by J. Roland Pennock and John W. Chapman

Copyright © 1974 by Lieber-Atherton, Incorporated

Address all inquiries to:
Lieber-Atherton, Incorporated
1841 Broadway
New York, New York 10023

Library of Congress Catalog Number 73-83018
ISBN 0-88311-008-3
Serial Publication Number US-ISSN-0078-0979

Printed in the United States of America

PREFACE

"The limits of law" is an exceptionally well-chosen topic for a meeting of the American Society for Political and Legal Philosophy because the majority of its members are legal scholars, philosophers, and political theorists. The subject of law is of interest to all of them, and the ambiguity of the word "limits" gives plenty of scope for both philosophical and political scientific approaches. The program of the meeting, which was held in conjunction with the American Association of Law Schools in Chicago in December, 1970, was arranged by a committee chaired by Professor David Haber of the Rutgers University Law School.

The volume is divided into three parts corresponding to the three sessions of our meetings. Each part opens with a chapter written by the individual who wrote the main paper for that session, followed by the contributions of two commentators in each case. In some instances both original papers and comments have been substantially revised and enlarged since their original presentation. Moreover, it has not always been possible to provide the commentator with the final product of the author whose paper he originally commented upon. In accordance with our custom, the editors solicited further papers following the meetings, with the purpose of providing a fuller and somewhat more rounded volume. These papers have been placed within the respective parts of the volume to which they seemed the most directly related, although the relationship in some cases is that of remote cousinship. The papers in Part I are of the most general nature, frequently touching on the connections between practical and ethical limits to law. Part II is perhaps even more difficult to describe. Dershowitz's paper, together with the two papers commenting upon it, deals with the limits of law as a preventive instrument. It has seemed to the editors not inappropriate to combine with these chapters those by Bayles and Regan that discuss, from opposing points of view, the ethical case for paternalistic legislation, specifically legislation designed to prevent people from doing injury to themselves. The papers by Dolbeare, Hall, Bedau, and Rosenblum, in Part III, are all related in one way or another to the application of behavioral studies to the law.

To all of the contributors, and to the Program Chairman, the editors wish to express their thanks.

J. R. P.
J. W. C.

CONTENTS

CONTRIBUTORS

MICHAEL D. BAYLES
Philosophy, University of Kentucky

HUGO ADAM BEDAU
Philosophy, Tufts University

JULIUS COHEN
Law, Rutgers University

SERGIO COTTA
Philosophy of Law, Università di Roma

DAVID J. DANELSKI
Government, Cornell University

ALAN DERSHOWITZ
Law, Harvard University

KENNETH M. DOLBEARE
Political Science, University of Washington

MARTIN P. GOLDING
    Philosophy, John Jay College of Criminal Justice

KENT GREENAWALT
    Law, Columbia University

JEROME HALL
    Law, Hastings College of Law

GRAHAM HUGHES
    Law, New York University

WILLIAM LEON McBRIDE
    Philosophy, Purdue University

DONALD H. REGAN
    Law, University of Michigan

VICTOR G. ROSENBLUM
    Law, Northwestern University

JUNE LOUIN TAPP
    Criminal Justice Studies, University of Minnesota

STEPHEN L. WASBY
    Political Science, Southern Illinois University

MICHAEL A. WEINSTEIN
    Political Science, Purdue University

INTRODUCTION

The phrase "the limits of law" perhaps most readily calls to mind two kinds of limits: practical limits and ethical limits. That is to say, there are limits to what law can do as well as to what it ought to be used to do. But the phrase can also be interpreted in other ways. For instance, law is limited by its very nature in the extent to which it can secure justice and other societal objectives. In these introductory remarks I should like to say a few words about each of four kinds of limits.

Volumes can be, and indeed have been, written about the subject of what law can and cannot do, particularly with respect to laws that attempt to influence behavior based upon widely held and deep-seated values and attitudes. The American experiment with Prohibition is frequently alluded to in this connection as an example of the failure of law to alter entrenched behavior patterns. On the other hand, the confrontation between federal law and local laws and practices in the case of racial discrimination presents a different picture. Here too the existence of deeply ingrained attitudes on the part of very large numbers of people in certain parts of the country led many to predict that the attempt to bring about change by court decision and legislation would fail. Certainly it had no immediate success, and its goal is still far from achieved. Yet no one would suggest that, as in the case of Prohibition, we are faced with the prospect of having to abandon the whole effort. On the contrary, great strides have been made and are being made. Why this great difference?

No attempt will be made here to answer this question in detail, but it may be fruitful to call to mind a few of the most obvious dissimilarities in circumstances that doubtless had much to do with the differing results. The manufacture or sale of alcoholic beverages could be carried on clandestinely. The operations themselves did not involve persons who were harmed by them, or at least not persons who believed they were harmed by them. At the same time, they involved great profit to certain of the participants. In the case of racial discrimination, whether in schools or elsewhere, the situation is quite different. No one gets rich by it (although it may advantage them); on the other hand, millions of people are educationally, psychologically, or economically impoverished by it. In short, there is a large class of victims too obvious to be overlooked and increasingly able to protest their victimization. Moreover, as Gunnar Myrdal so rightly pointed out, a deeply ingrained American ideal, that of equality, was a powerful force on the side of racial minorities. Indeed, it is at least arguable that the very nature of law itself embodies an ideal of equal treatment for persons similarly situated that was in the long run impossible to square with racial discrimination.[1] Whatever the case may be for the attack on the morality of the manufacture, sale, and use of alcoholic beverages, it clearly is a much less powerful force in terms of American ideology, and perhaps even in terms of some universal morality, than is the case with racial discrimination.

Law, it would appear, can be a powerful force for changing both behavior and attitudes when a large number of people will benefit by the change and when the change derives from a principle deeply embedded in our heritage—indeed, derivable from fundamental principles of justice widely if not universally recognized in the abstract. Law can have this effect even when it is opposed by widely held powerful prejudices and by contrary practices buttressed, if not sanctified, by time. In the case of the American Negro, then, it appears that law succeeded in changing behavior and attitudes, although thus far, of course, its success is far from complete. To be sure, the change in the law itself undoubtedly reflected changing attitudes on the part of a great many people.

One can find other examples where it is more clearly the case that changed attitudes led the way, where indeed changing attitudes led not to the creation of new law but to the nullification of old law. An example may be helpful. Between the college campus, which is my place of work, and the village of Swarthmore runs a railroad track, a double-tracked line. Many years ago these tracks were divided by an iron fence, forcing pedestrians to use an underpass. Apparently decades went by during which all or certainly nearly all pedestrians accepted this legalized barrier, which had been placed there by the railroad company, as a matter of course. In time, however, a few, and then many individuals, began to walk around the end of the fence and others, more venturesome, climbed over it in defiance of clearly posted signs prohibiting trespassing on this part of the railroad company's right of way. As this violation of the company's rights became notorious, the company decided to fight back. They posted guards. The guards warned students that they would be subject to arrest for trespass if they climbed over the fence or circumvented it. Threats failed. With the cooperation of local police a few arrests were actually made, including, as I recall, the son of the captain of the naval unit then undergoing training at the college. Readers can imagine for themselves the loud protests that followed. But for a while the company persisted in its efforts to enforce its legal rights. Then one morning, lo and behold, the fence was not there! It had been spread out on the grass of the lower campus by persons never identified. It was never re-erected. Thus ended the railroad company's attempts to enforce the law.

To all intents and purposes, the law in that particular application had been nullified. It had met its match. It had reached its limit, or rather, the limits of the law had retreated upon it. The law, once acceptable and enforceable, had ceased to be so. Possibly the law never could have been enforced against this kind of defiance. But why had it not previously been defied? Something had changed. Was it people's attitudes toward law in general? Was it rather their attitudes toward the law of trespass as it applied to crossing railroad tracks? Was it growing opposition to paternalism? Was it an increasing demand that law should appear to be functional and reasonable, combined with the belief that this law as applied was not? Had people's values changed? Their respect for property declined? Their unwillingness to climb a few steps increased? It would be hard to say, but perhaps all these tentative suggestions point to factors that are relevant to the limits of law.

Let me take still another example. A few years ago a generous alumna contributed to the college a valuable tapestry that she had commissioned a French artist to make. It was hung in the college library. A number of students found their tastes at variance with those of the donor and the artist. They wrote letters to the college paper that were embarrassing to the college. When the offending tapestry still graced the library walls, they, or some of them, or perhaps one of them, resorted to direct action. One night the tapestry disappeared, but after fervent appeals by college authorities it was returned. Somewhat later the incident was repeated. This time it was a period of months before the lost article was found. However, it did turn up, it was put back on the wall, and there it hangs today.

Once more there had been a confrontation between established authority and the action of individuals who disagreed sharply with the "law" of the college in this case and who were perhaps more willing to defy that law than a previous generation might have been. Yet this challenge failed. Perhaps the feelings of some were not shared so widely as in the case of the fence. Perhaps they were not felt so deeply. Perhaps college authority was respected more than that of the Pennsylvania Railroad. It is probably considerations of these sorts, rather than the generalized attitude toward law, authority, established procedures, formalism, or the like, that accounted for the different results. I say it was *probably* so; it seems to me plausible. But the considerations I have raised are intended less to point to conclusions than to suggest lines of inquiry that might be worthy of pursuit as applied to examples similar in nature but perhaps of greater import than those discussed above.

Several of the papers in this volume discuss the question of the *proper* limits of law. Apart from the fact that it is pointless, futile, and perhaps harmful to try to do the impossible, there are other ethical limits on the sphere of law. It is not simply a matter of deciding such questions as what should be done, what conduct is good, what it would be well that people should or should not do. Rather, it is a question of when it may be better to allow people to do what they should not do than to attempt to control their conduct by law. This is an old issue, but it is one on which neither John Stuart Mill nor Lord Devlin nor H. L. A. Hart has said the last word, as the papers in this volume by Messrs. Bayles and Regan demonstrate. Professor Bayles deals with criminal paternalism, that is to say, with paternalistic legislation that relies upon criminal sanctions, but he explicitly leaves open the question of whether legal sanctions short of punishment may properly be used in a paternalistic way. Professor Regan takes issue with Mill's utilitarian approach to the problem and in doing so deliberately opens the door to certain types of paternalistic legislation.

It is interesting to note that Regan's line of argument is based upon the principle of maximizing liberty on the whole and in the long run. A more traditional nonutilitarian approach that also stresses liberty is that of Kant and the British idealists. To them it is important that people should perform their duties for duty's sake. It is the good will that counts, and laws that coerce one into doing what he ought to do of his own volition deprive him of the opportunity, and perhaps of the incentive, to develop his moral self. Of course, where the interests of others are seriously at stake, we cannot afford to rely solely on morality. But in other cases we can and should, so the argument runs. This argument for limiting law is individualistic, as is Mill's, but the case for individual autonomy is differently grounded.

Finally we return to another area of things that law cannot do—of limits in the realm of "is" rather than "ought"—but that do not relate to the realm of compliance. This group of limits falls into two classes. The first is best exemplified by certain types of law that attempt to regulate the economic system. Take the matter of price control. Suppose that the regulations issued under President Nixon's inflation control program are universally observed and let us further assume that this results in holding the rate of inflation down to modest levels, say two or three percent a year. Conceivably the result might be recession and increased unemployment, yet certainly the objectives of the law as applied in this case were to control inflation without creating unemployment, and in general to make the economic system operate more justly rather than less justly, as would seem to be entailed by an increase in unemployment. If the law regulating minimum wages is applied in such a way as to raise those minima beyond a certain point, it may again be self-defeating, not in the sense that it will not be obeyed but in the sense that the economic consequences will be the opposite of those desired by the policy makers. Such examples could be multiplied ad infinitum.

In the cases just discussed it was not so much the nature of law as the complexity of the problem and the nature of the economic system that placed limits upon what law could accomplish. In other instances it is the very nature of law itself, specifically its generality, that is the limiting factor. Aristotle gave classic expression to this problem. One need not repeat or parallel his examples and arguments. The rule of law is essential to justice, yet the rule of law may defeat justice. Every legal system, except perhaps the crudest and most primitive, must in some way make provision for equity as contrasted with legal justice. Most modern industrialized countries like our own have been forced by the complexities with which the legal system must deal to resort increasingly to "administrative justice." One purpose in doing so is to get away from the strict rule of law and permit more discretion, the pressure for which is intense and proceeds from many sources. The discretion that is exercised by administrative agencies, moreover, is small compared to that which, under any system, is exercised by those who enforce the law and those who decide whether or not to bring charges or, having taken that step, whether to dismiss them. Today, while we take great pains to see that all individuals accused of crime receive equal treatment at every step of the way from first contact with law enforcement officers to final determination of guilt or innocence, we then hand over to a judge, parole board, or probation officer enormous discretion in determining and administering punishment. While all this takes place within the framework of law, it tends to lose the characteristics we associate with the idea of law. Formalism gives way to discretion, uniformity to variety, the nomothetic to the idiosyncratic. One finds no ultimate solution to the problem of law versus discretion. The regularity of law, as contrasted with the infinite variety of life, defies justice, and justice demands that law be limited. Yet the alternative to regularity, discretion, provides constant opportunity and invitation to arbitrariness, which brings us back to the original source of the demand for law.

A volume such as this makes no pretense to systematic coverage of the topic specified by its title, and in these few introductory remarks I have not attempted either to refer to all the topics discussed by our various authors or to outline the territory that would be covered by a comprehensive treatise. Rather, I have used my discretion, I hope not too arbitrarily, to mention and make a few remarks about aspects of the subject that seem to be worth giving thought to, whether or not they are dealt with in these pages.

J. Roland Pennock

REFERENCES

[1] See J. Roland Pennock, "Law's Natural Bent," *Ethics,* 79 (April 1969), 222-228.

PART I

1

THE LIMITS OF LAW

David J. Danelski

The limits of law may be empirical or ethical. Analytically, it is not difficult to distinguish one from the other. Empirical limits are determined by law's capability in fulfilling its functions. Ethical limits are determined by normative judgments indicating law's appropriate reach. Existentially, the questions "How far can law go in fulfilling its functions?" and "How far should it go?" are related. To answer the former, it is necessary to consider the ethical dimensions of human behavior; to answer the latter, it is necessary to consider the possibility and probability of certain kinds of human behavior.

I

At the outset it is necessary to indicate what is meant by law in the context of this discussion. My view of law comes close to Lon Fuller's. I regard it as a process in which human conduct is subjected to the governance of officially sanctioned rules.[1] The process, which is partly internal and partly external, consists of the following series of events: (1) awareness that a legal rule is applicable to one's own or another's conduct; (2) a judgment that the rule should and/or will be followed; (3) action consistent with the judgment. This conception of law is sufficiently general to apply to citizens, judges, police officers, and other officials who subject not only their own conduct but also the conduct of others to legal rules.

Perception of officially sanctioned rules (especially by laymen) is often imprecise and vague. It is connected with other images and is typically rich in symbolism. In regard to penal rules, the symbols evoked are usually those of the criminal process—arrest, trial, and punishment—and they mean not only life, liberty, and property may be in jeopardy but also exposure, shame, and disgrace.[2] Such images constitute a scenario of consequences of disobedience. Important in this process is one's self-concept.[3] Relatively little is known about the relationship of self-concept to rule perception and consequent conduct.[4] The same is true of the unconscious roots of legal perceptions. What is known indicates that fear underlies the general propensity to obey legal rules; the image of a world without law is for many a world of anarchy and chaos, in which the "rule of the tooth and claw must prevail."[5]

Judgments concerning legal rules may be normative and/or predictive. A person may conclude: (1) I should obey the rule, and I shall. (2) I should obey the rule, but I shall not. (3) Whether I should obey the rule or not is irrelevant, but I shall (or shall not) obey it anyway. (4) I should not obey the rule, and I shall not. (5) I should not obey the rule, but I shall. The statements recognize that legal obedience or disobedience may turn on moral and/or expediential considerations.

Action consistent with a judgment is the result of enforcement, which may be internal, external, or both. Usually when law enforcement is discussed, the referent is external enforcement—action by police and other officials subjecting the conduct of others to the governance of officially sanctioned rules. Although internal (or self) enforcement probably accounts for most legal behavior, it is difficult to assert that enforcement is purely internal even when it appears to be because knowledge and perceptions of rules often stem from external enforcement.

II

A discussion of law's limits implies that it has certain functions. Scholars are not in complete agreement concerning law's functions, but most would agree that among its principal functions are social control, which has as its purpose personal security and (in many societies) freedom, and dispute settlement, which has as its purpose interpersonal and intergroup harmony. A third function some would add is moral education, which is at times called law's declaratory function in that it shows "members of society what is regarded as undesirable conduct."[6] Bentham put it this way: "In many cases morality derives its existence from the law; that is, to decide whether the action is morally good or bad, it is necessary to know whether the laws permit or forbid it."[7]

In some societies law plays a small role in fulfilling the functions of control, dispute settlement, and moral education. A good example is the Arusha in Tanganyika. The dispute-settlement processes among them are mainly political. There is no intervention by an uninterested third party. Settlement is reached on the basis of the relative strengths of the parties to the dispute tested in social action. Dispute resolution, Gulliver has written, "is not a case of reaching a decision as to which disputant is supported by the norms, and to what extent. Neither party is willing to agree to a resolution of the dispute to which it is not compelled—and a party is not compelled only by an appeal to norms. A defendant may perhaps even concede that his behavior was a breach of the relevant norm, but he still attempts to avoid the normative consequences of it—and he may succeed."[8]

Traditional Japan provides a different example of a society in which law was quite limited. For the most part, social control was effectively accomplished by the community, using social rather than legal sanctions—criticism, ridicule, gossip, and, in extreme cases, ostracism. When a crime was committed, use of legal processes was the last resort, the preference being to dispose of the matter informally. Even when there was a resort to criminal law, rules were applied particularisticly. The whole previous history of the offender was taken into account; so were his intelligence, education, and motives; "and final judgment was decided by moral common sense rather than by legal enactment or precedent."[9] Particularistic justice prevailed also in the settlement of civil disputes. Litigation was not a socially acceptable means of dispute settlement. Hence, when there were disputes, conciliation was not only preferred, it was socially required. The purpose of conciliation was the repair of broken accord—the restoration of social harmony—not justice according to officially sanctioned rules, and it was a highly effective means of dispute settlement.[10] Statutes in Japan were regarded as *denka no hoto*, a sword handed down from generation to generation as a family treasure, perhaps important as a symbol but not something for actual use, except as a last resort.[11] Japan has had a long tradition of viewing legal codes as statements of morals. Kawashima has pointed out that "the government always used the codes as a basis of moral education—*shūshin*—and law is still so regarded today by the people."[12]

In Western societies, law is presently regarded as "the paramount agency of social control."[13] It is also the chief means of dispute settlement. That is not simply because litigation is in general socially acceptable and formal legal processes are extensively used; law underlies a considerable amount of dispute settlement that on the surface appears to be informal. I have in mind particularly the settlement of personal injury claims and disputes among businessmen in the United States. The vast majority of these disputes never reach a court; they are usually settled informally in lawyers' offices or elsewhere. Yet the settlement process usually involves subjecting conduct to the test of officially sanctioned rules—for example, ascertaining liability in a personal injury dispute—and in the background of settlement negotiations is at least the possibility of litigation. In the West, law also has the function of declaring morals. The Swedish criminology literature stresses the "moralizing" or "educational" function of penal law.[14] And in the United States, because some persons strongly believe in law's moralizing function, symbolic battles are sometimes fought over statutes dealing with controversial matters of morality, even though many of these statutes are seldom enforced.[15]

As societies passed from traditional to modern, law became more important in fulfilling the functions of social control and dispute settlement. In part this trand was due to the increased size and complexity of communities in modern societies. As traditional ties weakened in relating men to each other, relationships among individuals became increasingly legal. Nonetheless, traditional means of social control and dispute settlement tend to persist. This is the situation in Japan today. Conciliation is still preferred over litigation as means of dispute resolution, and there is still a tendency toward particularism in applying officially sanctioned rules. But with rapid economic development and an increased tendency toward urbanization in Japan, law has become increasingly more important.

Secularization of society has increased law's importance in the West. Religion was, and to some extent still is, an important agency of social control, but it is no longer as important as law. Although the vestiges of religious influence can still be seen in some officially sanctioned rules, law is becoming increasingly secular. The morality it declares today tends to be more social than religious. It is concerned more with keeping men from harming each other and with promoting harmony than with achieving religious goals. In other words, the moral ends of social control and dispute settlement are now among law's goals; hence, legal obedience takes on a moral character. In a secular age when law has a heavier functional burden, any increase in its morality tends to make it more effective.

Whether law will continue to carry its functional burden is problematical. It may be, as Mazor argues, that law has reached its zenith—at least in the West—and already is beginning to decline.[16] As men enter a postindustrial age, law begins to lose its importance in ordering economic relationships, and just as religion was displaced by law, law may be displaced by psychology and technology as more effective and desirable means of managing human behavior. The extent and pace of such displacement are difficult to foresee, but quite likely they will be related to law's empirical limits and perhaps also to its ethical limits.

III

The empirical limits of law appear to be related to (1) perception of officially sanctioned rules, (2) the development of a sense of obligation to obey them, and (3) their enforcement. Research findings upon which this formulation is based are slender and scattered; thus, the discussion that follows is necessarily tentative and is intended only to suggest hypotheses for future systematic research on the subject.

1. Law's effectiveness is directly related to the extent and nature of perception of officially sanctioned rules. This might be regarded as another way of saying what legal philosophers have long held—that promulgation is a necessary element of law. There is, however, a difference. For philosophers like Thomas Aquinas, promulgation is

a necessary condition for law's validity, but here perception is a necessary condition for its effectiveness. Ignorance of the law is often said to be no excuse for disobedience, but ignorance obviously limits law's effectiveness. Similarly, law is limited to the extent that rules are not stated precisely, and not only because men are uncertain about what the rules mean. Vague rules permit perceptions (or interpretations) of inapplicability, and thus the legal process may terminate at its initial phase.

Perceptions of rules vary with their sources. Important in this regard are a source's legitimacy, its position in the institutional hierarchy, and the responsiveness of enforcement agencies to it. Enforcement not only communicates rules; it also shows that the rules are taken seriously and that punishment for their violation is likely. Personal acceptance (self-enforcement) is as important as institutional enforcement in the perception of rules. If, for example, persons in a given community (especially those of high social status) generally obey traffic regulations, perceptions of such regulations and expectations concerning them will be different than in communities where scofflaws are common.[17] Rules regularly enforced tend to be perceived as more binding than they would have been if they were seldom enforced, apparently because enforcement establishes behavioral norms, and in time, as Hoebel pointed out, "the *norm* takes on the quality of the *normative.* What the most do, others should do."[18]

2. Some scholars take the position that "[i]n regard to most 'serious crimes,' the socialization process rather than the direct threat of a particular legal penalty keeps most people law abiding."[19] In other words, law abidingness stems in large part from a well-developed sense of obligation, which is the product of moral and legal socialization.

The ideas of scholars who take a developmental approach to moral judgment are useful in discussing the obligation phase of law. Piaget's work in this area is best known, but Kohlberg's more recent research on children in the United States, Mexico, Yucatan, Turkey, and Taiwan is heuristically more useful.[20] Based on that research and also on the findings of Piaget, Kohlberg sets forth a theory of moral development, consisting of three levels and six stages:

Level I. Premoral
    Stage 1.   Punishment and obedience orientation. Obey rules to avoid punishment.

Stage 2.   Naive instrumental hedonism. Conform to obtain
           rewards, to have favors returned, and so on.

Level II. Morality of Conventional Role-Conformity
Stage 3.   Good-boy morality of maintaining good relations,
           approval of others. Conform to avoid disapproval,
           dislike by others.
Stage 4.   Authority maintaining morality. Conform to avoid
           censure by legitimate authorities and resultant
           guilt.

Level III. Morality of Self-Accepted Moral Principles
Stage 5.   Morality of contract, of individual rights, and
           of democratically accepted law. Conform to main-
           tain the respect of the impartial spectator judging
           in terms of community welfare.
Stage 6.   Morality of individual principles of conscience.
           Conform to avoid self-condemnation.[21]

Children move from stage to stage as they grow older, some more
quickly than others, and seldom is a stage skipped. The development
of some persons stops, however, at one of the stages and goes no
further. Kohlberg found that teen-age delinquents were markedly less
mature in moral judgment than matched controls, usually having
developed no further than the first or second stage, which is normal
for children from eight to ten. He cites an example of a male
seventeen-year-old delinquent who told him: "Laws are made by
cowards to protect themselves. Everybody is a crook at heart. You
can take a child from birth and riase him to any type of character.
We raise people to kill rabbits, we could riase them to kill people.
As far as I am concerned what is right is to go by my own instinct."[22]
This statement, says Kohlberg, is not an expression of a ready-made
code of a juvenile gang but a view of life based on first-level thinking.

If Kohlberg's developmental theory is correct, law is more or less
limited depending on the stage of moral development of members
of a society. Here both qualitative and quantitative considerations
are important. One would want to know the modal stage of the
moral development of its elite members, of those who are not elite
but who serve as models for ethical behavior, of average citizens,
and of deprived groups. One would also want to know how many

persons were at each stage of development and their ages. If most persons were at the first and second stages, institutional enforcement would be crucial in maintaining security, order, and a minimum of harmony in society. Law would probably be least limited in a society in which most of its members were at the third and fourth stages of development. Law at the fifth and sixth stages is probably more limited than it is at the previous two stages, but it might be otherwise if it is perceived as democratically agreed upon and consistent with individual principles of conscience. If it is not, it is likely to be more limited. In other words, the limits of law in terms of moral development appear to be curvilinear. Of course it must be remembered that judgment, not behavior, is being discussed. Persons may acknowledge that they should obey legal rules and yet not do so, and some will say a rule violates conscience and yet obey it. Nonetheless, there is a positive relationship between moral judgment and behavior.[23]

Law itself plays a role in moral development of children, but it operates initially through their parents. Children move from one stage of development to another primarily by personal identification with their parents. Age is related to development because maturity is needed for the child to put himself psychologically in his parents' position for purposes of the latter stages of moral development. "In American children," writes Kohlberg, "there is a stage in middle and late childhood in which moral role-taking is primarily focused on his parents. This is probably due to the child's awareness that his parent is the legitimate and final authority for him within our society. As the adolescent moves into more complex and egalitarian role-taking systems, moral role-taking or identification with parents is largely replaced by tole-taking of those whom the social order, moral principles, and the moral situation then deem most relevant."[24]

In view of the importance of parents in moral socialization, it is not surprising that socioeconomic status is related to moral development. Kohlberg finds that working-class and middle-class children move through the same stages, "but the middle-class children seem to move faster and farther."[25] In response to the question, "Should someone obey a law if he doesn't think it is a good law?" two sixteen-year-old youths answered:

Lower-class boy: Yes, a law is a law and you can't do nothing about it. You have to obey it, you should. That's what it's there for.

Upper-middle-class boy: The law's the law but I think people
                            themselves can tell what's right or
                            wrong. I suppose the laws are made
                            by many different groups of people
                            with different ideas. But if you don't
                            believe in law, you should try to get
                            it changed, you shouldn't disobey it.[26]

The reasons for class differences in moral development of children
have been summarized by Aronfreed as follows:

> Parents of higher socioeconomic status generally behave in
> ways which would tend to induce an internal governor in
> their children. Along with their relatively close control over
> their children's behavior, they use a verbal medium of disci-
> pline and much explicit withdrawal of affection. They also
> concern themselves with the intentions behind their children's
> actions. Parents of lower socioeconomic status tend to exercise
> less immediate control over their children's activities, and seem
> to give their attention primarily to the visible manifestations
> of transgression. Their discipline more frequently takes the
> form of direct attack, with less explanation of their punishment,
> and is therefore more likely to sensitize their children to the
> punitive consequences of transgressions. Children from the two
> major social classes in our society do differ in their evaluative
> expressions of conscience, and in the orientation of their in-
> ternalized reactions to transgression, in ways that are predict-
> able from their predominant experiences of discipline.[27]

An experiment by Schwartz and Orleans concerning legal sanctions in the payment of taxes shows that socioeconomic status persists into adulthood as a relevant variable in moral judgment.[28]
They divided a sample of United States taxpayers earning more
than $10,000 in 1962 into four groups, three of which were inter-
viewed about the payment of income taxes. The first group was
asked questions that stressed legal sanctions; the second group was
asked questions that appealed to conscience; and the third (placebo)
group was asked general questions about taxes. High normative
response was correlated with high socioeconomic status in the sanction group but not in the other groups. In view of the literature

on class differences in moral judgment, the same correlation might have been expected in the conscience group. But the conscience questions had the greatest impact on tax behavior. The point of the experiment was to determine what effect, if any, the sanction and conscience questions had on the payment of income taxes the following year. The difference in payment of taxes between 1961 and 1962 was by group: sanction, +$11; conscience, +$243; placebo, -$40; and untreated control, -$57. Schwartz and Orleans did not report tax payment in relation to socioeconomic status or other variables.

The importance of parents in moral development of children and the significance of socioeconomic status to such development partly explain why moral and legal socialization vary from culture to culture and from subculture to subculture within a society. Generally, members of subcultures characterized by poverty not only move more slowly from stage to stage of moral development, but are also more likely, because of their economic situation, to violate certain laws than are members of more affluent segments of the same society. But even more important, moral judgments and behavior are learned from parents; hence, arrested moral development in parents tends to persist in their children. This is a plausible explanation for the high crime rates characteristic of certain ethical and racial groups. It is not, as Lombroso asserted, that certain ethnic and racial groups are prone to crime; rather it is that at a certain time in history these groups are economically deprived and inadequately socialized. An illustration of this point is contained in the study of a Nova Scotian county by Hughes, Tremblay, Rapoport, and Leighton.[29] In the moderately prosperous community of Lavallée, Acadian parents present their children with a model of hard-working, religious, law-abiding folk. They require strict obedience of their children but do not resort to physical punishment with any frequency. Lavallée mothers employ words, both reasoning and ridicule, and deprivation of privileges and desired objects tends to be used in place of physical punishment. The children grow up to be like their parents. Researchers could find no evidence of serious crime in the community for more than a generation. In the same county there are groups of poor settlements, inhabited by persons of mixed Acadian and English blood, in which a different pattern of private and public behavior prevails. In these areas there is considerable drunkenness, thievery, laziness, and sexual promiscuity. Liquor and game laws are frequently violated. In reference to the latter, one of the local people said; "What is the use of law if it can't be broken?" Contempt for authority is common; indeed, one way to acquire status in the community is to be contemptuous of authority and get away with it. Parents are generally permissive with their children. Children are allowed to jump on the furniture, mark the walls, play with another's property, etc.—things that Lavallée mothers would never permit. Mothers in these poor settlements seldom use words—and reasoning almost never—in disciplining their children. If they threaten to punish, however, they are quite likely to carry it out. Ridicule is used, and mothers and fathers resort to spanking as a means of discipline, though they believe it does little good. These settlements have had a history of crime, some of it serious, that can be attributed in large part to inadequate moral and legal socialization.

Personality is another variable related to moral judgment. Kohlberg's Moral Judgment Scale is negatively correlated (-.52) with the F Scale, and there is evidence that authoritarian attitudes decline in middle-class youths as they grow older. This may be related to the class variable, because there is also a negative correlation between authoritarianism and social class and intelligence.[30] Berkowitz and Walker designed an experiment to test the relative influence of knowledge of legal rules and peer group opinion on conceptions of morality of British university students.[31] They found that peer opinion was considerably more influential than legal rules, but the latter was not negligible except for those students who had high F-Scale scores and those who had low Social-Responsibility-Scale scores. For them, peer opinion was dominant. Students with low F-Scale scores, however, were significantly more influenced by law than by peer opinion, and those with high Social-Responsibility-Scale scores were slightly (though not significantly) more influenced by legal rules than peer opinion.

Civil disobedience is often a manifestation of a high level of moral development. Rawls has written that "civil disobedience in a democratic society is best understood as an appeal to the principles of justice, the fundamental conditions of willing social cooperation among free men, which in view of the community as a whole are expressed in the constitution and guide its interpretation. Being an appeal to the moral basis of public life, civil disobedience is a political and not primarily a religious act. It addresses itself to the common principles of justice which men can require one another to follow and not to the aspirations of love they cannot."[32] Civil disobedience is ultimately political, but the judgment upon which it is based is often moral. It becomes political when men act publicly on their moral judgments, especially when they seek to justify their judgments and actions by arguing that the law they are protesting is contrary not only to their consciences but to the fundamental moral and jural postulates of their society. An example is Gordon Hirabayashi's refusal during World War II to comply with regulations and orders that required all persons of Japanese ancestry living in the western part of the United States to be off the streets during curfew hours and to report to detention centers. Later, when he was asked why he violated these rules, he said that he had thought the regulations and orders were contrary to everything he had learned about basic American principles—especially equality for all citizens. As an American citizen, he felt his government was acting contrary to the Constitution. He pointed that, unlike Korematsu (who was later involved in a similar case),[33] he had not been furtive in his actions and had surrendered himself to lawful authorities. He did this, he said, because he wanted his case to be a test of basic American principles.[34] Throughout the legal proceedings in his case, he showed respect for law. This is typical in civil disobedience, for, as Rawls has pointed out, civil disobedience "manifests a respect for legal procedures" and expresses itself "within the limits of fidelity to law."[35] The typical person who resorts to civil disobedience would, under ordinary circumstances, scrupulously obey the law. Daniel Berrigan wrote that prior to his act of civil disobedience at Catonsville, Maryland, in May of 1968, he had never violated a civil law. "This," he added, "was one experience the nine [Catonsville] defendants shared in common."[36]

One could predict from Kohlberg's developmental theory that practitioners of civil disobedience would tend to have relatively high socioeconomic status. In view of the upper- and upper-middle-class backgrounds of men like Gandhi, Henry David Thoreau, Martin Luther King, Jr., A. J. Muste, David Dellinger, and Willian Sloane Coffin, the hypothesis seems plausible. One might predict also that they would have nonauthoritarian personalities, but research is needed to ascertain even the plausibility of this hypothesis. What appears to separate persons who practice civil disobedience from other men who are in most other respects similar to them is the intensity of their moral commitment and their willingness to act on it. Why they develop this intensity of commitment and willingness to act on it is perhaps the most interesting research question concerning them.

Although civil disobedience limits law, it can at the same time contribute to it, for those who practice it are potential agents of legal change. When they say, "Make the law just and we shall obey it," they are seeking to make law consistent with their own perceptions of its moral and jural postulates, and some of them have been successful.

Just as conscience in civil disobedience limits law, so do prejudice, passion, and ideological commitment in a number of instances, including civil disobedience. Whether these variables are correlated to the stages of moral development previously discussed is an important research question yet to be answered.

3. External enforcement communicates officially sanctioned rules, in some cases reinforces moral judgments to obey them, and in other cases persuades potential violators that, apart from any morality of the rules, it is expedient to obey them. Most external enforcement is done by government officials—police officers, prosecutors, lawyers, administrators, and judges—and perceptions and judgments to act according to officially sanctioned rules are necessary conditions for legal action by them. Their notions of obligation are (or should be) specifically related to their role conceptions. Of course, role conceptions alone do not determine sense of obligation for them; individual moral principles, ideology, and judgments about the limits of the possible are also important.

External enforcement in some cases turns on such variables as wealth and knowledge of the legal and social systems. For example, the rights of the poor often go unenforced because the poor usually have neither sufficient money nor knowledge of the legal system to employ lawyers or otherwise do what is necessary to receive justice under law.

Depending on the rule or person involved, law's effectiveness varies with external enforcement. This is demonstrated in situations in which, because of a war or a strike, the police do not perform their regular enforcement duties. In 1944, the Germans arrested the entire Danish police force, and for seven months police functions were performed rather ineffectively in Denmark by a volunteer watch corps. During that period the rate of thefts and robberies rose more than tenfold, but there was no noticeable increase in embezzlement, fraud, sexual offenses, or murder. Andenaes suggests that embezzlement and fraud did not increase because the perpetrators of such crimes are generally known;[37] hence, the primary sanction is social—embarrassment and shame of prosecution and possible imprisonment. The reason that sexual offenses and murder did not increase can be attributed to the fact that those offenses are perceived as *mala per se,* and thus their occurrence is related primarily to inadequacy of moral and legal socialization rather than to enforcement. This suggests that offenses that are *mala prohibita*— for example, tax evasion or traffic violations—are likely to occur in the absence of enforcement. There are some persons, however, who scrupulously obey legal rules whether they are *mala per se* or *mala prohibita.* What is needed is a typology of effectiveness of enforcement based on the type of offense and the person who is prone to commit it. Chambliss has devised such a typology.[38] He contrasted prohibited acts that are *expressive* (those that are impulsive and not easily controlled) and acts that are *instrumental* (those that are presumably rational). Examples of expressive deviant acts are most murders, offenses by drug addicts, sex offenses, and drunkenness. Examples of instrumental acts are murders committed by professionals, parking violations, shoplifting, and check forging and other white-collar offenses. Expressive acts are relatively unaffected by threats of punishment, whereas instrumental acts generally are affected. Effectiveness of threats of punishment also depends on a person's commitment to a life of crime. Those who have a high commitment are less likely to be deterred than those with a low commitment. By combining these two variables, Chambliss obtained the following typology:

Most likely to be deterred	Low commitment— instrumental	High commitment— instrumental	Low commitment— expressive	High commitment— expressive	*Least likely to be deterred*

According to the typology, persons who would be most deterred by police enforcement are nonprofessional shoplifters, parking violators, and white-collar criminals. In regard to the nonprofessional shoplifter and white-collar criminal, criminal sanctions alone are not what are feared but the social sanctions that are perceived to follow in their wake.[39] In regard to parking violations, certainty and severity of punishment appear directly related to effectiveness.[40] Chambliss' typology is heuristically useful, but another typology containing the variables of level of moral judgment, degree of self-control, perception of morality involved in certain prohibited acts, and perception of certainty and severity of punishment would appear to have more explanatory power.

IV

"[L]egislation," wrote Bentham, "has the same center with morals, but it has not the same circumference."[41] That is true of law generally. Where and why does one draw the line indicating law's ethical limits? I should suggest three principles: (1) Law should not seek to do what it cannot do. (2) It should not be used if the costs in using it (social, political, and economic) are unduly high. (3) It should not be used if it is not aimed at fulfilling law's functions.

1. The argument that law's capability should limit it is, of course, not new. Locke, for example, made it in opposing attempts to use law to change religious beliefs.[42] Law that is incapable of fulfilling its functions is not only useless; it is often dysfunctional. One reason is that it often provides reassurance that the problem it has dealt with has been solved, and reassurance leads to political quiescence.[43] The difficulty here is obvious. If law attempts to control antisocial conduct, and it is the kind of conduct that is beyond law's empirical limits, that conduct will continue. An example is the attempt to control drunkenness in the United States through the use of criminal sanctions. A large percentage of those convicted of drunkenness are compulsive drinkers, men and women who are run through the criminal process over and over. For them, law is simply not a deterrent, and "rehabilitation also proves illusory because a correctional regimen for these persons is largely nonexistent."[44] Another example is in the area of economic regulation; legislation may provide reassurance that threats to the economic environment are under control when in fact it exacerbates such threats by permitting greater claims on tangible resources by organized groups.[45]

In the West, law is viewed as having universal applicability, and justice under it is "impartial and pitiless as fire: whoever breaks the law must suffer the consequence, just as surely as the person who puts his hand into fire must experience pain."[46] But law has different empirical limits for different people, depending, among other things, on their stage of moral development. Subjecting a Gandhi or a King to the law for an act of civil disobedience will not change his behavior. Whether such prosecutions make others lawabiding is problematical; such men are often viewed as martyrs and become models for further disobedience. This is not to say

that the state should not act in some way in regard to civil disobedience, but whether it should act punitively is highly questionable.[47] This raises the general problem of the appropriate sanctions
for crime; for many criminals, imprisonment is simply ineffective
and hence its use in these instances is also questionable. Again,
this is not to say that criminals should not be dealt with by the
state or that the legal process should not be used. It is to say,
though, that if the legal process cannot be used effectively, other
means of dealing with problems it seeks to solve should be used
if such means can, consistent with basic social values, better fulfill
law's functions.[48]

2. In 1965, almost one-third of all arrests in the United States—
more than a million and a half—were for drunkenness. The time,
effort, and money expended in processing and trying these cases
cannot be justified in relation to the results. The costs, not only
in money but also in time and energy that could have been spent
by police officers, prosecutors, lawyers, and judges on other cases,
are obviously too high to justify dealing with this problem in this
way. Sometimes the political or social costs of using law to deal
with a particular problem are unduly high—for example, severe
polarization of a society caused by prosecutions related to an un-
popular or civil war. In such instances a government has several
choices, among them discretion not to prosecute, amnesty, and
pardon. Sometimes the costs involved in using law are so high that
the wiser course for government is to do nothing. When costs of
using law far outweigh its benefits, it is clear that other available
and appropriate means of handling the problem should be used.

3. Over time, the values of societies change, and legal regulation
of certain conduct no longer fulfills law's functions. This appears
to be the case in regard to the so-called offenses against morals
in Anglo-American countries. The ordinary justification for making
such conduct illegal—social control so that individual freedom and
security can be maintained—is usually not present.[49] And it is
difficult to justify laws regulating such "offenses" in terms of moral
education because there is no longer a consensus concerning morality
regarding such matters as private sexual conduct. The old rules
are no longer generally agreed upon, and those who feel that such
agreement is necessary for obedience are hesitant to support them,
even though they themselves abide by them. This was recognized
by the drafters of the Model Penal Code:

We deem it inappropriate for government to attempt to control behavior that has no substantial significance except as to the morality of the actor. Such matters are best left to religious, educational and other social influences. Apart from the question of constitutionality which might be raised against legislation avowedly commanding adherence to a particular religious or moral tenet, it must be recognized, as a practical matter, that in a heterogeneous community such as ours, different individuals and groups have widely divergent views of the seriousness of various moral derelictions.[50]

All this suggests Kohlberg's fifth stage of moral development—"the morality of contract, of individual rights, and democratically accepted law." As societies approach this stage of moral development, moral education alone is not enough to justify the use of law to regulate conduct unless there is a clear consensus that it should be used. When such consensus is lacking, government must choose between or among competing moralities and thereby needlessly run the risk of exacerbating conflicts and denying individual rights.

The main point in this section is that the ethical limits of law often turn on empirical considerations. Thus it is important that social scientists and legal scholars study law's empirical limits. Such studies will be useful in determining law's capabilities, its costs and benefits, and the extent to which it achieves its purposes. Such determinations provide a basis for circumscribing law's *outer* ethical limits. There are other arguments for setting more restrictive *inner* limits, but that is a matter properly in the realm of moral philosophy and beyond the scope of this paper. The fact that law cannot and should not be used to deal with certain problems (especially moral problems) does not mean that they should not be dealt with by other means. Recognition of law's empirical and ethical limits is a first step toward finding better means of solving such problems. It is also a first step toward better social control, dispute settlement, and moral education.

REFERENCES

[1] Cf. Lon L. Fuller, *The Morality of Law* (1964), p. 91.

[2] See Herbert L. Packer, *The Limits of the Criminal Sanction* (1968), pp. 42-44.

[3] Earl R. Quinney found that retail pharmacists who saw themselves as professionals were less likely to violate prescription laws than pharmacists who saw themselves as businessmen. Those who saw themselves as both professionals and businessmen or who were indifferent to either self-concept were more likely to be violators than professionals but less likely than business-oriented pharmacists. "Occupational Structure and Criminal Behavior: Prescription Violation by Retail Pharmacists," *Social Problems*, 11 (1963), 179-185.

[4] A beginning has been made by Robert Stover in his unpublished paper "Obedience toward Law Viewed from a Symbolic Interactionist Framework," which was presented at the 1971 American Political Science Association meeting. He found moderately strong relationships between verbal commitment to legal obedience and the following self-concepts: "I am equal to all others in the eyes of the law." "I am the kind of person who obeys the law." "As a citizen of the United States, I have a good chance to influence the decisions of government." "I am a person actively working to preserve law and order in this country."

[5] Learned Hand, *The Spirit of Liberty* (1954), p. 87. Cf. Frankfurter's statement in *Felix Frankfurter Reminisces*, ed. Harlan B. Phillips (1960), p. 189: "I do take law very seriously, deeply seriously, because fragile as reason is and limited as law is as the expression of the institutionalized medium of reason, that's all we have standing between us and the tyranny of mere will and the cruelty of unbridled, undisciplined feeling." June L. Tapp, reporting findings from a six-country study of legal socialization of children, wrote that in answer to the question "What would happen if there were no rules?" the children of all countries predicted the same result—"chaos, disorder and anarchy. In addition children in five cultures foresaw violence, crime and personal gain as outcomes. . . . Older children in all but two of the countries studied were more likely than younger ones to say that disorder and personal gain would prevail if rule and law failed." *Psychology Today*, 4 (December 1970), 62. See also June L. Tapp and Felice J. Levine, "Persuasion to Virtue: A Preliminary Statement," *Law and Society Review*, 4 (1970), 565-582.

[6] Nigel Walker, "Morality and the Criminal Law," *Howard Journal*, 11 (1968), 213.

[7] Jeremy Bentham, *Theory of Legislation* (1871), p. 64.

[8] P. H. Gulliver, *Social Control in an African Society* (1963), pp. 296-302.

[9] Lafcadio Hearn, *Japan: An Interpretation* (1955), pp. 352-353.

[10] See Dan Fenno Henderson, *Conciliation and Japanese Law* (1965); Takeyoshi Kawashima, "Dispute Resolution in Contemporary Japan," in Arthur Taylor von Mehren, ed., *Law in Japan* (1963), pp. 41-72. Conciliation was also the traditional means of dispute settlement in Korea and China. See Pyong-Choon Hahm, "The Decision Process in Korea," in Glendon Schubert and David J. Danelski, eds., *Comparative Judicial Behavior* (1969), pp. 19-47.

[11] Takeyoshi Kawashima, "The Notion of Law, Right, and Social Order in Japan," in Charles A. Moore, ed., *The Status of the Individual in East and West* (1968), pp. 429-447.

[12] *Law in Japan*, p. 190.

[13] Roscoe Pound, *Social Control Through Law* (1942), p. 20.

[14] Johs Andenaes, "General Prevention—Illusion or Reality?" *Journal of Criminal Law, Criminology, and Police Science,* 43 (1952), 179.

[15] For example, Connecticut's anticontraceptive statute, which, after prolonged litigation, was declared unconstitutional in *Griswold* v. *Connecticut,* 381 U.S. 479 (1965).

[16] Lester J. Mazor, "The Fate of Law," *The Center Magazine,* 4 (1971), 68-72.

[17] See Monroe Lefkowitz, Robert R. Blake, and Jane Strygley Mouton, "Status Factors in Pedestrian Violation of Traffic Signals," *Journal of Abnormal and Social Psychology,* 51 (1955), 704-706.

[18] E. Adamson Hoebel, *The Law of Primitive Man* (1954), p. 15.

[19] Frank Zimring and Gordon Hawkins, "Deterrence and Marginal Groups," *Journal of Research in Crime and Delinquency,* 5 (1968), 100.

[20] Lawrence Kohlberg, "The Development of Children's Orientations Toward a Moral Order," *Vita Humana,* 6 (1963), 11-33; "Moral Development and Identification," in Harold W. Stevenson, ed., *Child Psychology* (1963), pp. 277-332; "Development of Moral Character and Moral Ideology," in Martin and Lois W. Hoffman, eds., *Review of Child Development Research* (1964), pp. 383-431; "The Child as Moral Philosopher," *Psychology Today,* 2 (1968), 25-30. Some of Kohlberg's unpublished work is discussed by Eleanor E. Maccoby, "The Development of Moral Values and Behavior in Childhood," in John A. Clausen, ed., *Socialization and Society* (1968), 231-242. Jean Piaget's classic work, *The Moral Judgment of the Child* (1927), has had a great influence on scholars interested in law and justice. See, for example, Jerome Frank, *Law and the Modern Mind* (1930) and John Rawls, "The Sense of Justice," *Philosophical Review,* 72 (1963), 281-305.

[21] *Review of Child Development Research,* p. 400.

[22] *Ibid.,* p. 417.

[23] *Ibid.,* p. 408.

[24] *Ibid.,* pp. 415-416. The psychological literature on modeling in relation to the development of self-control is relevant to moral and legal socialization. See Albert Bandura and Richard H. Walters, *Social Learning and Personality Development* (1963).

[25] *Review of Child Development Research,* p. 406.

[26] *Ibid.,* p. 407.

[27] Justin Aronfreed, *Conduct and Conscience* (1968), pp. 318-319. He adds: "Cross-cultural comparisons suggest similar associations between orientation toward the control of conduct and the types of parental discipline which are characteristic of entire societies." *Ibid.,* p. 319.

[28] Richard D. Schwartz and Sonya Orleans, "On Legal Sanctions," *University of Chicago Law Review,* 34 (1967), 275-300.

[29] Charles C. Hughes, Marc-Adelard Tremblay, Robert N. Rapoport, and Alexander H. Leighton, *People of Cove and Woodlot* (1960).

[30] Kohlberg, *Review of Child Development Research,* p. 422.

[31] Leonard Berkowitz and Nigel Walker, "Laws and Moral Judgments," *Sociometry,* 30 (1967), 410-422.

[32] John Rawls, "The Justification of Civil Disobedience," in Hugo A. Bedau, ed., *Civil Disobedience: Theory and Practice* (1969), p. 248.

[33] *Korematsu* v. *United States,* 323 U.S. 214 (1944).

[34] Hirabayashi lost. *Hirabayashi* v. *United States,* 320 U.S. (1943). When his appeal was decided, he was permitted to hitchhike by himself from Spokane, Washington, to a federal prison in Arizona. After he served his sentence, he refused to submit to the draft on grounds of conscience and served another prison sentence. After the war, he received a Ph.D. in sociology and is presently teaching at a Canadian university. Interview of Gordon Hirabayashi by author, June 22, 1967.

[35] *Civil Disobedience: Theory and Practice*, p. 247.

[36] Daniel Berrigan, *No Bars to Manhood* (1971), p. 39.

[37] *Journal of Criminal Law, Criminology, and Police Science*, p. 187.

[38] William J. Chambliss, *Crime and the Criminal Process* (1969), pp. 368-372.

[39] A nonprofessional shoplifter, caught stuffing a dress into a shopping bag and carrying it out of the store, said: "I didn't intend to take the dress, I just wanted to see it in daylight. Oh, what will my husband do? I did intend to pay for it. It's all a mistake. Oh, my God, what will my mother say! I'll be glad to pay for it. See, I've got the money with me. Oh, my children! They can't find out I've been arrested! I'll never be able to face them again!" Mary O. Cameron, *The Booster and the Snitch* (1966), quoted in Chambliss, *Crime and the Criminal Process*, p. 367. During World War II businessmen were most concerned about the shame of imprisonment for blackmarket violations. Here are some of their statements: "A jail sentence is dishonorable; it jeopardizes the reputation." "It [jail] spoils the offender's reputation and frightens the other fellow." "The thing that puts a man to shame—closing his store and sending him to jail." Marshall B. Clinard, *The Black Market* (1952), quoted in Chambliss, *Crime and the Criminal Process*, pp. 365-366.

[40] William J. Chambliss, "The Deterrent Influence of Punishment," *Crime and Delinquency*, 12 (1966), 70-75. See also Charles R. Tittle, "Crime Rates and Legal Sanctions," *Social Problems*, 16 (1969), 409-423.

[41] *Theory of Legislation*, p. 60.

[42] John Locke, *A Letter Concerning Toleration* (1689).

[43] Murray Edelman, *The Symbolic Uses of Politics* (1964), chap. 2.

[44] President's Commission on Law Enforcement and the Administration of Justice, *Task Force Report: The Courts* (1967), p. 99.

[45] Edelman, *The Symbolic Uses of Politics*, p. 38.

[46] Hearn, *Japan: An Interpretation*, p. 352.

[47] See Roland Dworkin, "On Not Prosecuting Civil Disobedience," *The New York Review of Books*, 10 (June 6, 1968), 14-21. Use of the legal process may, however, be justifiable. One example is the use of law to remove persons who lie down on a highway before oncoming traffic to protest what they regard as unjust law. Another example is the trial of conscientious legal violators to show publicly the untenability of their moral positions. If the government is successful in such a trial, further action (e.g., punishment) is usually unnecessary.

[48] This is basically Hugo Bedau's argument in regard to economic regulation. He states that economic life is beyond the reach of law because "economic allocation of goods, services, and resources . . . cannot be done as effectively through adjudicative—and, to this extent, legal or governmental—devices as it can be done in other ways." "Law and Society: Necessities, Impossibilities, Obscurities," *The Philosophy Forum*, 8 (1970), 68.

[49] Louis B. Schwartz, "Morals Offenses and the Model Penal Code," *Columbia Law Review*, 63 (1963), 669.

[50] Quoted, *ibid.*, p. 674.

2

AN OVERVIEW OF FUTURE
POSSIBILITIES: LAW UNLIMITED?

William Leon McBride

The present essay was first prepared as a set of comments
on Professor Danelski's original paper. Although the latter has since
undergone very substantial revisions, I think that it still remains
within a certain perspective that, leaving minor critical points aside,
first occasioned my most fundamental misgivings about it. The
perspective in question is one of comparative optimism and of
taking the historical present state of affairs—the characteristics of
"modern" legal and moral systems as we know them today—as
a standard against which to measure the practices of other types
of societies and, despite the paper's frequent references to past
and present non-Western societies, as the effective basis upon which
to construct an analysis of our subject matter. I have tried in my
title to evoke an alternative perspective, upon which I shall proceed
briefly to elaborate.

I shall begin by tentatively accepting, as a useful though very
rough and ultimately problematic distinction, Professor Danelski's
division between ethical and empirical limits. If one denies, as I

do, that the sphere of "ethics" consists of a set of eternal and unchangeable rules, and stresses instead the historically relative character of rules of conduct and perhaps even, at the limit, of the entire phenomenon of "ethics" as we now know it, then one is committed to a view of the interrelationship of ethical and empirical factors in law that casts doubt on the distinction itself. Nevertheless, it retains some use as a scheme of classification.

1. My first set of remarks, then, has to do with the meaning of the empirical kind of limits. It seems to me that we ought not take the concept of law's empirical limits to refer only to the various—often, as Danelski is quite right to emphasize, highly diverse—legal practices that have obtained or do obtain in societies up to the present time. For an adequate discussion of empirical *limits* must, I think, also deal with real present and future *possibilities*. In fact, it is precisely this aspect of the question of law's empirical limits that is or should be of most concern to those involved in legal and especially judicial *practice*, as opposed to those with merely an academic interest in the law. For the "can" of the law has been and is being vastly extended by modern technological developments. Not all these developments, of course, have direct and automatic effects on legal procedures, nor is law as such to be identified with the techniques of social control. But social control is one of the functions of law that Professor Danelski lists, and the fact is that certain new techniques have greatly extended the optential future empirical limits of the law in this respect. One obvious example is the technique of wiretapping or, more broadly speaking, of "bugging," which, as we all know, has raised numerous new questions for judges, lawyers, and legislators by permitting the law to deal with a whole range of human activities that were beyond its empirical limits only a short while ago. A second familiar example of the expansion of law's empirical limits through technology is the new data-collecting machinery that makes the idea of a legally sanctioned control of eugenics practices for a nation of 200 million, for instance, a real possibility. Once the electronics and chemistry of brains become a little better understood, it is no longer wildly speculative even to imagine techniques of total thought control that could be applied with due process and in strict accordance with established legal procedures.

Now I am not, of course, advocating any of these developments; I am quite horrified by some of the possibilities that occur to me. But my point is that no adequate discussion of the
empirical limits of law can afford to neglect them. When we
consider areas of human activity in which legislators have tried,
in the past, to exert control and have been ineffective in doing
so, presumably because of law's "empirical limits" up to now,
we must remember that this observation provides us with no sure
guide about what might be done in the future.

I suggest that we reconsider, in light of modern technology,
the validity of Thomas Hobbes' statement to the effect that "the
greatest liberty of subjects, dependeth on the silence of the law."[1]
This is often urged, with good reason, as evidence against the
contention that Hobbes' legal philosophy can be regarded as an
ideological justification of contemporary totalitarianism. Hobbes was
enough of a man of his own times to regard it as unfeasible, for
practical, empirical reasons, for the law to deal with many broad
areas of private human conduct. This is no longer the case. Although we may all acknowledge, when pressed, that it is not the
case, we too often continue to speak and act as if we accepted
Hobbes' easy and unaccustomed optimism in this regard.

It is possible, of course, to ask whether a state in which both
the technology supporting law enforcement and the range of human
activities subject to law's control had evolved to their conceivable
limits could properly be called a "state of law" any longer.[2] This
question is, to a considerable extent, a terminological one, hinging
on familiar, ultimately bootless, and yet ever-recurring problems
concerning precisely how we are to define "law." Certainly the
envisaged state of nearly total technological control is a far cry
from the ideal *"Rechtsstaat"* of early twentieth-century liberals.
(In certain *formal* respects, it is closer to the allegedly desirable
community in which the Platonic Statesman would "sit beside"
every citizen to direct all his actions toward the common good;
the complete technological unfeasibility of this in his time was
advanced by Plato as the major reason for requiring general rules,
i.e., laws, as a kind of second-best arrangement.[3]) Terminology
aside, however, it is crucial for us to recognize and identify even
the most extreme possibilities that are present in existing legal
systems. Just as a case can be made in support of the thesis of
constitutional continuity between Weimar and Nazi Germany (by
virtue of the *Ausnahme- und Notverordnungsrecht*, Article 48 of

the Weimar constitution, which sanctioned the passage of the law
by which Hitler was granted extraordinary powers in 1933), so
there is no reason in principle why the law as we know it in, let
us say, the contemporary United States, could not be remolded
into the instrument of total social control to which I have been
pointing, without the occurrence of an overtly violent revolution
or other sudden and dramatic rupture.

2. In any likely future evolution toward a system of unlimited social control, the intensification of the sense of obligation
to obey the law would certainly be crucial. At the conceptual
limit, obedience to the law would become purely habitual, and
one would again be forced to ask the terminological question
whether a state in which obedience to the law was totally habitual
could properly be called a state of law at all.[4] Short of that
limit, more attention ought to be paid, in discussions of the
empirical limits of law, to the manipulative techniques whereby
the sense of obligation to obey the law can be, and is, intensified.

Among the most successful of such techniques is the mystifying
hypostatization or fetishizing of the laws—the raising of them, in
the words of Konrad Lorenz, "to sacred ends in themselves."[5]
The use of the religious term "sacred" is quite significant. Laws
are the products of human convention; unless these products are
continually subjected to re-evaluation and criticism, they come to
dominate their producers. The socialization process whereby this
comes about is a complex one; only very seldom and in scattered
instances[6] does it exhibit the features of a deliberate plan or
organized conservative "conspiracy." The concept of "law"—or, more
frequently in contemporary discussions, of "law and order" (to
be read as one word)—is treated, both in ordinary language and
in the language of politicians and sometimes even of political
theorists, as if it referred to a real entity that existed independently
of the members of society. It then becomes possible to speak of
the fetishized concept, in its empirical manifestations (i.e., the
enforcement of a particular set of laws by means of a particular
set of institutions, such as courts and police), as if it possessed
a rigid and specific configuration that was permanent and not
subject to dispute. "The preservation of law and order" can then
be treated as if it were a social imperative of greater magnitude
than that of meeting the real needs of society's members, and

any attempt to question its meaning can be condemned as a sort of social blasphemy.[7]

This is a useful state of affairs for those who are aided by the laws in retaining positions of privilege over others in society (such as, perhaps, the more prosperous citizens of Lavallée, whom Professor Danelski mentions, by comparison with their poorer, "insufficiently socialized" neighbors), but it is irrational. Laws are *in fact* instruments, not "sacred ends." When they are regarded as the latter by their subjects, as they have been often enough in history, then their effective force does indeed become virtually unlimited, in the sense that all questioning concerning the subjects' alleged obligations to obey the laws has been eliminated.

It is for this reason that we ought to maintain a considerable skepticism about both the social meaning and the value of any empirically discernible trend toward the intensification of the sense of obligation to obey "the law." With respect to specific laws and legal institutions, the meaning and value of such a trend will depend on the specific laws and legal institutions in question. With respect to "the law as such" (to the rather modest extent to which this phrase has any specifiable meaning at all!), a trend toward the intensification of the sense of obligation to obey implies that the law is in the process of becoming both an object and an agency of habituation. It is for this reason too that our original topic of "the limits of law" must be conceived in normative as well as in empirical terms.

3. I have thus far argued that we are now able to conceive of a vast possible future extension of the empirical limits of law, and I have mentioned a common technique for intensifying the popularly felt sense of obligation to obey the law, by means of which the path to such an extension may be rendered comparatively smooth. What remains for me to discuss, in this very brief overview of the future possibilities of the law, is the ethical or normative question proper, namely, whether an extension or, alternatively, a preservation or retraction of law's present limits is desirable. This question, it seems to me, does not permit of a simple, unqualified answer.

A widely held belief with which I concur is that law is justifiable only as a means for promoting certain fundamental human social values.[8] It might seem to follow from this that law should not attempt to do what can be done more effectively by other means[9] and that, consequently, we ought to favor the elimination of law from any area of social behavior in which such more effective means can be discovered. This would be plausible if we were to consider effectiveness both as an unambiguous quality and as the highest value to be achieved. But these premises are themselves indefensible, as the briefest reflection will suffice to illustrate. From a certain point of view, for instance, a vigilante group can often be more effective in doing away with suspected criminals swiftly and decisively than legal procedures could ever be. (From another point of view, of course, one could argue that vigilante practices will necessarily prove ineffective in the long run; this may or may not turn out to be true, depending on the circumstances.) But the admission of this possibility does not mean that the more effective means of vigilantism ought therefore to be substituted for the law. (The same considerations may be applied, by the way, to the choice between unilateral police actions and the development of *international* law.) The reason, of course, is that the law can and often does promote many other, more fundamental human values than that of effectiveness, narrowly understood. Effectiveness is only one of many important social values, and it is not always a particularly good one to use as a criterion for deciding when legal and when extralegal procedures should be followed.

These considerations show that the extreme anarchist ideal of substituting other means for legal institutions immediately and universally is a false ideal. Nevertheless, some of the arguments that are advanced by the advocates of antinomianism are surely very cogent ones. The law as we know it, it is said, has an alienating or even a repressive effect on the members of society, especially on those who occupy subordinate social roles. Although legal processes often do serve to right wrongs and to facilitate social amelioration, even on such occasions the inherently institutional character of law results in the interposition of the massive, impersonal machinery of statute and precedent, time delay and ritual, and a whole "middle-man" class of legal professionals between the individuals and groups in society who are involved in the struggle to obtain what each of them considers his or its due; this is the meaning of the alleged "alienation," whereby social actions and events cease to bear a direct relationship to intentions and projects. Moreover, no one can seriously deny that the law as we know it frequently acts to the special advantage of those who occupy positions of dominance within the existing social order; this is one definition of "repression." To the extent to which such considerations do indeed have force, it must be conceded that the desirability of a vast extension of the limits of law, which I have depicted as a possible societal future, is highly dubious. How, then, are we to reconcile this conclusion with the assertion that other means should not necessarily be substituted for the law simply because they are more effective?

The example of greater effectiveness that I chose, vigilantism, like its suggested analogue of international vigilantism, is characterized above all by the direct and overt employment of *coercion* by one individual of group against others. (Its perpetrators will, to be sure, justify their employment of coercion by reference to alleged previous coercive actions on the part of their adversaries.) However, the historical fact that law has sometimes, though not always, served the civilizing function of mitigating the most brutally coercive elements in human societies implies no positive conclusions concerning the value of typical contemporary forms of law in social situations, or even in conceivable entire future societies, in which coerciveness is an irrelevant or very minimal element.[10] In *such* situations, as opposed to those, still far more prominent in our world, in which overt or covert violence and coercion prevail, the position of those who advocate substituting other social means for the law as we now know it might well become an acceptable one.

In short, it is true that society is, generally speaking, better off under the rule of law than under the rule of force or *Diktat,* but can we not also conceive of a form of society existing under a more desirable order than that of the rule of law as we now know it? Earlier, I pointed to the possibility of a totally coerced future society, in which, at best, certain legal trappings might be maintained, but there would be no choice about whether or not to observe the laws, and hence no real law at all. Such a state of affairs might be regarded as one extreme in a spectrum or range of possible future states, the opposite pole of which should now be brought into focus. This would be "a society of individuals so enlightened that, while they would still be confronted with rules of conduct of all sorts, they would constantly be making conscious choices as to whether to accept or to reject any one of these rules, and no coercion would be exerted over any member's choice."[11] It seems to me that this is an ideal limit toward which legislators, judges, philosophers of law, and others ought to work, since this state of affairs would accord most completely with such human values as responsibility, free choice, and respect for persons.

But in such a state of affairs, the law as we know it today would disappear, just as it would, as we saw, in its polar opposite, the totally coercive state. For in the state of universal, uncoerced free choice, individuals would presumably never choose to abide by a law *simply* because it was "the law," since to do this would be to succumb to mystification, but rather because it was a better rule than any alternative.[12] In such a state there would, *ex hypothesi*, be rules of social behavior, and hence law in *this* sense; society would still be structured or "ordered." But if one comes down (as Danelski, for example, does) on the side of the debate about the nature of law that takes coerciveness to be an essential feature of it, and if one's concept of "law" remains largely rooted in the set of institutions and procedures that ordinarily go under that name today, then the state that I have depicted as an ideal limit toward which legislators and all citizens ought to work could *not* be considered a state of law as we know it.

Some developments in this direction have already begun to take place. For instance, in the discussion following the original presentation of Professor Danelski's paper and this commentary, mention was made of the growth of procedures of mediation, regulated by the disputing parties themselves, in the field of labor-management relations, and of the substitution of administrative processes for litigation in many areas of social activity. A significant current example of this is the trend toward "no-fault" systems of automobile insurance, which obviate the need to rely on most of the ponderous legal machinery of the past in this sector. The meaning of all such developments can be interpreted in a variety of ways, of course, but I choose to see them as at least pointing to a general desire to get away from certain forms of social straitjacketing that have been imposed by our traditional legal institutions.

At the same time, it should be recognized that the decline of legal institutions in a socially liberating, rather than a totalitarian, direction has only become possible in modern times. It is precisely the evolution of technology, to which I referred in a context of deep concern about its baneful possibilities at the beginning of this paper, that also begins to make available the material resources needed to transcend the antisocial individualsm and class dominance characteristic of societies in which endless litigation is the rule.

For instance, the private ownership of property, which is the basis of so much of our traditional legal theory and remains the leitmotif of so many of our present-day legal processes, is anachronistic when the property in question is the very large-scale industry upon which our modern life depends. Similarly, the evolution of advanced techniques of automation, which at the limit render large work forces totally superfluous in entire vast sectors of industrial production, makes imperative the rethinking and critical reworking, the beginnings of which we are witnessing, of such traditional social and legal concepts as "employment" and "unemployment," "contract," and "welfare." Without modern technology, the emergence of what Marx called a "society of associated producers," in which the rules of social interaction would be very differently configured from present-day legal systems, would be unthinkable; with it, such an event is possible, though by no means inevitable.

Thus, even the ethical limits of law, and not just its empirical limits, are seen to be relative to historical circumstances, and there are good reasons for not treating the present state of affaris in law as in any sense a standard for analyzing these limits. The *Rechtsstaat* was originally conceived of as, among other things, a defense against arbitrariness and tyranny; now its retention in areas in which it is no longer needed may serve as a block to the development of human potentialities.

This, then, it seems to me, is the ultimate *ethical* limit of law: a possible future society that, far from regarding the extension of law's limits as desirable, would have succeeded in dispensing with the law as we now know it in favor of social rules and practices less pervaded by coerciveness. But we have a long, long way to go before we reach that point, and meanwhile we face the constant threat that the trend away from reliance on the legal machinery of the past may be pre-empted by the advocates of what is euphemistically called "law and order," who would simultaneously eliminate much of that machinery (e.g., warrants, bail, the jury system) and yet extend the empirical limits of law, in the sense considered at the outset of this essay, in the interests of coercion and political repression.

REFERENCES

[1] *Leviathan,* Oakeshott ed. (Oxford: Basil Blackwell, 1960), p. 143.

[2] Commenting on Mazor's essay at the end of his Part II, for example, Danelski speaks of the possible eventual *displacement* of law "by psychology and technology as more effective and desirable means of managing human behavior." There are conceptual difficulties with this way of putting the matter. Law, psychology, and technology are three quite different and incommensurable types of categories. Certain aspects of the legal process today make considerable use of modern technology, and certain theories about human psychology play an important part in determining, for example, criminal responsibility. A more accurate and illuminating way of conceiving of the eventualities to which Danelski and Mazor here wish to point would be, I think, to imagine a system of social rules within which the special knowledge and skills possessed by members of the legal profession as we know it today would no longer be employable.

[3] *Statesman,* 295 a-b.

[4] I know that there is an old tradition going back at least to Aristotle to the effect that it would be most desirable if obedience to the law were to become purely a matter of habit. But I tend to agree with Professor Hart and many others that, in order for behavior to be characterized as "law-abiding," there must remain the real possibility of violations of the rules—violations that might be morally as well as legally unjustifiable, in the case of good laws, or violations that might be morally justifiable or even obligatory, in the case of bad laws—on the part of subjects.

[5] Konrad Lorenz, *On Aggression* (New York: Bantam Books, 1967), p. 79. This phrase was cited in the paper originally presented by Professor Danelski. The full sentence reads as follows: "If social norms and customs did not develop their peculiar autonomous life and power, if they were not raised to sacred ends in themselves, there would be no trustworthy communication, no faith, and no law."

[6] Probably the 1970 United States Congressional election campaign of the vice president can be cited as one such instance.

[7] I find the word "mystification" a useful shorthand for expressing the outcome of a complex, circular linguistic and social process of the sort that I have just briefly described. But I admit that my choice of word is perilous. In particular, it is important to note that "mystification" means nothing so simple as "obfuscation" or "confusion," and it is equally important to prevent it from becoming an object and an instrument of mystification in its own right.

[8] For an extended current argument *against* this commonly held position, see Charles Fried, *An Anatomy of Values* (Cambridge, Mass.: Harvard University Press, 1970), especially chap. VIII, pp. 116-136. Fried's use of comtemporary marriage legislation as an example intended to illustrate his point seems to me especially poorly chosen. Robert S. Summers, in his review of Fried, gets to the heart of the matter when he shows that Fried's valid recognition of law as a promoter of certain "process values" with an intrinsic significance that is independent of the *outcomes* of the processes is by no means identical, as Fried tries to make it seem, with the designation of law as "an end in itself." See "A Critique of Professor Fried's Anatomy of Values," *Cornell Law Review,* 56:4 (April 1971), 622.

⁹ This contention figured prominently in the final main section of Professor Danelski's original paper.

¹⁰ For some further discussion of such possibilities, see my article "Non-Coercive Society: Some Doubts, Leninist and Contemporary," in *Nomos XIV, Coercion,* ed. Pennock and Chapman (Chicago: Aldine-Atherton, 1972), pp. 178-197.

¹¹ I have developed this same idea in my article "The Abolition of Law as a Standard in Legal Decision-Making," in *Legal Reasoning (Proceedings of the World Congress for Legal and Social Philosophy),* ed. H. Hubien (Brussels: Etablissements Emile Bruylant, 1971), pp. 313-318. The description cited is taken from this article, p. 317.

¹² In the cases of certain seemingly arbitrary but practically necessary kinds of rules, of which the requirement that traffic keep to the right-hand side of the road is at once one of the most familiar and most extreme examples, the reasons for observance would of course be very simple and uncomplicated, involving a universal recognition of the need to agree upon conventions in such matters involving the entire collectivity. But even this sort of reasoning is by no means identical with passive acquiescence to the slogan that the law must be obeyed simply because it is the law.

3

PERSPECTIVES ON THE LIMITS OF LAW

Julius Cohen

I

      Law shares with other social mechanisms—some with strong family resemblances—the task of controlling and giving direction to human conduct. To discourse meaningfully on the limits of law requires at the outset a determination of those distinguishing marks that in themselves constitute a form of delimitation—those that give law its identity and differentiate it from other instruments of social control. There have been many candidates for the mark of the "legal"; there have been many claims that without the presence of such elements as "rules," "legitimacy," "justiciability," "inner morality," "reasoned elaboration," "sanctions," etc., the imprimatur "legal" would be counterfeit. It is not necessary to postpone inquiry into the limits of law until such an unlikely time when a final theoretical definition will emerge. But it is necessary to make clear the particular meaning that one ascribes to "law" is a discussion of its limits is to have communal focus.

A stipulative definition of law "as a process in which human conduct is subjected to the governance of officially sanctioned rules"[1] has the advantage of providing a broad working conception that reflects some minimal linguistic agreement; it has the disadvantage of not making clear whether "officially sanctioned rules" include those self-imposed obligations that a nation recognizes as legally binding but that are not subject to the orders of an international public body backed by threats of force.[2] To exclude such rules from the concept of law would, to that extent of course, narrow the area of inquiry concerning the limits of law. Greater clarity would also result by keeping the concepts of law and government separate and distinct. The repeated references in literature to "government of law," and "government of men but not of law" would suggest a reflective awareness that there can be government without law, and that, whatever the limits of law, they are not necessarily the limits of government.

As in the case of the proverbial elephant whose outlines became clearer when the different perspectives of the blind men were pieced together, so a clearer conception of the limits of law might well emerge from a composite of views taken from different observation points. Take, for example, the view from the top—from the perspective of the wielder of legal authority concerned with his subjects only to the extent that they could be utilized as means to secure his selfish ends. From this perspective, the limits of law loom primarily as a problem of determining the extent of the restraints that it would impose on the free exercise of his will over his subjects. As Kelsen and others have made abundantly evident, the distance between gangster authority and legal rule can be as short as a few formal, procedural notches. There are prescribed validating procedures that the rules must follow if the rules of the wielder of authority are to satisfy the requirements of "legality." In addition, his subjects must be accorded procedural justice under the rules—in the main, impartial, unbiased treatment to all members of the class or classes that the rules demarcate. There need be no minimal requirement that slaves be treated as human beings, but only that one slave be accorded the same treatment as the other members of the same generic class. To the cynical tyrant impervious to the needs and aspirations of his subjects, save as they relate to their efficiency as means, this is not too steep a price to pay for respectability. As history has painfully shown, the difference between a tyrant and a legal tyrant, measured on a substantive scale, can be very small. What distinguishes the two concepts is an adjective whose function, it is well to remember, is merely to modify and not to eliminate the noun.

II

The view from the bottom looking up—from the perspective of those who would wish to harness law to the ideal of achieving maximum satisfaction to all the competing interests that enter into a social life—presents the problem of the limits of law in a somewhat different light. The limits are those that, in the main, stem from an insufficiency of knowledge. The age-old ethical problem of determining the ideal goals or ends to which law should be harnessed in order to function ideally as a means still remains and most likely will remain a problem; whatever limits ethical theory encounters in grappling with ideal goals or ends inevitably become the same limits within which law must be confined in functioning as a means. Agreement quickly dissipates when discussions of the problem move away from such abstractions as "the good life" to the earthier level of empirical content. Beyond the task of determining what the expressed values are that seek satisfaction through the instrumentalities of law is the more essential and more difficult normative task of determining the values that, on calm reflection, are really *worthy* of satisfaction. And even beyond this task lies another, that of translating them into some fungible measuring unit that would take the "in" out of the term "incommensurable." There are further limits to knowledge especially germane to law—of how justly to ration and distribute the competing satisfactions seeking fruition when the demand for material and other resources for implementing them is, in the nature of things, greater than the supply. For example, greater rewards to inventive minds would most likely contribute to the discovery of ways to increase the general wealth of the community, but it would, at the outset, lessen the already limited amount of buying power that is available to the poor. Or take the case of a labor strike that is threatened because of the decline in real wages for the working man. Suppose that, if it succeeds, it would fuel inflation and harm the rest of the community. If law is to intercede, which of the competing interests should justly prevail? The number of imponderables and "it depends" is not inconsiderable. The content of substantive justice, geared to time, place, and circumstance, still remains, in considerable part, indeterminate; such formulas as "giving every one his due" are merely question-begging devices that postpone the real and difficult dimensions of the problem. In seeking direction toward substantive justice—both on the legislative and judicial levels—law is thus often limited by the inadequacies of the instruments that it has at its command for determining in which of many competing directions it should go. Much of its flying is, accordingly, blind; and if it often succeeds in achieving order at the expense of justice, it usually is a consequence of avoiding what would be worse when the alternative is simply not knowing what direction is best. Indeterminacy is scarcely a condition unique to the field of law. It is a condition shared by the nonomniscient in all fields of endeavor, be they normative or empirical. But because of the complexity of the human problems that are involved, the wherewithal for coping with and reducing the indeterminacies that would plague the ideal law-maker is in painfully short supply. At moments of crucial decision-making, when determinate guidance is needed, ethical principles like moral maxims and legal precedents are known for their capacity to point in different directions at the same time, leaving to intuition the task of balancing them and determining which way the ideal law-maker ought to go.

III

From the perspective of the law-maker who is fairly clear on the objectives to be achieved by law, the limitations of knowledge extend to the problem of means. How, for example, to cope effectively with the production and sale of narcotics, with drug addiction, with overpopulation, with corruption in government, with the hardened recidivists and the other hardy perennials of the legal order? They still defy adequate solution. Each is not a single problem but a complex of problems; each generates a host of countervailing considerations—moral, economic, and otherwise—that compound the complexities. Further limitations flow from the inherent clumsiness of the instrument of the rule of law. One cannot easily foresee and take into account the situations to which a rule might apply. An illustration is the classic example of the soldier given strict orders by his commanding officer to stand squarely in front of the door of a building and to guard it with his life; he stands dutifully for a while, but then observes what he suspects to be a time bomb ticking relentlessly but twenty feet away. As in medicine, the side-effects of a confident legal prescription often come as an unwanted surprise. How many advocates of rent control for the poor would have anticipated the extent to which it would contribute to the perpetuation of the ghetto? How many legislators would have foreseen that subsidies to help farmers would result in reducing the number of farmers? The enactment of a law is often, thus, like a game of chess—it is difficult to know in advance what one move will ultimately do to the rest of the board. There are limits also to what law can possibly control. Its power can readily extend to property, to things, and, to a limited extent, to persons. It can, as in the case of the Sabine women, implement their acquisition, but it cannot secure their affection. It cannot erase hurt feelings, restore lost limbs, or bring back to a family a life that has been inhumanly snuffed out. For such pains and deprivations, compensatory palliatives are, at best, woefully inadequate.

IV

From the perspective of those who are to apply and enforce the law—even assuming an impartiality that is stretched to its human limits—"fact skepticism" has become as significant a symbol of the pitfalls in ascertaining the facts to which law applies as "rule skepticism" is to the indeterminate structure of many of the legal rules to which the facts are to apply. These are built-in limits that are to be added to the varied limits of fallible human beings—of the judges, jurors, administrators, and police in whose hands the day-to-day operations of the legal machinery have been placed. As Pound observed quite some time ago,[3] there are areas in which the need for redress is undisputed, as in the case of mental suffering, but the complexities of proof and the opportunities for deception are so great that for law to undertake to correct an injustice might well result in an injustice. And with respect to the problem of indeterminacy that faces the judge in searching for the proper rule and the proper application of the rule, the sensitive reactions of Mr. Justice Cardozo are worth repeating:

> I was much troubled in spirit, in my first years upon the bench, to find how trackless was the ocean on which I had embarked. I sought for certainty. I was oppressed and dis-

heartened when I found that the quest for it was futile. I was trying to reach land, the solid land of fixed and settled rules, the paradise of a justice that would declare itself by tokens plainer and more commanding than its pale and glimmering reflections in my own vacillating mind and conscience. I found with the voyagers in Browning's 'Paracelsus' that "the real heaven was always beyond." As the years have gone by, and as I have reflected more and more upon the nature of the judicial process, I have become reconciled to the uncertainty, because I have grown to see it as inevitable.[4]

V

Finally, the limits of law take on another dimension when viewed from the perspective of those from whom the law seeks compliance. Compliance is obviously a crucial measure of law's effectiveness, but how it is to be ascertained and measured is not so obvious. All behavior consistent with law clearly cannot be attributed to compliance with law. Those entirely ignorant of it often behave consistently with it on moral or other grounds. To those aware of the law, the extent to which compliance is a function of self-interest, force, fear, inertia, habit, moral feelings, etc., is a matter that varies with time, place, circumstance, and subject matter. Those who insist that for law to be law there must be some external public force capable of imposing sanctions are often surprised at the extent to which national commitments under "international law" are nevertheless honored without such sanctioning authority.

In the eyes of those who are both aware of the law and wish to comply, law is limited to the extent that it is often difficult, if not impossible, to make clear just what is proscribed or permitted in the concrete instance. It is an unavoidable consequence of the inherent abstractness of many rules and of the fact that some degree of ambiguity or vagueness in language is an ineradicable human condition. It is not uncommon, therefore, for those who behave according to the clear letter of the law or what they in good faith otherwise assume its meaning to be, to be informed subsequently by a court that they were wrong in their interpretation and must suffer deprivations for not having had the intelligence to anticipate what a court, acknowledging the law's vagueness or ambiguity, later would say it would mean.

There is still another limitation that is inherent in the very concept of "rule of law." Resort to rule implies law-making by generic class, and, therefore, law-making wholesale rather than re-tail. It is not geared at the outset to deal with the unique or special situations that are the concerns of justice. These must await consideration and refinement, often at considerable cost and discomfort to those concerned, by courts and other refining agencies long after the enactment of the original rule. Once enacted, the need for order and predictability bestows on it a presumption of correctness and imposes on those adversely affected the heavy burden of proving it wrong or unjust.

Save for the certain knowledge that law cannot secure the impossible, there are no easy formulas for determining in advance just what types of measures would result in noncompliance, although it is tempting to offer quick generalizations from limited and local experience. Many matters thought beyond the sphere of legislative effectiveness have been subjected to effective control—polygamy in the United States, dress and religious practices in Turkey, suttee in India. Reflection on those instances in history in which successful revolutionary movements have accomplished changes in behavior patterns previously thought out of reach of legal control should give one considerable pause.

VI

Dwelling merely on the limits of law as an instrument of social control does not, of course, imply the absence of an inner core of functioning effectiveness. To the contrary—an inquiry into the upper and lower limits of law would have no meaning were there nothing of substance sandwiched in between.

REFERENCES

[1] See Danelski, "The Limits of Law," p. 8 in this volume.

[2] In Hart, *The Concept of Law* (1961), chap. X, the author argues persuasively for the position that such self-imposed obligations should be included within the purview of "international law."

[3] Roscoe Pound, "The Limits of Effective Legal Action," *American Bar Association Journal*, 3 (1917), 55, 66.

[4] Cardozo, *The Nature of the Judicial Process* (1921), p. 166.

4

THE PSYCHOLOGICAL LIMITS
OF LEGALITY

June Louin Tapp

THESIS AND TASKS

"Limit" and "limits": these are the concerns of current rule system analysts whether in law or psychology. These control and capacity notions are juxtaposed against goals and principles of dignity and volition, reason and responsibility, order and freedom. Any examination of contemporary crises (self-destruction, environmental pollution, mob violence) calls into question present laws of behavioral control—personal or social. Any further examination of contemporary crises reveals unprecedented revolutions and counterrevolutions in

I wish to acknowledge Felice J. Levine and Robert B. Tapp for their invaluable assistance and advice in the completion of this chapter. Some of the ideas on human legal development will appear in my forthcoming book with Felice J. Levine, *The Jurisprudence of Youth*. Although this present writing was finished during my tenure as a Fellow in Law and Psychology (1972) at the Harvard Law School, I also wish to thank the American Bar Foundation for its support and Brenda Smith, who typed the final version.

civil rights (women and ethnics), education (community control and student representation), crime control (no knock and preventive detention), and traditional "morality" (abortion and pornography). Just as important, they disclose too that both the legal and the psychological pervade the social issues dominating modern cultures.

Thus, any assessment of the limits of the law must consider the limits imposed by the configuration and impact of human legal development. The necessity of exploring the relationship of the psychological to the legal in defining the limits of the law was succinctly captured in Roscoe Pound's recognition of "the inapplicability of the legal machinery of precept and sanction to many phases of human conduct, to many important human relations, and to some serious wrongs."[1] The vitality of the position reappears in Lon Fuller's recent charge: "The pressure of our present predicament pushes us—as we have not been pushed for a long time—toward an effort at comprehension. We must come to perceive and understand the moral and psychological forces that underlie law generally and give it efficacy in human affairs."[2] Consistent with these theoretical assertations and my own research, I submit that the "true" limits of the law are psychological—and empirically describable. While the law can hamper realization of those limits (i.e., capacities), they are more readily attained insofar as the law (1) is congruent with them and (2) facilitates movement to higher levels of legality. Under such conditions both the limits of the law and the psychological legal limits are appropriately extended.

In sum, through comprehending the relationship of psychological variables to legal ones, the limits of principled. efficient, and just rule-guided behavior can be clarified. Ultimately the determination of the ethical limits of law (how and how far should the law go?) rests on answers to questions about the psychological limits of humans (how far can individual legal reasoning go?). So, briefly, read the theses and tasks of this chapter.

SOCIALIZING OR EDUCATIVE ROLE OF THE LAW

Value of Socialization

Effective communication about the law and its limits requires comprehending the legal worlds—the structures of legal reasoning—of children and adults. It is no longer necessary to draw information about the cognitive maps of individuals and legal cultures from casual conversations or conceptual debates.[3] No longer need we work in the dark regarding the characteristics of legal development, the origins of compliance, or the ethical utilization of rule systems and the law. Scientific studies are available which provide this information and insight.

Fellow contributors to this symposium, Daniel Danelski and Kenneth Dolbeare, also speak to the necessity of extending legal research efforts to attitudes and values, especially youth's. Dolbeare argues that such research is essential to (1) understanding "current concepts and uses of the law," (2) moving beyond purposes of "social management and 'rehabilitation,'" and (3) transcending "existing conceptual assumptions."[4] He is surely correct that studies of preadult socialization offer a new perspective on the relationship between value change and the current status of the law.[5] Similarly, Danelski accurately maintains that legal socialization is a key to understanding law and its limits but may overstate the case by claiming that "relatively little is known" about it.[6] While there is still a paucity of hard data, the recent work of several developmental social psychologists provides some of the requisite knowledge. To that reported in my colleagues' papers, I add other equally relevant work within these pages and by citation on the socialized and socializable limits.[7]

Indeed, the legal socialization process vitally determines the course of human legal reasoning.[8] With few exceptions, the "traditional" shapers of individual moral and social education in all cultures are the home, the church, the peer group, and the school. The burgeoning "legal" nature of civilization—a by-product of cultural complexity and modernity—necessitates inclusion of a fifth: the law.[9] For example, recent research stresses the impact of the legal network on conceptualizations of law, justice, and authority and derivative acts of compliance or deviance.[10] Accompanying this increased visibility of law is a reinterpretation of the law's educative or socializing functions, not only in the East but in the West as well.[11] Edwin Schur describes this functional trend of the law as a socializing mechanism as "a general feature of legal development in modern industrial societies."[12] The respective legal and psychological works of Harold Berman[13] and Urie Bronfenbrenner[14] on the U.S.S.R. provocatively corroborate the allocation of "social" education to more than the traditional socializing agents. Evidently in complex societies, the maintenance and refinement of social values concentrate in a set of institutions which includes the courts, the police, and many other structures of the legal system. Therefore, increased attention must be paid to the role of the law in the socialization process and to the impact of its contexts (courtrooms, administrative agencies), agents (judges, legislators), and strategies (reform goals of legal services agencies, family courts) on extending the psychological limits of legality.

Reciprocity of Legal Socialization

The strategic importance of the law as a legal socializing agent is preeminent. While legal socialization encompasses role orientations to various legal or rule systems, this chapter particularly focuses on the interaction between the institution of law and the structures of human legal reasoning. Through its decisions and directives, the law socializes and is affected by socialization—a reciprocal process in which it is both an independent and dependent variable. Thus, if society's agents are not merely to institutionalize blind obedience but are to stimulate the evolution of an ethical legal system, they must understand more fully the process of developing and crystallizing legal values. They must willingly see that the laws of a society as much as its child-rearing practices reflect hypotheses about the nature of humans. Both are telling commentaries.

The searing issue is whether adult authorities have presented a socializing framework in their most venerable, specialized rule system (i.e., the law) which is both philosophically and psychologically sound.[15] Is the law as presently interpreted consistent with acknowledged principled positions such as the "official morality" of the U.S. Constitution and congruent with psychological assessments of ethical ideological growth? Basically, the problem facing law makers and legal socializers alike is whether current styles and statutes will encourage individuation and expression, reason and order, justice and independence *or* court dehumanization and repression, impulse and chaos, bias and dependence. The former constellations are the avowed goals of both a law and a psychology pledged to educating a rational, efficient, democratic, compassionate, justice-seeking society. If the law as a prime educating force is incompatible with these goals, modes of deviance, dissent, and distrust will prevail, and the probability of effectuating a high-order sense of legality will be substantially reduced.

While exploring the limits of the law is difficult, my premise is that the task can be eased through familiarity with psychological investigations of youth's attitudes toward laws, rules, authority, and justice. An empirical assessment of the development of ethical legal reasoning should facilitate elaborating the conditions that accelerate or retard such growth in both the law and its citizenry. In sum, then, the psychological contributes both a measure of and a mode for creating new boundaries for the limits of law. In order to elucidate this point, I shall: (1) undertake to dispel the myths of dissociation, lawlessness, and legality, (2) build a cognitive map of legal development utilizing theoretical and empirical evidence from psychology, and (3) consider the implications for the role of the law. Throughout I shall draw heavily from jurisprudential and psychological sources, convinced that both perspectives are necessary to achieve a full understanding of the ethical utilization of the law.

MYTHS IN THE LAW

Many myths obfuscate considerations about the limits of the law as well as determinations about the limits of individual legal reasoning. While myths or legal fictions may be viewed by system sustainers as necessary, they are usually counterproductive paradigms for growth and development.[16] For this reason, definitions and limits must be examined for their logical and psychological veracity or their mythical and fictitious quality. If in the face of evidence—psychological or legal—empirical assumptions are found wanting, they should be dispelled and dismissed. Only by incorporating an empirical scientific base can we move beyond conceptual debates and legal fictions.[17] Ultimately such examination is essential to testing and extending the limits of law and attaining the limits of human nature. In short, unless psychological limits are assessed empirically, perspectives on the potentialities of legal development, legal reasoning, or the law are limited.

The Myth of Dissociation

The real issue of this chapter is the myth of the separateness of psychological and legal limits. Both are inextricably interwoven.

Psychological limits constrain the law; legal limits place boundaries on psychological growth. For example, legal limits restrict psychological growth through statutes governing many victimless crimes or ordinances perpetuating discrimination.[18] While the attainment of a fully matured, sophisticated, and ethical legality *is* limited by the organism's capacity, that capacity can normally extend much beyond what is anticipated by ordinary and/or conventional state law.

The possibilities for ethical utilization of the law that knowledge about psychological limits could provide remain to be explored. There is evidence in our culture and others that individuals are capable of reaching highly principled stages of legality, e.g., Socrates, Asoka, Jesus, Thomas Jefferson, Mahatma Gandhi, Albert Schweitzer, Martin Luther King, and Daniel Ellsberg. Our belief in the relatedness of principled psychological and legal limits, however, does not preclude recognition that the dominant or modal reasoning in most societies reveals a less principled, conventional posture. But the presence of exemplary historical figures in many cultures and the empirical psychological evidence in my own and colleagues' work certainly suggest the potentiality of legal growth for more persons and the eventuality of a legal system dependent on justice and compassion rather than on uncritical rule maintenance and distrust.[19] In sum, the point is simple: the development and institution of the law are bound by the capacities—the "legal quotients"—of the human animal.[20] But, the law functions as socializer and creator of the contexts necessary to extend the legal quotient (LQ) in human legal development.

Since—within the framework of this biosocial, interactive model—the legal system in a very real sense can limit one's legal quotient, the "legal" level of the system is eminently important. When, for example, it embodies an uncritical, law-and-order approach, psychological evidence shows that a majority of the population expresses the same level of reasoning. In order to achieve the highest principled levels of human legal development, a system needs to esteem such values as life, reciprocity, trust, and impartiality and provide channels for their expression by more than a modest group of persons.

One merely needs to examine legislation on victimless crimes (homosexual relations between consenting adults, drunkenness, and use of marijuana) to realize the association of the legal with the psychological and the moral with the legal.[21] Laws that are incompatible with ethical values or psychological capacities create confusion regarding the meanings of compliance and deviance, independence and obedience, obligation and loyalty. Harold Berman puts the problem succinctly: "The official law of the state, with its authoritative technical language and its professional practitioners, cannot do violence to the unofficial law-consciousness of the people without creating serious tensions in society."[22] True, the law is limited by human capacities and needs otherwise known as psychological limits, but more importantly these "limits"—when developed to their limit—have been shown empirically to encompass ethical principles of justice. Ultimately, the law's role and efficacy will be measured by its success in moving humankind to attitudes and acts of justice in administering justice, achieving law and order, and engendering legal compliance. To attain these ends, the law must be consonant with the limits of human legality.

The Myths of Lawlessness and Legality

The difficulty in defining law is historical. From fellow contributors to this volume (Danelski and Dolbeare) to other commentators on the legal scene (Selznick and Shklar) to outstanding jurisprudents (Fuller and Llewellyn), the law has been variously described as bewildering, wretched, inchoate, abstract, and erratic. Frequently the same persons describe it as never neutral, evocative, authoritative, inclusive, interactive, and as a baseline for morality and legality.[23] Any consideration of the limits of the law is affected by the broadness or narrowness of these descriptions as well as by the willingness of law makers to believe in the myth of humankind's lawlessness and the fiction of the law as the only font of legality. My approach and the research reported herein are concerned with *nomos* defined as the. study of human rule systems and human rule-guided potentialities for obeying, maintaining, and creating law. For me, the law reflects two overarching human needs also evident in all other rule systems: (1) a nomotic—rule-guided or law-consciousness—ability and (2) a legal justice quest.[24]

1. In describing the nomotic quality of the human organism, the tendency is to focus solely upon individuals as inherently rule breakers and as optimally only rule obeyers or rule maintainers, not rule creators. Even in Zimbardo's psychological experiments, in which he investigated the willingness of subjects to wreck an unattended car, he discusses only tangentially the fact that the number

of people *not* willing to wreck the car was twice that of those prepared to engage in vandalism.[25] The wish to describe people as lawless creatures incapable of becoming lawful and ethical stems from a cynicism about basic needs. However, empirical evidence from Mead's and Piaget's observations on game rules,[26] through Weyrauch's NASA penthouse experience,[27] to Kohlberg's replication of Piaget's report on children's moral development[28] should dispel the myth of lawlessness perpetrated by the law-and-order cult. The search for rules and rule dependency appears early in human life and is visible across all activity from games to government and language to law.[29] In fact, rule-guided behavior is so prevalent that it is hard to imagine a group without some type of order.[30] In essence, no community is truly lawless.[31]

Inherent in the myth of lawlessness seems to be the desire to see mortals as irrational, the post-Freudian rendition of demonic. This view tends to encourage, breed, and perpetuate a legal system with a law-and-order mentality that seeks to restrain, repress, and depersonalize humanity. Rather than push for expression and explanation, its enacted laws demand blind obedience as well as physical deference and total conformity. To the psychological observer, the myth of lawlessness is almost the converse of or reaction formation to the myth of legal certainty criticized long ago by Jerome Frank.[32] Both fear a loss of control; both infer irresponsibility. In dismissing the myth of lawlessness, we take one step further toward liberating both humankind and law from the labels that restrict attainment of a truly ethical legality.

2. Another stumbling block impeding this growth is the myth that the law is the major institutional source of rule-guided behavior. Perhaps the desire to make legalities the exclusive property of the law is related to the belief that binding authoritativeness can only occur where force is assured.[33] Decidedly, "the rules" in various realms diverge, but certain elements appear common to all systems, e.g., the structuring quality, the expected compliance, and the overriding ethic of justice. Since the need for rules is present in all human social relations, all social systems—not just the law—are in some sense legal. Such continuity speaks for a broader definition of law than the more common but restrictive focus on government (i.e., state) law. This perspective is congruent with Lon Fuller's contention that the word "law" be "construed very broadly . . . to include not only the legal systems of states and nations, but also the smaller systems— at least 'law-like' in structure and function—to be found in labor

unions, professional associations, clubs, churches, and universities."[34]
In treating law as an interactional process found in many settings,
Fuller generates a conceptualization of the law not as an exercise
of authority for effectuating social control but as a framework for
facilitating human interaction.

The crippling aspect of the legality myth is the assumption that
legality and its correlates of justice, obligation, and responsibility
reside only in the law. Such a stance ignores the reality that humankind operates in a network of rule systems which guides behavior and
is experientially "legal." This myth results in the belief that only
the law can create law and order, produce a rule of law, and procure
the administration of justice. If contemporary humanity continues
to see legality as resident only in the law, then the emergence of an
authoritarian repressive law is more likely. If instead legality is seen
as the property of all rule systems, then the law is more likely to
emerge as an expressive, participatory instrument of social change.

The promise of the law in the twentieth-century crisis lies in its
ability to (1) articulate laws that will reflect the powerful rule-guided
and justice-seeking needs of the human psyche and (2) incorporate
the legal component from experiences in other rule systems into
the structure and functioning of the law. Such an incorporation
should simultaneously move society toward a more dynamic and
more enduring rule of law because it is congruent with the psychological capacities of developing human organisms. The current scene
presents stark testimony to the jeopardy inherent in considering the
property of legality the estate only of the law.

A COGNITIVE THEORY OF LEGAL DEVELOPMENT

In view of the damaging impact of these myths in the law,
the legal socialization process is most insightfully *logical* and *psychological* when it circumscribes the limits of law while remaining
cognizant of individual and institutional capacities. The recitation
of the problem and promise of socialization—whether moral, political,
or legal—is a tedious task.[35] But, while the reiteration of stated aims
is a monument to human purposiveness, idealism, and rationality,
the repetition of history's failures remains a glaring testament to the
inadequacy of past methods.

Theoretical Model of Psychological Limits

A cognitive theory of legal development provides a new approach. A developmental analysis of the growth of attitudes in normal children from kindergarten to college elucidates the real psychological limits of the law and the psychological origins of legality. Information on how youth's emergent jurisprudence affects perceptions of a rule system and interactions with its authorities yields an analytic description of human legal reasoning founded on empirical data, not on intuitive assumptions or conceptual debate.

Legal development, as elaborated in recent social psychological research, is influenced by the cognitive theories of moral development introduced by Jean Piaget and refined by Lawrence Kohlberg.[36] In a recent exercise in crossing theories and methods,[37] Tapp's empirically derived interview categories were analyzed in terms of Kohlberg's moral development levels.[38] Paralleling evidence on universal moral levels, the development of individual legal orientations reveals consistent movement from obedience to conformity to principled perspectives. Such a cognitive theory of legal development continues to be useful for assessing the dynamics of legality.

The limits of the law can best be determined by understanding the limits of human legal development as structured by the three major progressions: the preconventional (I), a law-obeying (punishment) deference stance; the conventional (II), a law-and-order maintaining (conformity) posture; and the postconventional (III), a law-creating, principled perspective. Of these three, the second or conventional system maintenance level is modal cross-culturally.[39] Nevertheless, there is evidence cross-culturally and developmentally that individuals have the cognitive ability to reach the third level of legal reasoning. Sufficient though modest numbers of individuals achieve this highest legality wherein they exercise ethical utilization of the law.

Characteristically, preconventional and conventional individuals respond primarily to the fixed rules and values of a society. However, while the former is rigidly oriented to avoidance of physical punishment and unquestioning deference to power, the latter is rigidly oriented to systems of law as identified with and at the core of social order and social welfare. In contrast, those with a postconventional perspective require principles that offer universal and rational criteria for *maintaining* as well as *changing* laws. Thus, for example, the rule-maintaining and rule-making perspectives toward law and society are best distinguished by determining whether one justifies an action because it falls under a practice or justifies the practice.[40] By the third level particularly, the values of justice, communication, and compassion emerge as preeminent criteria for choices—both personal and social.

This cognitive theory approach to human legal development also necessitates a fuller description of the methods of legal socialization. As I previously noted, the demanding reality for the adult authority is to recognize that, while individuals have the cognitive ability to reach the highest level of reasoning, the surrounding educative environment may not be conducive. Since stimulating awareness of ethical legalities on the part of youth and authorities is paramount, if not tantamount, to the development of a just legal order, adults must also attend to their own levels. Socialization agents in courtrooms, on police forces, or in probation offices who themselves are at the modal law-and-order level rather than the ethical utilization-of-the-law level are unlikely to cultivate a preponderance of constitutional or higher ethical legal reasoning. Yet that plane of judgment is precisely the avowed goal or "official morality" of this society.

Jurisprudential Congruence

Philosophically, such a goal for legal socialization incoroprates a morality of aspiration, but it is not devoid of a morality of obligation. The authority of a rule, then, is not wholly determined by formal criteria or external stimuli but also by the inner psychological limits of the human organism. As a foremost proponent of legal naturalism, Lon Fuller appreciates this interactional process and strongly recognizes the basic reciprocity of the moral, legal, and psychological.[41] For Fuller the law is ultimately inspired by a morality of aspiration subsuming a morality of duty. Furthermore, his discussion of the relationship between the morality of aspiration and the morality of duty implies a developmental progression, most clearly evident in his "invisible pointer that marks the dividing line where the pressure of duty leaves off and the challenge of excellence begins."[42] In moving from duty to aspiration, Fuller's analysis bears resemblance to Piaget's shift

from an amoral to a juridical position.[43] It is also congruent with the
Kohlberg moral growth paradigm[44] and the Tapp model of legal
development.[45] In all, philosophically and psychologically, there is
an advance from a dependent, hedonistic, and uncritical mode to
an independent, altruistic, and rational manner.

John Rawls provides another congenial jurisprudential perspective.
While an extensive list could be compiled for the ambiguous term
"justice," Rawls' articulations seem most penetrating and apt.[46] To
him, a sense of justice (or ethical utilization of the law) is a psychological and logical developmental phenomenon. In using an empirical,
developmental social psychological orientation, Rawls attempts to
demonstrate how a "sense of justice may be viewed as the result of
a certain natural development."[47] Drawing heavily upon Piaget's
model, his detailed construction of the three developmental stages
of justice (authority, association, and principle) highlights the requisite
experiences of trust and love, cooperation and friendship, role taking
and empathy. Rawls recognizes that the ethic of justice, although
part of the individual's human capacity (natural), requires the nour-
ishment (social) of love and trust, and participation and mutuality.
In addition to characterizing the developmental process for acquiring
a sense of justice, Rawls identifies justice as a prerequisite for a
constitutional democracy as well as a universal ethic. He portrays
an efficient, just society as "evolving in a morally right direction,
toward a condition of greatest equal talent, composed of men who
can cope with complexity. It is a picture of . . . equilibrium . . . in
which human development once again displays moral direction and
structure."[48] Rawls' approach is both pluralistic and individualistic,
thus permitting analysis of the interactive and communicative processes
involved in developing senses of justice. More than that, it recognizes
that cognitive and affective as well conative experiences are instrumental to the development of principled states of both legality and
morality.

Strengths of a Cognitive Legal Theory

The intent of this chapter is precisely to demonstrate through
empirical evidence a way to encourage the exercise of intelligent,
ethical legal judgment in democratic personalities. Historically, different psychological approaches—each essaying a view of man—have
been used to study rule acquisition. Briefly, for example, social group

or role theory portrays the individual as a mirror of others' expectations; psychoanalytic theory depicts a struggling ego balancing id and superego; and social learning theory perceives a network of trained "moralities." Though one should be highly suspicious of an explanation of legal development in terms of any one theory, the heuristic advantages of the cognitive developmental approach over other learning theories are well and extensively documented.[49]

A cognitive developmental analysis of the emergence of legal judgment most cogently reveals the human animal's protoethical need. This ability, which biologists report as well, is mediated through environments: "Such behavior is 'inherited' and becomes to some extent built into each individual through the 'conscience' mechanism and it is reinforced and maintained in society by a range of devices from informal sanctions to the formal threat of law."[50] The cognitive developmental approach accounts for both the logical and psychological. Evolutionary in perspective, it emphasizes the importance of intelligence and interaction.

This approach to legal development—when broadly conceived—has the capacity to incorporate other theoretical systems without doing violence to either its own assumptions or those assimilated. For example, although both cognitive development and social learning theories—which respectively emphasize "natural" development and "societal" training—try to comprehend the legal socialization process, the cognitive developmental viewpoint concentrates more clearly on changes in organized thought as affected by a biosocial interaction. Social learning theory, like psychoanalytic theory, emphasizes the critical nature of the affective relationship between children and parents; cognitive theory argues this as only one important context and aspect. While both cognitive and social learning theorists study the formation of attitudes and actions, the latter group stresses that social development essentially reflects the influence of training, modeling, and identification with agents, such as parents and teachers.[51] In so doing they dismiss the strengths of cognitive theory. By minimizing the individual's capacities for differentiating, integrating, generalizing, and conceptualizing, the social learning theorists view the acquisition of norms more as a passive than a participatory activity.

Cognitive developmental theory allows for individual creativity in devising rules, irrespective of the rules of authority but respectful of the interplay between the "natural" rules of development and the "social" conditions that minimize of maximize intellectual development. While from the perspective of internalizing legal values and behaviors "both formulations are right to a degree,"[52] cognitive theory pays greater heed to the creative (i.e., intellectual capacity, originator of ideas), adaptive (i.e., interactive, conflict-resolver), and commitment (i.e., obligatory, justice-seeker) capacities of the human species. Built upon an assumption of cognitive control of motivation, a cognitive theory of development neither negates nor ignores the impact of social forces or the force of the interaction between the internal and external, the natural and social, the given and acquired.[53] But, in this biosocial, interactive perspective, the locus of control is shifted from external to internal stimuli. Thus, the final appeal of a cognitive developmental explanation of ethical legal thought is its refusal to accept the preeminence of irrationality. Law built on an hypothesis of humankind as demonic (irrational) must be repressive; law built on an hypothesis of competence (rational) is more likely to be expressive.

Empirical Evidence for the Limits of the Law

To illustrate the strengths of cognitive developmental assumptions, I present analyses of answers to four interview questions excerpted from my forthcoming book *The Jurisprudence of Youth* (with Felice J. Levine).[54] My goal herein is twofold. First, I want to describe the progressive levels of legality and demonstrate that higher levels are attainable by normal individuals. Second, instead of solely presenting a theoretical proposition that might be regarded by some as mythical, I intend to examine its empirical validity.

Assessments of the purposes of rules and laws, motivations for legal compliance, and criteria regarding justice are some of the dimensions of a jurisprudence that influence the limits of an individual's legal judgment. For example, an uncritical, law-and-order image of the law (II) may form the basis of a decision to kill "the enemy" or not to steal drugs for a dying wife. Conversely, evaluation of the internal morality of a rule (III) may provide sufficient justification for legal compliance even when the possibility of detection for violation is remote.

According to cognitive developmental theory, with increasing maturity children—though cognizant of the purpose of rules—see them as less divine and immutable. Even by the primary grades most children recognized the legitimacy of rule changing. Their

estimate of the legitimacy of rule breaking, another aspect of the
fixity and authoritative power of rules, was probed by asking "Are
there times when it might be right to break a rule?" While 55
percent of the youngest children equated rule breaking per se with
badness (level I), there was marked developmental progression toward
greater flexibility so that only 7 percent of the middle schoolers
retained such a preconventional posture. Furthermore, by preadolescence significantly more children described the conditions pre-
cluding compliance. This pattern reflected augmented skills of legal
reasoning and broadened moral judgments. Rules were less likely to
be portrayed as inevitable, irrevocable, or infallible by older youth;
simultaneously, there was evidence of internalized baselines which
guided determining conditions for obedience.

One condition cited at the conventional level of legal judgment
was the *morality of the circumstance* (level II): Transgressions are
legitimate under emergency circumstances, especially where potential
harm to others may be averted. This mode of reasoning was typically
a middle school approach (73 percent), and decreased significantly
by college age (35 percent). As a grade 8 preadolescent boy observed,
"Well, it depends on what's going on. If it's a matter of life and
death or you know something pretty important, then it's all right.
But it should be followed as much as possible."

By college, circumstantial rationales were superseded by serious
ethical concerns about the *morality of the rule* (level III, 54 percent).
The majority of college students argued that expected compliance
must be weighed against the inherent rightness or morality of the
rule, independent of the particular circumstance. Rather than hardship
justifying deviation, the internal morality or justice of the rule was
the primary condition for disobedience, its inherent illegitimacy
sufficient cause for repudiation. A college woman's response was
typical of this position: "[I would break a rule] when the rule is
immoral or unjust. Because I believe that people are morally accountable for their actions, and this is above the law or rules." The
earlier concern with the morality of circumstances rather than with
the morality of the rule suggests a lower-level psychological limit
that emphasizes the accommodation of rules rather than the revocation
of a bad, wrong, or unfair rule. While these older youth recognized the
essential value and role of rules, they were increasingly committed to
a dynamic view of norm building guided by ethical and moral
concerns—the highest limit of legality.

Since rule deviation is a possible consideration in legal reasoning, it is crucial to explore how developing youth variously define the issue of obligation to legal systems. For example, more extensive inquiry should tell us whether repressive or punitive approaches are compatible with realizing the psychological limits of legality or whether most individuals evolve roles vis-à-vis the legal system that are not predicated on fear or expectation of sanctions. Though enforcement of sanctions may be instrumental in gaining overt compliance, neither certainty nor administration of punishment is necessarily a force for engendering obedience. To probe more fully these dynamics of legal compliance, we asked youth "Why should people follow rules?" and "Why do you?"

In explaining the reasons why people ought to obey, the primary school children sought to *avoid negative consequences* such as punishment or harm (level I). A grade 2 girl reasoned, "Because people would be doing anything and the police would try to catch them and it would be bad." By middle school and college this preconventional rationale significantly decreased. Also, a substantial minority of primary schoolers—already equating compliance with *personal conformity* (level II)—were motivated to maintain authority's expectations regarding good behavior. A second-grade boy's comment ("Not to be bad; not doing things they are not supposed to do") exemplified the "being good" view.

By middle school, personal conformity explanations significantly decreased. Instead, a majority—still at the conventional level—offered a broader *social conformity* motive emphasizing law and order. Still a conventional stance, this perspective maintained that compliance with law prevents societal chaos and is, therefore, the best way to behave (level II). Such a social conformity orientation was typically preadolescent, increasing significantly at middle school (53 percent) and decreasing again by college (25 percent). In the words of a grade 8 boy, "Well, sometimes it's for their own good. Or, well, they should follow rules because, well, like you go back to where you had confusion again if you didn't have any rules."

Unlike primary graders (5 percent), a sizable minority at middle school age also gave *rational-beneficial-utilitarian* reasons (level III, 27 percent). A grade 8 girl observed that people ought to obey "for the benefit of everyone, and it makes everything easier actually and easier to live with." This explication generally implied a postconventional legal compliance based on rational choices and utilitarian considerations of individual and social welfare. In contrast to the fixed obligation to obey apparent in personal and social conformity responses, the rational-beneficial-utilitarian explanation supported an obligation based on balancing competing claims and consequences. By college, significantly more students, slightly over half, answered from this vantage. A few also took the postconventional position that internal commitment to underlying *principles* (level III), not conformity per se to concrete rules, should dictate obedience. "People should only follow those they think are fair and just," said a college woman.

While youth's reasons for their own obedient behavior ("Why do you follow rules?") disclosed the same cognitive developmental progression, their responses also differentiated between what ideally should motivate them to obey and what realistically often does. Illustratively, on the ideal "should people" question, 45 percent of the primary schoolers expressed a conventional orientation; in response to the real "do you," only 20 percent attained this limit of legality. Likewise, even at college, although there was generally a significant increase in the postconventional position, more students expressed a conventional orientation on the real; in the ideal situation, 51 percent expressed postconventional rational-beneficial-utilitarian values while in the real only 22 percent did. It is important to note that, by their own self-assessment, these youths generally recognized that their daily behaviors were guided predominantly by a law-and-order maintaining frame, although they realized that purpose and principle should determine compliance and their sense of obligation to rule systems.

If we take both obedience questions together, it appears that youth from kindergarten to college primarily perceived the dynamics of legal compliance not in terms of a simple punishment model but rather in terms of respect for and obligation to maintain rule systems. While only a small minority defined obligation in terms of postconventional compliance to a fundamental ethic of justice overriding all rule systems, preconventional limits of legality based on enforcement and sanction concerns were equally as rare. Clearly, with maturity youth developed a jurisprudence that rejected a punishment-authority stance. While the prevailing limit exhibited by middle school age and crystallized thereafter was one of conventional conformity to the collectivity, achieving a principled legal development is apparently well within normal human potential.

Since optimally a key reason for compliance with a rule is its morality, discerning the requisites of a fair rule and the dynamics of a just system is vitally important to extending the limits of the law. Consistent with previous findings, those with a preconventional orientation predictably will accept all authoritative directives as sacred and just per se, but those who achieve a postconventional reasoning will assess and make rules in terms of fundamental interpersonal rights. To probe the development of a sense of legal justice, the rather simple open-ended question "What is a fair rule?" was asked.

Developmentally, four dimensions (equality, beneficial-rational, consensual-supportive, and human rights-freedom) were crucial to youth's conceptions of justice. Since of these four dimensions only that of human rights strongly implied evaluating a rule against universal, independent, and prior principles, it is singularly postconventional. In terms of conceptualizing the limits of legal development, however, it is probably more accurate to view all these concepts as having a cumulative or additive effect on legal judgment. A grade 8 boy's response illustrated *equality:* "A rule that would apply to everyone equally. It wouldn't put one person out and another person in." On *beneficial-rational,* a kindergarten boy explained: "A fair rule is to be good and nice to everyone because you'll get along better." The *consensual-supportive* aspect appeared in this preadolescent boy's answer: "When somebody suggests a rule and everybody thinks it's right, then it's fair." Finally the *human rights-freedom* component was evident in this college man's reply: "One which allows much individual freedom of behavior yet protects rights of others."

The configuration of these responses at each age level revealed several striking developmental patterns. First, indicating a preconventional, uncritical acceptance of authority, only primary schoolers (20 percent) maintained that *all* rules are fair (level I). (In addition, almost none were willing to see a rule described as fair solely because of its creation by an *authority.*) Second, for all three groups, conventional concerns about equality and rationality were the most frequent responses (level II). In the main, equality answers oriented toward uniform and regular administration of the law; beneficial-rational considerations focused on fair law serving social functions of helping everyone. Both concepts were expressed in system-maintenance terms for the given legal order; few moved beyond to emphasize that an ethical consideration of rights must guide the making of rules as well. Although equality significantly decreased between middle school and college, both equality and rationality were anticipated early and retained their primacy across the age spans.

The emergence of the consensual-supportive dimension (level II) at preadolescence was a significant indicator of developing expectations for participation, social acknowledgment, and group effort. The wish for cooperative involvement, autonomy, and constitutionalism was less strong in the more authority-oriented, heteronomous younger group. However, youth's interest in popular agreement is likewise viewed as conventional. While consensual support is an important procedural component of fairness, for youth to focus on this component—without simultaneously acknowledging that laws must also reflect, serve, and be evaluated independently by justice principles—is to elevate the general will into a sacred entity.

By college, the fourth dimension—human rights and individual freedoms—emerged as essential for a small number of youth (level III). Nor was this additional aspect included at the expense of dismissing the other dimensions characterizing a fair rule. Rather than denying the other three elements, the college group's focus on guarantees of civil liberties further elaborated their perception of a fair legal system.

From the foregoing responses, it is clear most youth from kindergarten to college feel that neither absolutist positions nor authoritative fiats can insure legal justice. Instead, justice may be guaranteed through infusion of equality, rationality, consensus, and respect for individuals. In essence, the emergent assessment of fairness revealed a focus on components that are substantively and procedurally essential to a just jurisprudence. The jurisprudence of youth at its best envisions justice as the goal of law, not law at the expense of justice. But that only a small minority even at college age assessed rule fairness in terms of human rights and individual freedom again underscores the contention that conventional legality is dominant among youth. In considering these results and other data analyzed over some 50 questions, surprisingly—given a sloganized Bill of Rights emphasis—relatively few children associated civil liberties with depicting rule fairness.[55] Evidently, abstract teaching of a concept without experience-based activity in personal interactional situations is insufficient for developing values to the limtis of human potential.

As must be apparent, part of what seems to be occurring in the development of legal reasoning is a changing conception of rights and roles vis-à-vis authoritative rule systems. Basically, the largest proportion of this sample of U.S. youth are rule maintainers in orientation, decidely conventional and uncritically compliant in their estimates of the legal process. However, it is not preconventional punishment avoidance that primarily motivates or reinforces their obedient orientations. Most individuals apparently stablize at a law-and-order conforming level wherein there is no distinction between basic, underlying principles of justice and the legal system itself. Such a position confuses loyalty and obedience, and commitment to law with commitment to legal justice. Only the modest number who reach a postconventional stance are truly able to accept that they can internalize the values and principles of a system and, simultaneously, in judging the system by these standards, not be obligated to obey an unfair rule. To encourage these higher limits of legality, agents of socialization may need to define new goals and appraise old values.

IMPLICATIONS FOR THE ROLE OF THE LAW

Julius Stone has observed that, while the law cannot produce creative thought, it can foster the conditions necessary for its appearance.[56] In order for the law to help achieve that constellation of values, attitudes, and behaviors coincident with human psychological limits, the law must accept its educative (socializing), experimental (reform), and principled (ethical) roles.

For some the law is a primary vehicle for effecting change; for others it is a mechanism for deflecting efforts toward change. Implicit in these goals are inferences about the educative, experimental, and control purposes and roles of the law. For many the law has been more parochial and less stimulating than anticipated. Such a narrowness accomplishes only an insularity that avoids scientific empirical examination and experimental endeavors. Dismissing an interdisciplinary, cosmopolitan orientation, the law has frequently failed in its socializing and reform missions. The result is a state of conventionality that sanctifies tradition and limits the law from moving to more expressive, sophisticated, and ethical levels.

Explicit findings now available from systematic empirical studies multiply propositions about the possibilities of change in legal education. This presence of a body of knowledge must be reckoned with the law's purpose and role *and* be absorbed into the structure and functioning of the law. Viewing reforms in legal socialization as experiments suggests one way of utilizing the law to effect change and attain ideals through legal enactments.[57] After all, what makes a brave new world is that it has brave people in it!

In essence, the aim of socialization, be it legal or otherwise, is to elevate individuals (and society) above the dominant conventional plateau and to urge them to go beyond the satisfactory to the excellent and the just. This approach to legality builds on the common characteristics of human beings—their nomotic and justice-seeking qualities. Commenting on this need for "perfectibility," Richard Flathman notes: "it is a morality that urges man to press beyond a satisfactory life to a life of excellence, to aspire to the achievements of saints and heroes."[58]

The stress on the possibility of human "perfectibility" is not only the wish of legal and/or moral philosophers. Philip Zimbardo's definition of "individuation" reflects it as well: "To be singular, to stand apart from other men and to aspire to Godhead, to honor social contracts and man-made commitments above family-bonds. . ."[59] The possibility of "perfectibility" and "individuation" is recognized particularly among clinical and personality psychologists also concerned with describing the mentally healthy, the self-actualized, the identified, and the mature.[60] Pervading these ideal aims are such qualities as empathy, cooperation, self-esteem, and autonomy, which have juridical parallels in such concepts as reciprocity, mutuality, respect, and independence. Since deviant behavior can be labeled as delinquent, criminal, emotionally disturbed, and/or psychologically immature, not only the law or the justice systems are involved with the problem of defining the highest principled level of human interaction. And that which was formally and formerly seen as the domain and goal only of the religious or the psychological is now also seen as the domain and goal of the legal, i.e., living together harmoniously with justice and compassion.

The goals of rule systems bear a startling similarity that would suggest that the limits of one find congruence in the limits of another. As the law takes on more of the socializing functions of the other major institutions, its efficacy will be enhanced if it considers and incorporates knowledge about psychological limits. Fortunately, human development can potentially display as its goal a just society. One question remains: can the law socialize its own limit sufficiently to guarantee the greatest ethical extension of this human limit?

REFERENCES

[1] Roscoe Pound, *Jurisprudence* (St. Paul, Minn.: West, 1959), vol. III, p. 359. Pound presented his ideas on "The Limits of Effective Legal Action" as early as 1916 and 1917 (*ibid.*, p. 353, n. 1). In his discussion of "the socialization of law," Pound further expounded the necessary absorption of social science ideas into the law (*ibid.*, vol. I, p. 431).

[2] Lon L. Fuller, "Human Interaction and the Law," *The American Journal of Jurisprudence*, 14 (1969), 1.

[3] Legal culture, a key concept for the law, is defined by Lawrence M. Friedman as "the network of values and attitudes relating to law, which determines when and why and where people turn to law or government, or turn away [as well as determining] the place of the legal system in the culture of the society as a whole" in "Legal Culture and Social Development," *Law and Society Review*, 4 (August 1969), 34.

[4] Kenneth M. Dolbeare, Chap. 14, pp. 225-226, of this volume.

[5] *Ibid.*, p. 226.

[6] David J. Danelski, Chap. 1, p. 9, of this volume.

[7] For legal socialization, see the entire symposium "Socialization, the Law, and Society," June L. Tapp, issue ed., *Journal of Social Issues*, 27:2, (1971); in particular therein, June L. Tapp and Lawrence Kohlberg, "Developing Senses of Law and Legal Justice," pp. 65-91. See also June Louin Tapp and Felice J. Levine, "Persuasion to Virtue: A Preliminary Statement," *Law and Society Review*, 4 (May 1970), 565-582; Joseph Adelson, Bernard Green, and Robert P. O'Neil, "The Growth of the Idea of Law in Adolescence," *Journal of Developmental Psychology*, 1, (July 1969), 27-32; Joseph Adelson and Lynnette Beall, "Adolescent Perspectives on Law and Government," *Law and Society Review*, 4 (May 1970), 495-504. For an excellent overview of political socialization, see David O. Sears, "Political Behavior," in Gardner Lindzey and Elliot Aronson, eds., *The Handbook of Social Psychology*, 2d ed. (Reading, Mass.: Addison-Wesley, 1969), vol. V, pp. 315-458. Also for exemplary relevant research, see Fred I. Greenstein, *Children and Politics* (New Haven: Yale University Press, 1965); Robert D. Hess and Judith V. Torney, *The Development of Political Attitudes in Children* (Chicago: Aldine, 1967); David Easton and Jack Dennis, *Children in the Political System: Origins of Political Legitimacy* (New York: McGraw-Hill, 1969). For a comprehensive bibliography and analysis of several research strategies in moral development, see Derek Wright, *The Psychology of Moral Behavior* (Baltimore: Penguin, 1971). For the cognitive developmental approach, see, e.g., Jean Piaget, *The Moral Judgment of the Child* (New York: Kegan Paul Trench, Trubner, 1932); Lawrence Kohlberg, "The Development of Children's Orientations Toward a Moral Order: I. Sequence in the Development of Moral Thought," *Vita Humana*, 6 (Winter/ Spring 1963), 11-33; *id.*, "Development of Moral Character and Moral Ideology," in Martin L. Hoffman and Lois W. Hoffman, eds., *Review of Child Development Research* (New York: Russell Sage Foundation, 1964), vol. I, pp. 383-431; *id.*, "Stage and Sequence: The Cognitive Developmental Approach to Socialization," in David A. Goslin, ed., *Handbook of Socialization Theory and Research* (Chicago: Rand McNally, 1969), pp. 347-480; Lawrence Kohlberg and Elliot Turiel, "Moral Development and Moral Education," in Gerald Lesser, ed., *Psychology and Educational Practice* (Chicago: Scott, Foresman, 1971), pp.

410-465; Kohlberg and R. Kramer, "Continuities and Discontinuities in Child-hood and Adult Moral Development," *Human Development*, 12 (Spring 1969) 93-120.

[8] For a more detailed perspective and analysis of the legal socialization process, see Tapp, issue ed., "Socialization, the Law, and Society," *Journal of Social Issues*. In that issue both psychologists and lawyers address them-selves to various nuances of this important topic. For example, Lawrence M. Friedman in "The Idea of Right as a Social and Legal Concept," p. 189, reaffirms the crucial importance of knowing "how children learn about the legal culture; how they learn about law and authority, about rules, punishments, and norms," Friedman particularly focuses on the socialization of the concept of rights, convinced it is basic to understanding legal orientations.

[9] Concomitant with modernization are feelings of psychological mobility, I use the term "psychological mobility" to describe the new boundaries for self experienced with social, economic, and geographic mobility. The greater probability of "achieving" and "developing" experiences in the twentieth century, enhanced by urbanization and technology, can produce more oppor-tunities to achieve self-hood (or self-actualization). The difficulty in accepting autonomy is exemplified in expressions of alienation frequently found in the "mobile." I will further explore this idea as well as the notion of the law as a "mobility belt" to the socialization of rights in subsequent research on ethnic legal cultures.

[10] See, e.g., Albert Reiss, "Social Organization and Socialization: Variations on a Theme about Generations," Center for Research on Social Organization, University of Michigan, Working Paper No. 1 (Ann Arbor, 1965); David Matza, *Delinquency and Drift* (New York: John Wiley, 1964); Robert M. Carter, "Upper-Class and Middle-Class Delinquency," *Medical Arts and Sciences: Journal of Loma Linda University School of Medicine*, 22:1 (1968), 3-17; Norman Lefstein, Vaughan Stapleton, and Lee Teitelbaum, "In Search of Juvenile Justice: *Gault* and Its Implementation," *Law and Society Review*, 3 (May 1969), 491-562; Herbert Jacob, "Black and White Perceptions of Justice in the City," *Law and Society Review*, 6 (August 1971), 69-89, Paul D. Lipsitt, "The Juvenile Offender's Perceptions," *Crime and Delinquency*, 14 (January 1968), 49-62; "The Challenge of Crime in a Free Society," *President's Commission on Law Enforcement and Administration of Justice*, Nicholas deB. Katzenbach, Chm. (Washington: U.S. Government Printing Office, 1967).

[11] See Harold J. Berman, *Justice in the U.S.S.R.* (Cambridge, Mass.: Harvard University Press, 1963), and his "The Educational Role of the Soviet Court," *International and Comparative Law Quarterly* (in press). For additional per-spectives on Western legal cultures, see also Johannes Andenaes, "The General Preventive Effects of Punishment," *University of Pennsylvania Law Review*, 114 (May 1966), 949-983; *id.*, "The Moral or Educative Influence of Criminal Law," *Journal of Social Issues*, 27:2 (1971), 17-31; Paul A. Freund, *On Law and Justice* (Cambridge, Mass.: Harvard University Press, 1968). For another vignette, see Donald Eugene Smith, *India as a Secular State* (Princeton, N.J.: Princeton University Press, 1963).

[12] Edwin M. Schur, *Law and Society: A Sociological View* (New York: Random House, 1968), p. 120.

[13] Berman describes the law's function (especially through the court) as an agent of socialization for the entire citizenry, educating the public to societal values and legal expectations; see *Justice in the U.S.S.R.* and "Educational Role." In a revealing comparison in *Justice in the U.S.S.R.*, pp. 333-334, he reports similar ordinances in the U.S.S.R. (from the mid-thirties) and the state

of Oregon (from the forties) which prescribe parents' moral and legal responsibility to bring up (i.e., socialize) their children for honesty and law-abidingness.

14 Urie Bronfenbrenner, *Two Worlds of Childhood: U.S. and U.S.S.R.* (New York: Russell Sage Foundation, 1970); see also his "Soviet Methods of Character Education: Some Implications for Research," *Religious Education-Research Supplement*, LVII (July-August 1962), 345-361.

15 John Dewey, in 1895, articulated the necessary relationship between philosophy and psychology. For present purposes, I suggest substituting the terms "adult authority" for "educator," and "the law" for "the school" or "education": "To the educator, therefore, the only solid ground of assurance that he is not setting up impossible or artificial aims, that he is not using ineffective and perverting methods, is a clear and definite knowledge of the normal end and the normal forms of mental action.... Briefly, only psychology and ethics can take education out of its purely empirical and rule-of-thumb stage. Just as a knowledge of mathematics and mechanics have wrought marvelous improvements in all the arts of construction . . . so a knowledge of the structure and functions of the human being can alone elevate the school from the position of a mere workshop, a more or less cumbrous, uncertain, and even baneful institution, to that of a vital, certain, and effective instrument in the greatest of all constructions—the building of a free and powerful character. . . . Summing up, we may say that the teacher requires a sound knowledge of ethical and psychological principles. . . . *Only knowledge of the order and connection of the stages in the development of the psychical functions can, negatively, guard against these evils, or, positively, insure the full meaning and free, yet orderly or law-abiding, exercise of the psychical powers. In a word, education itself is precisely the work of supplying the conditions which will enable the psychical functions, as they successively arise, to mature and pass into higher functions in the freest and fullest manner, and this result can be secured only by knowledge of the process—that is only by a knowledge of psychology.*" John Dewey, *On Education: Selected Writings*, ed. Reginald Archambault (New York: Modern Library, 1964), pp. 198, 202, 207-208.

16 According to Jerome Frank in *Law and the Modern Mind* (Garden City, N.Y.: Doubleday, 1930), p. 37, lawyers, as professional rationalizers, find the use of myths important and necessary. Frank applied the theories and findings of psychology (e.g., Piaget, Freud) to the processes of legal reasoning and judicial decision in order to dispel the myth of their unrelatedness to the formation of a mature legal system. In an earlier work, *The Paradoxes of Legal Science* (New York: Columbia University Press, 1928), pp. 33-34, Benjamin N. Cardozo wryly noted that "[t]he law is no stranger to the philosophy of the 'As If.' It has built up many of its doctrines by a make-believe that things are other than they are." For a contemporary, empirical illustration of the impact of legal myths, see James Marshall, *Psychology and Law in Conflict* (New York: Bobbs-Merrill, 1966).

17 For arguments on the need "to empiricize the study of law," see June L. Tapp, "Reflections," *Journal of Social Issues*, 27:2 (1971), 3; Jack P. Gibbs, "Definitions of Law and Empirical Questions," *Law and Society Review*, 2 (May 1968), 429-446. For a critical analysis of the meanings of "empirical" and "research" for both law and psychology, see Paul E. Meehl, "Law and the Fireside Inductions," *Journal of Social Issues*, 27:4 (1971); Tapp, "Reflections."

18 See Johannes Andenaes, "Deterrence and Specific Offenses," *University of Chicago Law Review*, 38 (Spring 1971), 537-553. Also see Andenaes, "General

Preventive Effects", *id.*, "Moral or Educative Influence"; Freund, *On Law and Justice,* Chaps. 1 and 2; Schur, *Law and Society,* p. 127.

[19] While studies show the centrality of a conventional conformity posture, normal individuals reason principled decisions too. See the cross-cultural and longitudinal work of Kohlberg and associates; e.g., Kohlberg, "Stage and Sequence"; Kohlberg and Turiel, "Moral Development and Moral Education"; Kohlberg and Kramer, "Continuities and Discontinuities." Also see the work of Tapp and associates, e.g., Tapp and Kohlberg, "Developing Senses," and Tapp and Levine, *The Jurisprudence of Youth,* vis-à-vis legal development. Adelson's research is relevant too; e.g., Adelson, Green, and O'Neil, "Growth of the Idea of Law." Further evidence of the possibilities of principled reasoning in college youth is systematically presented in Norma Haan, M. Brewster Smith, and Jeanne Block, "Moral Reasoning of Young Adults: Political-Social Behavior, Family Background, and Personality Correlates," *Journal of Personality and Social Psychology,* 10 (November 1968), 183-201.

[20] I am suggesting here that there may be a "legal quotient" (LQ) for individuals similar to the intelligence quotient (IQ). Like IQ, the legal quotient (while problematic) is changeable and rarely fully measured, developed, or utilized. Moreover, the extension of its dimensions, like that of the intelligence quotient, is dependent on conducive factors in the environment—in this case the law of the land and the limits of that law.

[21] That these are as much the insights of behavioral scientists as legal deterrence theorists is evidenced, for example, by the work of Edwin M. Schur, *Crimes Without Victims* (Englewood Cliffs, N.J.: Prentice-Hall, 1965); Andenaes, "Deterrence and Specific Offenses"; *id.,* "General Preventive Effects"; *id.,* "Moral or Educative Influence"; Leonard Berkowitz and Nigel Walker, "Law and Moral Judgments," *Sociometry,* 30 (December 1967), 410-422; Franklin Zimring and Gordon Hawkins, "Deterrence and Marginal Groups," *Journal of Research in Crime and Delinquency,* 5 (July 1968), 100-114.

[22] Berman, *Justice in the U.S.S.R.,* p. 279.

[23] In addition to Danelski, pp. 8-27, and Dolbeare, pp. 211-229 *passim,* in this volume, and Fuller, "Human Interaction," p. 25, see also Lon L. Fuller, *The Morality of Law,* rev. ed. (New Haven, Conn.: Yale University Press, 1969); Henry M. Hart, Jr., and John T. McNaughton, "Some Aspects of Evidence and Inference in the Law," in Daniel Lerner, ed., *Evidence and Inference* (Glencoe, Ill.: The Free Press, 1959), pp. 48-49; Karl N. Llewellyn, *Jurisprudence: Realism in Practice and Theory* (Chicago: University of Chicago Press, 1962), pp. 3-4; Judith N. Shklar, *Legalism* (Cambridge, Mass.: Harvard University Press, 1964), p. 32; Philip Selznick, *Law, Society, and Industrial Justice* (New York: Russell Sage Foundation, 1969), Chap. 1 *passim.*

[24] Robert Hogan and Nancy Henley in their provocative "Nomotics," *Law and Society Review,* 5 (August 1970), 135-146, describe the appeal of rule-guided behavior to the human psyche. They explore as well the relationship between achieving morality and internalizing rules of conduct. Their work, like mine, emphasizes the rule-oriented foundations of morality and the morality-oriented foundations of law. Selznick, in *Law, Society, and Industrial Justice,* p. 18, elaborates this perspective further by contending that "in its richest connotation, legality evokes the Greek view of a social order founded in reason whose constitutive principle is justice." These psychological and sociological views are generally consistent with Fuller's jurisprudential ones. Specifically, for example, on the matter of law and morality's shared concerns, Fuller, in *The Morality of Law,* p. 131, writes, "it is as these concerns become increasingly the objects of an explicit responsibility that a legal system is created."

25 Philip G. Zimbardo, "The Human Choice: Individuation, Reason, and Order Versus Deindividuation, Impulse, and Chaos," in William J. Arnold and David Levine, eds., *Nebraska Symposium on Motivation* (Lincoln, Neb.: University of Nebraska Press, 1969), pp. 237-307. Zimbardo's research and analysis of the social conditions (crime control methods) that encourage deindividuated behavior, result in dehumanization, and augment violence are particularly congenial to my ideas on the role of cognitive motivation vis-à-vis choice and control.

26 George Herbert Mead, *Mind, Self, and Society* (Chicago: University of Chicago Press, 1934); Anselm Strauss, *George Herbert Mead on Social Psychology Studies* (New York: Random House, 1967); *id.*, *Moral Judgment.*

27 Walter O. Weyrauch, *The Law of a Small Group: A Report on the Berkeley Experiments with Emphasis on Penthouse V*, Space Sciences Laboratory Social Sciences Project, University of California, Berkeley, Internal Working Paper No. 54 (Berkeley, 1967); *id.*, "Law in Isolation: The Penthouse Astronauts," *Trans-action*, 6 (June 1968), 39-46; *id.*, "The 'Basic Law' or 'Constitution' of a Small Group," *Journal of Social Issues*, 27:2 (1971), 49-63.

28 Kohlberg, "Development of Children's Orientations"; *id.*, "Development of Moral Character"; *id.*, "Stage and Sequence."

29 In addition to references in *supra* notes 24, 26, 27, and 28, see other nomotic or rule structure analyses; e.g., Noam Chomsky, *Aspects of the Theory of Syntax* (Cambridge, Mass.: Massachusetts Institute of Technology Press, 1965); Claude Lévi-Strauss, *The Elementary Structure of Kinship* (Boston: Beacon Press, 1968); *id.*, *Structural Anthropology* (Garden City, N.Y.: Doubleday Anchor Books, 1967); Ludwig Wittgenstein, *Philosophical Investigations* (New York: Macmillan, 1953).

30 See, e.g., psychological research on small groups by Muzafer Sherif, *The Psychology of Social Norms* (New York: Harper, 1936); Solomon E. Asch, *Social Psychology* (Englewood Cliffs, N.J.: Prentice-Hall, 1952); Robert F. Bales and Philip E. Slater, "Role Differentiation in Small Decision-making Groups," in Talcott Parsons and Robert F. Bales *et al.*, *Family, Socialization and Interaction Process* (Glencoe, Ill.: The Free Press, 1955), pp. 259-306; Dorwin Cartwright and Alvin Zander, eds., *Group Dynamics*, 2d ed. (Evanston, Ill.: Row, Peterson, 1960); Barry E. Collins and Bertram H. Raven, "Group Structure: Attraction, Coalitions, Communication, and Power," in Gardner Lindzey and Elliot Aronson, eds., *Handbook of Social Psychology*, 2d ed. (Reading, Mass.: Addison-Wesley, 1969), vol. IV, pp. 102-204; John R. P. French, Jr., and Bertram Raven, "The Bases of Social Power," in Cartwright and Zander, eds., *Group Dynamics*, pp. 607-623. Robert T. Golembiewski, *The Small Group* (Chicago: University of Chicago Press, 1962); A. Paul Hare, Edgar F. Borgatta, and Robert F. Bales, eds., *Small Groups*, 2d ed. (New York: Alfred A. Knopf, 1965).

31 This prevailing "legal" need has been described historically and cross-culturally; see, e.g., Llewellyn, *Jurisprudence*; Pound, *Jurisprudence*, vol. I. Likewise, such a component is apparent both in Berman's "law-consciousness" concept in his *Justice in the U.S.S.R.*, p. 279, and in his noting of Leon Petrazhitskii's views, *ibid.*, pp. 420-423 *passim*, described as well by Shklar, *Legalism*, pp. 58-59. This nomotic need is observable in developmental and cross-cultural studies of children's answers about what would happen if there were no rules; see Adelson, Green, and O'Neil, "Growth of the Idea of Law"; Tapp and Levine, "Persuasion to Virtue."

32 Frank, *Law and the Modern Mind.*

[33] Extending the view further, Selznick in *Law, Society, and Industrial Justice*, p. 7, maintains that "[c]oercion does not make law. . . . [whether in] private or public agencies, the legal element is not the coercion itself but the invocation of authority." Underscoring this perspective on the role of force, Fuller in *The Morality of Law*, p. 108, contends that "[m]ost theories of law either explicitly assert, or tacitly assume, that a distinguishing mark of law consists in the use of coercion or force. That distinguishing mark is not recognized in this volume."

[34] Fuller, "Human Interaction," p. 1; see also his *The Morality of Law*, p. 106, where law is defined as "the enterprise of subjecting human conduct to the governance of rules."

[35] I prefer to distinguish between the legal socialization process and the moral and political socialization processes. While legal socialization overlaps the political and moral, the three realms differ somewhat vis-à-vis interactive "learning" contexts (jail vs. political party), indicators of authority (police vs. president), and topics of emphasis (compliance vs. voting behavior). Legal socialization delineates that aspect of the total socialization process dealing with the network of values, attitudes, and behaviors that constitute the legal in a culture. Not intending to embrace uncritical compliance to legal rules, a legal socialization perspective focuses on individuals' standards used in socio-legal judgments and their role preceptions in relating to systems of law. While legal socialization involves learning about the institution of the law specifically, its orientation extends to the "legal" in all human rule systems generally. See also Tapp, "Reflections"; Tapp and Levine, "Persuasion to Virtue"; Tapp and Levine, *The Jurisprudence of Youth*. The latter work attempts to explore human legal development from childhood to adulthood using theoretical and empirical formulations from law and psychology to analyze responses to classic jurisprudential questions.

[36] Tapp and Kohlberg, "Developing Senses"; Tapp and Levine, "Persuasion to Virtue"; *id.*, *The Jurisprudence of Youth*.

[37] Tapp and Kohlberg, "Developing Senses."

[38] Kohlberg's three levels of moral development (preconventional, conventional, and postconventional) were derived using cross-cultural, developmental, and longitudinal samples. Within each level there are two distinct stages. Immediately following are descriptions of these levels with stages, as they appear in my article with Kohlberg, "Developing Senses," p. 69.

"At the preconventional level (I), the cultural labels of 'good' and 'bad' are interpreted in terms of physical consequences (e.g., punishment, reward, exchange of favors) or in terms of the physical power of those who enunciate the rules and labels. The Physical Power stage (1) characteristically orients toward punishment, unquestioning deference to superior power and prestige, and avoidance of 'bad' acts. Regardless of value, physical consequences determine goodness or badness. The Instrumental Relativism stage (2) is basically hedonistic. Right action consists of that which instrumentally satisfied one's own needs and occasionally the needs of others. Elements of fairness, equality, and reciprocity are present, but interpreted pragmatically, not as a matter of loyalty, gratitude, or justice.

"The conventional level (II) is characterized by active support of the fixed rules or authority in a society. Maintaining the expectations and rules of the family, group, or nation is valued in its own right. The Interpersonal Concordance or good-boy/good-girl stage (3) orients toward pleasing others and gaining approval. There is conformity to stereotypical images of majority behavior. Also behavior is frequently judged by intention: 'He means well' becomes important for the first time. The Law and Order state (4) is typified by doing one's duty (obeying fixed rules), showing respect for authority, and maintaining the given social order. Respect is earned by performing durifully.

"The postconventional level (III) is characterized by a clear effort toward autonomous moral principles with validity apart from the authority of the groups or persons who hold them and apart from individual identifications. The Social Contract stage (5) has legalistic and utilitarian overtones; strong constitutionalism pervades. Right action is defined in terms of individual rights, critically agreed upon by the whole society. Awareness of the relativism of personal values is attended by an emphasis upon procedural rules for reaching consensus. The stress is on the legal point of view, but with the possibility of changing law in terms of rational, social utility rather than freezing it in terms of law and order. The Universal Ethic stage (6) moves toward conscientious decisions of right based on principles that appeal to logical comprehensiveness, universality, and consistency. These principles are abstract and ethical; they include justice, the reciprocity and equality of human rights, and respect for individuals."

[39] In cross-cultural studies in England, Canada, Mexico, Taiwan, Turkey, and the U.S., Kohlberg reports this phenomenon. For a graphic presentation of his findings, see Lawrence Kohlberg, "The Child as a Moral Philosopher," *Psychology Today*, 2 (September 1968), 24-31. To this reference add also Kohlberg, "Development of Children's Orientations"; *id.*, "Development of Moral Character"; *id.*, "Stage and Sequence"; Kohlberg and Turiel, "Moral Development and Moral Education"; Kohlberg and Kramer, "Continuities and Discontinuities"; Elliot Turiel, Lawrence Kohlberg, and Carolyn Pope Edwards, "Development of Moral Judgments in Turkish Village and Urban Children," in Lawrence Kohlberg and Elliot Turiel, eds., *Research in Moralization* (New York: Holt, Rinchart and Winston, in press). For further evidence of this phenomenon in other cross-cultural settings and more directly related to systems of law, see also Tapp and Kohlberg, "Developing Senses." Additional relevant law perspectives from Denmark, Greece, India, Italy, Japan, U.S. (black, white) can be found in June L. Tapp, "A Child's Garden of Law and Order," *Psychology Today*, 4 (December 1970), 29-31; Tapp and Levine, "Persuasion to Virtue."

[40] John Rawls, "Two Concepts of Rules," *Philosophical Review*, LXIV (January 1955), 3-32.

[41] In addition to Fuller's already cited "Human Interaction" and *The Morality of Law*, see "The Justification of Legal Decisions," a paper presented at the World Congress for Legal and Social Philosophy (August 30-September 3, 1971). To that paper Fuller adds this note, "Had I attributed a title to it that would indicate the content of my own contribution I would have chosen something like *Interaction Between Law and the Social Context into Which It Is Projected*" (p.i.).

[42] Fuller, *The Morality of Law*, pp. 9-10.

[43] Piaget, *Moral Judgment*.

[44] Kohlberg, *supra* note 28.

[45] Tapp and Kohlberg, "Developing Senses"; Tapp and Levine, *The Jurisprudence of Youth*.

[46] *Supra* note 40; see also John Rawls, "Justice as Fairness," *Philosophical Review*, LXVII (April 1958), 164-194; *id.*, "The Sense of Justice," *Philosophical Review*, LXXII (July 1963), 281-305; *id.*, "Legal Obligation and the Duty of Fair Play," in Sidney Hook, ed., *Law and Philosophy* (New York: New York University Press, 1964), pp. ´3-18; *id.*, "Distributive Justice," in Peter Laslett and W. G. Runciman, eds., *Philosophy, Politics, and Society* (Oxford: Basil

Blackwell, 1967), pp. 58-82. See particularly Rawls' seminal, comprehensive *A Theory of Justice* (Cambridge, Mass.: Belknap Press of Harvard University Press, 1971).

[47] Rawls, "The Sense of Justice," pp. 281-282. Roscoe Pound also used a developmental framework in *Jurisprudence*, vol. I, pp. 406-428, to describe the emergence of legal systems. In his model, the mature states parallel the psychological and/or philosophical highest states of morality and legality.

[48] John W. Chapman, "The Moral Foundations of Political Obligation," in J. Roland Pennock and John W. Chapman, eds. *Nomos XII, Political and Legal Obligation* (New York: Atherton Press, 1970), p. 170. The equilibrium notion—pendulum or action-reaction—involves conflict and balance as well as ambivalence and complexity. In this instance, justice is seen as an equilibrating concept. This approach is as much a part of psychology (see Piaget, *Moral Judgment*) as law (see Pound, *Jurisprudence*, vol. I, pp. 418-419) and philosophy (see Rawls, *supra* notes 40 and 46). In all, it is basic to developmental and purposive models about human nature and "perfectibility," For further explication of my ideas on the dynamics of conflict and balance in public and private contexts, see June Louin Tapp and Fred Krinsky, *Ambivalent America* (Beverly Hills, Calif.: Glencoe Press-Macmillan, 1970), especially pp. 1-14.

[49] In addition to Kohlberg, "Stage and Sequence," see also Sheilah R. Koeppen, "Children and Compliance," *Law and Society Review*, 4 (May 1970), 545-564, esp, 559: "The cognitive-developmental interpretation [over psychoanalytic and social learning theories] has much to recommend it to a legal system based on premises about individual accountability. Cognitive-developmental theory proposes that by adolescence, an individual can be expected to discern right from wrong and to value the social utility of laws that punish misconduct." For a careful weighing of the various theoretical frameworks, read too Eleanor E. Maccoby, "The Development of Moral Values and Behavior in Childhood," in John A. Clausen, ed., *Socialization and Society* (Boston: Little, Brown, 1968), pp. 227-269; Richard M. Merelman, "The Development of Political Ideology: A Framework for the Analysis of Political Socialization," *American Political Science Review*, LXII (September 1969), 750-767.

[50] F. J. Ebling, ed., in *Biology and Ethics* (New York: Academic Press, 1969), p. xxxvi. For another view of the biopsychological relationship to values, see Elizabeth Leonie Simpson, *Democracy's Stepchildren* (San Francisco: Jossey-Bass, 1971). For social psychological analyses of both the mediating processes in the internalization of conscience and the socializing contexts as well as devices, see Clausen, ed., *Socialization and Society*.

[51] See e.g., Justin Aronfreed, *Conduct and Conscience* (New York: Academic Press, 1968); *id.*, "The Concept of Internalization," in Goslin, ed., *Handbook of Socialization*, pp. 263-324; Albert Bandura and Richard H. Walters, *Social Learning and Personality Development* (New York: Holt, Rinehart and Winston, 1962); Leonard Berkowitz, *Aggression: A Social Psychological Analysis* (New York: McGraw-Hill, 1962); *id.*, *The Development of Motives and Values in the Child* (New York: Basic Books, 1964), esp. 44-96.

[52] Maccoby, "Development of Moral Values," p. 253. For additional observations on the integrative possibilities of cognitive developmental and social theories, see Tapp and Levine, "Persuasion to Virtue," pp. 566-567, 573, 576-578, 580-581.

[53] Indeed, as Zimbardo, "The Human Choice," p. 240, has suggested, this assumption may help "gain freedom from the behavioral proscriptions imposed by . . . history, physiology, and ecology." This assertion is consistent also with Koeppen's observation in "Children and Compliance."

54 To demonstrate the psychological limits of law and the empirical psychological origins of legality. I report data based on the responses of 115 white youths at various grade levels from kindergarten to college, most of whom come from professional families living in a large city in the United States. For analytic purposes, subjects were divided into three groups: (1) primary, spanning kindergarten through grade 2; (2) middle school, covering grades 4, 6, and 8; and (3) college, containing lower classmen. The preadolescent data were collected in 1965 as part of a six-country study (Robert D. Hess and June L. Tapp, *Authority, Rules, and Aggression: A Cross-National Study of the Socialization of Children into Compliance Systems: Part I* [Washington, D.C.: U.S. Dept. of Health, Education and Welfare, 1969]; Leigh Minturn and June L. Tapp, *Authority, Rules, and Aggression: A Cross-National Study of Children's Judgments of the Justice of Aggressive Confrontations: Part II* [Washington, D.C.: U.S. Dept. of Health, Education and Welfare, 1970]); the primary school material was gathered in 1967 as part of a student research project under my supervision; and the college information was obtained in 1970 as part of an impact study of an undergraduate course. Responses from all three groups to open-ended interview questions were analyzed in terms of empirically derived cross-national and developmental categories. The overall reliability averaged 83 percent. Differences between category response percentages for the age levels were tested using t-tests. Significant differences at the p $\angle$ .05 level or better from the primary to the middle school to the college sample groups are reported and discussed comparatively as developmental changes.

55 See Gail L. Zellman and David O. Sears, "Childhood Origins of Tolerance for Dissent," *Journal of Social Issues*, 27:2 (1971), 107-136; Samuel Stouffer, *Communism, Conformity, and Civil Liberties* (Garden City, N.Y.: Doubleday, 1955).

56 Julius Stone, *Social Dimensions of Law and Justice* (Stanford, Calif.: Stanford University Press, 1966), p. 788.

57 Donald T. Campbell, "Legal Reforms as Experiments," *Journal of Legal Education*, 23:2 (1971), 217-239, presents the creative practical suggestion that experimental research models be utilized for testing the impact of innovations, easing administrative burdens, and developing sound policy positions.

58 Richard E. Flathman, "Obligation, Ideals, and Ability," in Pennock and Chapman, eds., *Nomos XII, Political and Legal Obligation*, p. 96. Similarly, John W. Chapman's hint—in the same volume—at the universality of the ideal of human perfectibility is congenial to my reasoning about the equivalency of psychological and legal limits. To wit, it is "both moral and psychological, dynamic or developmental, and institutional, implying that there is a way of life which human beings can recognize as appropriate to their nature." See "Moral Foundations," p. 148.

59 Zimbardo, "The Human Choice," p. 249.

60 See, e.g., Erik H. Erikson, *Childhood and Society*, 2d ed. (New York: W. W. Norton, 1963), id., *Insight and Responsibility* (New York: W. W. Norton, 1964), id., *Identity, Youth and Crisis* (New York: W. W. Norton, 1968); Marie Jahoda, *Current Concepts of Positive Mental Health* (New York: Basic Books, 1958); Salvatore R. Maddi, *Personality Theories, A Comparative Analysis* (Homewood, Ill.: Dorsey Press, 1968); Abraham H. Maslow, *Toward a Psychology of Being*, 2d ed. (Princeton, N.J.: Van Nostrand, 1968); Carl R. Rogers, *Counseling and Psychotherapy* (Boston: Houghton Mifflin, 1942); id., *Client-Centered Therapy* (Boston: Houghton Mifflin, 1951); id., *On Becoming a Person* (Boston: Houghton Mifflin, 1961).

5

SOME RELATED LIMITS OF LAW

Kent Greenawalt

The "limits of law" is an elusive subject in part because of the different senses in which law may be considered limited. This piece is essentially an effort at categorization; it suggests a variety of kinds of limits, and some ways in which they are related.

Only to a limited extent does law accomplish the goals that those who make law (or others) intend (wish) it to accomplish. The statement "The laws against drunk driving in this state don't stop drunks from driving" describes the limited effectiveness of present laws in achieving their purpose. A second broad sense of the limits of law is the extent to which the character of law or generally accepted restrictions on its operation reduce law's effectiveness or make it impractical to employ the law to accomplish certain goals. "Attempts to outlaw gambling are ridiculous because gambling is in the nature of man" is a statement identifying a limitation on what law can accomplish. A third sense of the limits of law concerns moral limits on the kinds of goals for which law should be used.

A statement such as "It is wrong for the law to restrict 'self-regarding behavior' " asserts a moral limit to the use of law.

In addition to my primary purpose of sorting out different kinds of limits, I suggest that the limited effectiveness of law is largely a consequence of limits on what it "practically" can accomplish and that many of these "practical" limits have a moral aspect that blurs the distinction between "practical" and "moral" limits.

I. THE LIMITED EFFECTIVENESS OF LAW

The ineffectiveness of law in accomplishing an intended result is most easily understood in the context of laws, such as criminal laws or tax laws, that forbid or require certain behavior. One measure of their effectiveness is the extent to which persons act in the legally prescribed way because of the law. A law of this kind is ineffective whenever it is not obeyed; behavior in accord with the law, however, does not necessarily mean effectiveness, for it may be the product of something other than the legal prohibition or command.[1] Typically these laws are accompanied by sanctions for their breach, and another measure of effectiveness is the extent to which the sanction is actually imposed on violators. Thus, it can be asked of a criminal statute how effectively it prevents the forbidden behavior and how effectively violations are sanctioned.

Relative objectivity can be attained with respect to relevant measurements, at least in theory. The number of additional abortions after repeal of a prohibitive law provides a fair indication of the impact of the earlier prohibition.[2] Statistics can be, and are, maintained on the percentage of classes of crimes that are solved and for which persons are punished.[3] Even if relatively objective measurement is practically as well as theoretically possible, a judgment on overall "effectiveness" cannot be value free, since that requires, among other things, evaluation of the comparative importance of stopping behavior and sanctioning it, evaluation of the comparative importance of stopping or sanctioning subclasses of the forbidden behavior (for instance, suppose a law forbidding all gambling stopped all professional gambling but it did not touch gambling between friends), and estimation of the costs to society of achieving a given degree of effectiveness.

Effectiveness in respect to other kinds of laws is trickier conceptually. Provisions for civil damages may be meant[4] to prevent the behavior that leads to harm or to allocate losses, or both. Insofar as prevention is an end, it could be measured as with laws that forbid behavior. In respect to allocation of loss, rules allowing recovery may not be meant to allocate losses in all situations but only when parties do not satisfactorily settle on an allocation between themselves. For example, it would be strange to speak of the law as being ineffective if a victim of an accident declined out of kindness to recover damages from a friend who incurred legal liability to him. An accurate measure of effectiveness, perhaps, would be in terms of how many persons who are entitled to recover and who want to recover (or would want to if they knew their rights under a law and could recover effortlessly) do in fact recover.

Other legal provisions allow persons to give legal effect to their wishes.[5] The rules for a valid will tell persons how they may determine disposal of their property after their death. Ineffectiveness with respect to such provisions would relate to how many persons fail in their attempt to form valid wills, how many persons fail to draw a will from ignorance or supposed burdensomeness, and how many apparently valid wills are forged or coerced. The law of wills is not necessarily ineffective simply because a valid will is not formed, because some persons may be satisfied with an intestate disposition of their property or may not wish to think about or decide on the disposition of their property after death.[6]

Apart from ineffectiveness through nonobservance (in the various senses discussed above), law may be limited in its effectiveness in achieving goals to which it is assumed, or hoped, that observance will contribute.[7] Occasionally, there may be a clear miscalculation that particular behavior will produce a desired result. For example, a law against hunting deer, passed solely to protect deer, would be ineffective in this sense if its consequence was overpopulation of deer, depletion of their food supply, and finally the starvation of them all. Much more common is ineffectiveness with respect to less clearly defined goals of social harmony and human happiness.

Law is, among other things, an instrument for resolving social conflict and for preventing conflicts from arising. But it does not always have that effect, and it may be that "advanced" Western legal systems are generally less effective in this respect than many "primitive" systems in which the goal of reconciliation is given more prominence.[8] If after full civil recovery an accident victim murders the negligent driver who injured him, that might reflect the limited effectiveness of tort law as well as the law against murder. The law of wills may be ineffective insofar as a valid will does not prevent long legal wrangling over an estate and sharp personal hostility between survivors. When enforcement of the law of contract leaves two long-time business associates so embittered they refuse to deal with each other, it has failed in that instance to promote commercial harmony and intercourse. If a law forbidding discrimination produces increased rather than reduced animosity between groups, it has not been effective in one of its goals. Thus, when its dictates are followed, a law may not resolve or even improve the human problem that gives rise to its intercession.

II. THE "PRACTICAL" LIMITS OF LAW

There is a variety of reasons why laws are not fully effective in causing persons to act in the ways prescribed or in helping the underlying human situation.

A. Costs of Ascertaining Observance

Any system including official determinations of whether law has been observed involves costs, which may be borne by the state or the parties involved. Some of these costs are calculable in terms of time and money; some relate to sacrifices of other social values. In innumerable circumstances the rational economic man would not pursue his legal rights because the time and expense of vindication outweigh the highest possible recovery. And given the expenses of the other litigant and the state, it would be a gross misallocation of economic resources to have legal resolution of very minor disputes. It is true that the possibility of authoritative legal settlement will often encourage private disputants to settle on the basis of their prediction of what a court would decide, so the average cost of settling a class of claims according to a legal rule is much less than the cost of a case that goes all the way through trial. Still, in many situations the amount involved is so small that neither party expects the other to seek legal redress; then the basis of resolution is likely to be something other than legal principle, except insofar as legal principle is accepted as embodying a fair resolution. A government would be mistaken in removing altogether monetary and other impediments to legal action, for then a society would tend to expend considerable resources to settle disputes in which little is at stake.[9] A special problem is posed by the repetitive infliction of damage, injuring no one very much but causing a substantial total injury, as with some consumer frauds. There it is important to have a credible threat of legal action, and, in different ways, government-financed and public-interest law offices and expanding concepts of class actions help meet this need.

With respect to criminal and regulatory laws the government plays a much more active role in enforcement than adjudicating authoritatively the competing claims of private parties. Investigation and prosecution of crimes are expensive, and one obvious limit on effective enforcement of laws requiring or prohibiting action is the cost society is willing to bear to ascertain and prosecute violations.[10]

Criminal law enforcement reflects most sharply a different kind of cost, a sacrifice of other social values. No doubt a policeman at everyone's elbow would reduce crime, but it would also make life intolerable. Generally allowing searches without probable cause would uncover additional evidence of criminal activity, but personal privacy would be more frequently invaded. One reason laws are limited in effectiveness is because it is thought that more thorough-going measures to ascertain violators would impair other values to an unjustified degree.

This limitation affects not only the effectiveness with which given laws are enforced but also the range of behavior that should be prohibited or compelled. If it is usually unwise to have laws that are not effectively enforced, because they may breed disrespect for other laws and a sense of injustice and create undesirable side effects,[11] then society should not maintain laws that could be enforced at a minimally acceptable level only through unacceptable expenditures or intolerable methods of investigation.[12]

B. Uncertainty of Facts

Unlike moral injunctions that may affect behavior through the operation of conscience or belief in a higher Judge who can probe the hearts of men, law can be effective only when men can reasonably make judgments about other men, since it depends on the readiness of state officials to determine whether law has been observed. The ascertainment of some kinds of facts seems impossible or very difficult, and the need for reliable judgment greatly affects the development of legal rules and principles. For example, the standards for testing the validity of a will are relatively objective, because a simple inquiry to determine whether the will truly represents the desires of the deceased would be so difficult to make. General reliance in the law on standards of reasonableness rather than subjective belief is, in part, the product of the difficulty of gauging a particular person's state of mind.

Although the uncertainty of certain kinds of facts may seem inherent, a great increase in expenditures or vastly different techniques of enforcement might make some facts ascertainable that now seem beyond reach. For example, the difficulty of probing subjective feelings not evidenced by some overt action is one reason why criminal laws are framed in terms of overt acts, but extensive, frequent, mandatory psychological testing might conceivably yield fairly reliable insights into the propensities of individuals. Such testing on a wide scale, however, would be regarded as abhorrent to notions of individual privacy. Thus, other social values impose limits not only on acceptable methods of investigation and the extent of their employment but also on the kinds of facts that can reliably be discovered.

C. Modes of Inducing Compliance

The effectiveness of law is limited not only by the difficulty or cost of determining the relevant facts but also by the methods available to induce observance. Education of citizens, lawyers, and officials is one aspect of inducing observance, since that depends on awareness of what laws provide.[13] Such education may go beyond information about laws and include more or less explicit attempts to promote a favorable disposition toward law that will induce obedience to legal rules proscribing antisocial behavior and employment of rules for facilitating private wishes.[14]

In this society, the primary techniques for compelling compliance with the criminal law are imprisonment and fines, with some use of mandatory supervision through parole or probation. When persons are confined for violations of the criminal law, efforts are made, in theory at least, to rehabilitate or reform them through education, psychological help, and so on. Apart from prohibiting behavior, a government may try to discourage it by taxes or provisions for civil law recovery. These depend primarily on the transfer of money or other property and are backed by the power of the state to effect

the transfer itself or imprison someone who refuses to make a
required transfer.

Inducing observance of law costs time and money, and as with
methods of ascertaining observance, what society is willing to spend
in this endeavor limits law's effectiveness. For example, treatment
in penal institutions could be improved if the state hired more and
better qualified personnel and provided improved living conditions.

There may be some core of human behavior that law cannot
alter no matter what methods are employed to induce observance,
but many methods that might enhance effectiveness are rejected
because of competing social values. Rigid thought control of all
members of a society or the organized shunning of antisocial actors,
as apparently occurs in mainland China, might well produce a more
law-abiding society, but here it would be deemed unacceptable to
put in the hands of public authority every possible method for
affecting attitudes and behavior, both because of the inevitable price
in liberty and because of the danger of misuse of such power for
undesirable ends.

D. The Nature of Rules

Any method of regulating behavior that relies on rules has
certain limits, and rules are a central element of a legal system. One
can conceive theoretically of an individualized standard, like a private
act passed by Congress, for every human situation to be covered by
law, but individualized standards are possible practically only when
the group to be affected is very small. Parents can manage a family
without laying down many general rules, but the governors of a
large political entity cannot manage in that fashion. Not only
practical demands but also interests of actual and perceived justice
require that most rules be stated in general form, so that classes
of like actions are afforded the same treatment. The use of general
rules could be reduced by giving more extensive power to officials
so low in the hierarchy of government that they have close personal
contact with persons under their governance,[15] but most persons in
this society would resist the multiplication of differences in treatment
and of occasions for arbitrary exercises of power that such a system
would entail, and in any event personalized government by cell
leaders may be unworkable in a society in which human interrela-

tionships are very complex and persons are not neatly subdivided into simple social groupings.[16]

Though the tolerable degree of fuzziness varies depending on the kind of rule involved, generally applicable rules in a legal system should be relatively clear both in their meaning and in their application to particular facts. When a purpose of a legal rule is to inform persons that certain actions are undesirable and that adverse treatment will be visited upon violators, the rule should be formulated so that citizens and officials will understand it to apply to the same behavior.[17] Clear rules are also essential in rules of law, such as those governing the formation of wills or contracts, which tell persons how they may regulate their affairs in a desired way. Clarity is somewhat less essential when the law operates primarily after the fact rather than guiding initial behavior, as when particular sentences are imposed in criminal cases and damages are allocated after an automobile accident.[18] Some clarity is still needed, however, so that officials can deal with cases expeditiously and fairly, and, in the civil area, so that private individuals and their lawyers can predict official responses and settle their cases without requiring official intervention.

General rules focus on some aspects of an event to the exclusion of others. Although many of those excluded may be morally irrelevant, such as the hair color of the actor, workable rules must also exclude factors that are morally relevant. Thus, it would not be legally relevant that the victim in an auto accident had received a gift of $100,000 from the negligent driver one week before the accident, or that a family on whom a mortgage is to be foreclosed has a great need to stay in the home, or that if a detailed confession can be beaten out of a kidnapper, a young child's life will probably be saved. Each of these factors would have considerable weight for a moral judgment as to the proper course of action. Clarity and efficiency, as well as the limited capacity of rule makers to predict, restrict the number of morally relevant factors that may be taken into account legally.

General rules, thus, cannot produce an optimal result from a moral perspective in every circumstance to which they apply.[19] More significantly, many kinds of human activities cannot profitably be made the subject of such rules. Some human relationships are so complex, involving so many possible acts in different combinations, that rules giving clear directions for most situations would be a painfully restricting Procrustean bed. Spouses or parents may be required to meet certain minimal and irreducible obligations, such as refraining from physical attack, but other obligations, such as being considerate to one's spouse or spending time with one's children, cannot comfortably be subjected to rules of clear applicability. The problem is not simply one of whether the state should be interfering in such matters; it is also a matter of the difficulty of formulating moral rules for such relationships that provide clear directions. Most of the relevant "thou shalt's" or "thou shalt not's," such as "a parent should spend considerable time with his children," must be cast in a form that will leave room for disagreement as to whether almost any particular parent is living up to the rules.[20]

III. MORAL LIMITS OF LAW

It is frequently asserted that, apart from practical limits on what law can effectively do, some areas of human behavior should not, from a moral perspective, be subject to legal control. These moral arguments often coalesce with practical arguments against certain kinds of control, such as criminal punishment of drug use, and the threads are not always easy to separate. Perhaps the question that flushes out the moral limits that go beyond the practical ones is: Assuming that a rule can be well formulated to reach particular behavior and that compliance can be induced and noncompliance ascertained by acceptable methods and at acceptable cost, is there still some reason why the behavior should be left free of legal control?

Most assertions about spheres of behavior that should be beyond the reach of law focus on criminal prohibition and punishment. This focus tends to obscure whether the fundamental objection is to coercion or to the use of state power, a distinction that may be clarified by a brief consideration of some of the ways that persons and institutions seek to influence human action. One person may move another in the following ways: by providing new information ("the canal road is under six feet of water"), by nonrational persuasion ("you'd be foolish to vote for Nixon"), by incentives or disincentives ("I'll give you a dollar to cut the grass"; "if you watch television your allowance will be cut"), and by coercion ("your money or your life"; "go to bed or I'll thrash you"). Most human interactions do not, of course, reduce themselves neatly to these categories; for example, the explicit or implicit threat to withdraw affection or respect may sometimes be experienced as a disincentive, but when it is directed in strong terms at a vulnerable member of a close relationship, such as a child, it is likely to be felt as coercive.

Public authority can employ similar modes of influence. For example, it can try to reduce cigarette smoking by providing information about the physical harm it may cause, by financing advertisements that promote negative emotional associations with smoking, by taxing the sale of cigarettes heavily, or by forbidding smoking.[21] When it is urged that it is wrong for the state to control "self-regarding acts" such as drug use, cigarette smoking, or consenting homosexual acts, it is not always clear whether it is thought wrong to coerce persons with respect to these acts or wrong to employ state power. In some circumstances, it is morally wrong to apply strong private pressures to get others to do things. For example, parents would not be justified if they threatened to disinherit a child for choosing to go to a college other than their alma mater or for choosing to be a doctor instead of a lawyer. If the contention about "self-regarding acts" is that one person cannot make a judgment about what is good for another, or that, despite objective criteria of good, self-learning in these areas is the only useful learning or the only learning consistent with personal dignity, then strong private pressures with respect to such acts are wrong. Thus, the debate about "self-regarding acts" has a good deal to do with private choices to influence behavior, as well as state power.

There are, however, significant differences between state and private attempts to influence behavior, and governmental action may be inappropriate even when parallel private action would be justified. At least when the government acts through generalized rule of policy, as contrasted with the personal advice or direction of a publicly paid social worker, it must be less closely involved with someone making a choice than a friend or associate, less able to consider individual factors and to tailor attempted influence accordingly. Since the overall influence of the state is so great, its weight on one side of the balance is of much more moment than that of private individuals, and misdirected private influence is much more easily corrected by countervailing private influence.[22] The state should, therefore, be much more cautious and certain than private persons before it seeks to influence behavior in a particular direction. Finally, given the abhorrence most people have for jail and for being branded criminals, the state's coercive power is truly frightening, and only very powerful reasons justify its use.[23] But, as with private attempts to influence behavior, other forms of influencing behavior may be appropriate for the state, even if criminal sanctions are not. Education, for example, does not impair individual choice as does coercion, and required advertising (as against smoking) may be thought necessary to offset the influence of private advertising for economic profit. Although heavy taxes on cigarettes may restrict the range of choice, they do not foreclose the exercise of a strong choice to smoke. Thus the moral limits may vary depending on the kind of law or other form of state action that is involved.[24]

IV. CONCLUSION

Examination of some of the "practical" limits on what law can accomplish suggests the extent to which existing limits on law's effectiveness are a consequence of explicit or implicit judgments about acceptable methods for ascertaining noncompliance and inducing compliance, and about the desirability of generality and clarity in legal norms. Most ways in which law could be made more effective would involve at least an arguable sacrifice of other social values. For example, greater emphasis on human reconciliation in civil disputes would require dispositions more sensitively tailored to the many facets of a particular conflict. This would necessitate a sacrifice in generality and clarity, would make it much more difficult for private parties to predict the likely official settlement, and thus, by inhibiting private settlement, might be more costly. Arguably these drawbacks might outweigh the value of likely gains in reconciliation, a goal that may be more urgent in a closely knit society than one, like ours, in which parties to a legal controversy often do not have a continuing personal relationship.

In two significant senses the "practical" limits of law are also moral limits. An inefficient or wasteful use of law disserves other social values. When ascertaining and inducing observance become too expensive, resources devoted to the legal system might be employed more profitably elsewhere. When legal rules are unclear, or cannot be or are not effectively enforced, frustration, perceived injustice, and opportunities for the arbitrary exercise of power arise. But many of the "practical" limits are also moral in the sense that they derive directly from deeply held moral values. Unclear rules not only cause perceptions of injustice; they cause injustice. Pervasive and constant searches to ascertain compliance are morally unacceptable, and so is systematic thought control to induce compliance.

Focus on what have been treated here as the "moral" limits also suggests that they are not easily divorced from the "practical" limits. Two reasons for not subjecting self-regarding acts to state coercion are the inappropriateness of controlling such acts by rules not responsive to individual circumstances and the frightening character of the sanctions the state imposes; these reasons, in turn, relate to accepted limits on the character of legal rules and the kinds of methods of inducing compliance properly within the state's power. Thus, in the complicated inquiry into whether and how law should be employed for certain ends, the "moral" limits on law are not easily disentangled from many of the "practical" limits.

REFERENCES

[1] If an automobile is capable of doing only 30 miles per hour, it is not the law that keeps the driver from exceeding a speed limit of 35 miles per hour.

[2] Because of the multiplicity of variables that affect social behavior, precise measurement of the impact of a law is not possible. Moreover, to some extent laws influence moral outlook; for example, persons who do not commit murder because they find it morally abhorrent may be affected by the fact that murder has always been legally forbidden in their country. Thus, even if the precise impact of repeal of adoption of a law could be discovered over a short period of time, the more indirect long-term effects of the law would not be measurable.

[3] These statistics are, of course, not fully reliable because of unreported or inaccurately reported crimes and uncertainty whether all those punished (or recorded as guilty) for reported crimes are in fact guilty. Many more crimes are "solved" than "punished," largely because a prosecutor, when faced with a person admitting fifteen burglaries, is likely to accept a guilty plea to, or prosecute for, only one or a few of the crimes.

[4] The word "meant" connotes a more clearly formulated purpose than underlies the development of most such legal principles, and it is used here as a shorthand for possible ends against which effectiveness may be measured.

[5] H. L. A. Hart refers to these as power-conferring rules in his *Concept of Law* (Oxford: Oxford University Press, 1961), pp. 28-38.

[6] No doubt some persons do not make wills because the contemplation of death that making a will involves is painful, but that unpleasant association seems a fixed characteristic of wills under any legal provisions.

[7] It does not seem apt to speak of law as being ineffective in circumstances in which the goal asserted to be desirable has not been accepted at all, or accepted only in part. For example, it is not helpful to say that the tax laws of the United States are ineffective to equalize usable income if that has never been one of their purposes.

[8] See, e.g., M. Gluckman, *The Ideas in Barotse Jurisprudence* (New Haven, Conn.: Yale University Press, 1965), p. 9; T. O. Elias, *Nature of African Customary Law* (Manchester: Manchester University, 1956), p. 269.

[9] It may be desirable for the state to afford the possibility of redress even for isolated claims of this sort, because sometimes these carry a heavy emotional freight that makes legal "satisfaction" far more important than the actual monetary recovery.

[10] The vested interests, and inertia and other human foibles of the police and others actually enforcing the law, impose further limits on methods of enforcement. Not every decision made by a legislature or high officials can be converted into appropriate action.

[11] For example, a ban on abortions makes abortions more expensive and less safe. See H. L. Packer, *The Limits of the Criminal Sanction* (Stanford, Calif.: 1968), pp. 277-282.

[12] The unpalatability of necessary investigative measures was a crucial factor in the Supreme Court's conclusion that a state ban on contraceptives unconstitutionally restricts the sexual practices of married couples. *Griswold v. Connecticut*, 381 U.S. 479 (1965).

[13] Persons may, of course, do what the law requires for reasons unrelated to the law's provisions.

[14] In regard to officials performing their functions in the manner directed by law, their own sense of performing properly or working effectively is typically much more significant than any legal consequences to them of improper action. A trial judge has the power to dispose of criminal cases in a number of ways without possibility of review, but he is unlikely to do so on grounds that his brethren would regard as insupportable. The premise of the exclusionary rule for the fruits of illegal seizures is that the police will not want to have prosecutions of guilty persons undermined by their use of improper tactics.

[15] By giving parents extensive power over their children, the law, in a sense, does allocate power within families in this way.

[16] A person may work with one group, live with another, socialize with yet another, and purchase goods and services from wholly different groups.

[17] This assumes that it is not desirable to increase the leverage for arbitrary exercises of power by officials.

[18] The implicit assumptions of this sentence are (1) that it is less important for deterrence and fairness that precise punishment be fixed in the criminal law than that the precise behavior covered be clear, and (2) that the allocation of civil damages does not have a great effect on driving practices.

[19] For persons who unlike myself (see Greenawalt, "A Contextual Approach to Disobedience, in J. R. Pennock and J. C. Chapman, eds., *Nomos XII, Political and Legal Obligation* [New York: Atherton, 1970], p. 332), would define an optimal result from a moral perspective as one in which relevant moral rules were followed, even though observance of those rules occasionally and predictably produces less beneficial consequences than their breach, legal rules could produce optimal results except insofar as they did not track relevant moral rules.

[20] If I correctly understand Lon Fuller (*The Morality of Law* [New Haven, Conn.: Yale University Press, 1964], chap. I and p. 42) as believing that actions governed by a "morality of duty," as contrasted with a "morality of aspiration," are necessarily subject to relatively precise designation in rule form, I disagree. Human beings experience moral demands as duties even though they are not subject to precise definition. Given various conjunctions of circumstances, I may feel an obligation to wash the dishes or change the baby, but I would be hard put to define in advance when those actions seem

to me obligatory, rather than actions I might do if I were feeling particularly generous (that is, actions called for only by my morality of aspiration).

21 Another possibility is a direct prohibition on any advertising of cigarettes on television, the hoped-for indirect effect of which is to reduce smoking.

22 This may not be true with respect to particular persons making decisions, who may be more subject to the influence of one or a few individuals than to that of the state, but it is true if the whole range of persons making similar decisions is considered.

23 Some state prohibitions, however, such as those covering traffic violations, are not especially frightening to most people.

24 I avoid trying to define when the state acts through law and when it acts in some other way. Legitimate executive acts have, at least, legal authorization and could be required by a specific or general legislative mandate.

6

LAW BETWEEN ETHICS
AND POLITICS:
A PHENOMENOLOGICAL APPROACH

Sergio Cotta

I

The problem of the limits of the law is made all the more complex by the number and heterogeneity of these limits. It will be useful, therefore, to classify them, even if roughly. To begin with, there are *factual* limits, which may be subdivided into two principal subclasses. First, the law being a product of human activity, it meets those very limits to which every human product is subject, owing to the fact that man is limited in his material capacity. As a famous dictum says, the British Parliament can do everything except to change a man into a woman. The existence of such limits is, I think, uncontroversially admitted; science can move them forward, law certainly cannot. Second, there are those factual limits arising from environmental conditioning, both physical and human.

These last limits are sometimes forgotten, or their importance undervalued, under the influence of the supposed legislator's omnipotence, which finds lively expression in another well-known dictum: *lex facit de albo nigrum* (the law makes black of white). But legislator's omnipotence is less a reality than a myth, which cannot conceal its theomorphic nature as it transfers to the human ruler attributes which are generally ascribed only to God—in our case, His almightiness. This myth finds support also in the fact that the human capacity of pure imagination and of purely rational reasoning appears unlimited, both having a universal scope. That is why such a myth flourishes especially in ages, or in doctrines, inspired by an extreme rationalism (as the age of Enlightenment) or by an extreme voluntarism (as certain revolutionary messianic doctrines).

But such extremes have no real existential basis; they are mere abstractions. As Karl Jaspers has efficaciously reminded us, human existence is, and develops itself, always in a *Grenzsituation* (limited situation). And in fact law is neither an act of pure and unlimited rationality,[1] nor an act of all-powerful will. Montesquieu has penetratingly written, *"la loi n'est pas un pur acte de puissance"*[2] (the law is not a pure act of power), and has devoted a book of his *Esprit des lois* (book XIX) to demonstrate that it is never expedient, and often not even possible, to legislate against *"la manière de penser d'une nation"* (a nation's way of thinking), against its *"moeurs et manières"*[3] and its *esprit général.* One may even say that the essential aim of the *Esprit des lois* consists in finding out the structural, environmental, and historical conditionings both of the law and of the legislator. Montesquieu's views can be connected with a realistic tradition traceable back to Aristotle and renewed in our days by the sociology of law and by the legal theory of the "nature of things."[4]

Moreover, law meets with another important class of limits, which I would call *relational.* This comes from the fact that jural activity is not the only human activity, since it does not exhaust the totality of experience, either in its practical side or, even less, in its theoretical one. Therefore, in its development, law comes always in close contact with other activities, so that obviously reciprocal limitations arise. The activities with which law comes more frequently in contact are ethics and politics, but also economy and even art; let us remind ourselves of the crucial question whether art is free from any legal interference. These activities correspond to human needs, which jural activity appears unable to satisfy. They are, namely, existential activities not reduceable to law; for each of them rightly arises, therefore, the problem of its relational limits vis-à-vis law.

Notwithstanding the relevance of the factual limits, I shall restrict the present analysis to the relational ones, and specifically to the limits that ethics and politics might put to the law. Yet I shall not deal with the factual but only with the theoretical question, i.e., whether, and for what reasons, law as a whole, as a specific kind of human activity, is limited by ethics and by politics, understood in the same sense.

II

Let us consider first the case of ethics. The idea that law should not violate the so-called sanctuary of conscience (whatever this might historically mean) is undoubtedly present in the course of history since the remotest ages. A few well-known examples will help to point out its continuity.

The words and behavior of Antigone and Socrates when confronted by death, and of the Christian martyrs, gave full expression to that ideal. Later it found a successful theoretical formulation within the theory which—from Aquinas to modern authors (e.g., John Dewey)—considers the law as an "ethical minimum." This theory states, as is well known, that law has a moral content, but that such content is limited, as Aquinas said, to virtues and vices concerning only social, and not interior, life. For that very reason, the scope of the law is ethically limited, since it does not reach the so-called internal forum, where on the contrary ethics finds its full development.

In modern times, the doctrine of inviolable rights and fundamental liberties of the individual and social groups—as freedom of religion, liberty of thought, respect for human dignity aside from every racial discrimination, etc.—has clearly confirmed the view that law is limited by principles of moral order. Indeed, such principles are often regarded as the very foundation of legal order, and therefore represent the basic criteria of its interpretation.

Law being held as limited by ethics, it logically follows that when law exceeds its province, conscience is no more under the obligation to obey, but is free (not to say bound) to deny its assent. On this ground rest the theories and the behaviors which, from the Middle Ages till our day, have analyzed and practiced the denial of obedience to the law in its various forms, ranging from passive disobedience to active resistance.

All the views I have recalled find their explanation in the fact that jural activity is related to a specific level of the human structure, above which there is, in a value-scale, the structural level of the moral activity. From this axiological hierarchy originate the relational limits of the law, which could therefore be better called relational-hierarchical. The well-known Kantian distinction between law, as external legislation, and ethics, as internal legislation, sums up perfectly the dominant view of the relational-hierarchical limits imposed upon the law by ethics. The pragmatic (in the Kantian sense) imperative of the law is submitted to, and consequently limited by, the categorical ethical imperative as the exterior is submitted to the interior. In no different direction runs Hegel's legal doctrine. In the Hegelian system, law—which represents the interindividual and external moment of the life of the objective spirit—is dialectically submitted to morality *(Moralität)*—which represents the internal moment of the same spirit—and finally to ethics *(Sittlichkeit)*, that is, to the fully conscious political life in which the objective spirit reaches the perfect union of universality with historical concreteness.

In short, law is held as limited by ethics both because it regulates only the external behavior of man and because it is an abstract (in the Hegelian sense) imperative.

Let us turn now to the relations between law and politics. Here too we can see that the former is very often thought of as subordinate to the latter. This is particularly evident in the "revolutionary mind," but not only there. The principle *salus reipublicae suprema lex* (the welfare of the state is the highest law) has been frequently invoked to legitimate the suspending of some legal procedures, statutes, or rights during wars or troubles threatening public order. Moreover, law in its international aspect has been often and is often held to be subordinate to the supreme requirements of safety and welfare of a nation. This conception of the internal and international supremacy of politics upon law (and even upon ethics) has found a very important expression in the well-known doctrine of the *raison d'état*, as much as in the Hegelian theory of the state.

The fact that law is generally considered a mere instrument of politics can well explain such doctrinal and practical trends. Through legal norms and jurisdiction, political communities organize themselves and secure their internal peace. Being a mere instrument, law has no peculiar aim but the aim itself of politics: the welfare and good organization of the community. Therefore, if a contrast arises between law, or the legal mind, and political necessities and ends, the latter must prevail. In a certain sense, law might be called a "political minimum," which cannot be a hindrance to common good in its whole.

To sum up, one could state that the limitation of law by ethics and politics is traditionally justified by three orders of interrelated reasons: (a) in comparison with ethics and politics, law is held as necessary but not sufficient, not reaching the fullness of the former. It is thought of as a sort of ethics, or politics, of an elementary and inferior kind. Generally, in fact, one does not think that it is enough to observe laws to be a moral man or a good citizen. As law is only an ethical or a political minimum, or a mere instrument, it seems logical that its limits be fixed by what is superior to it or represents its aim. (b) Law is represented as a rule concerning merely external behavior. This view is usually asserted in order to show its subordination to ethics, but it applies also to politics. In fact, no political society can be strong, well organized, and harmonious if it rests merely upon a system of legal rules and sanctions. It needs above all what Aristotle called political friendship[5] and we call today civic solidarity: a solidarity among fellow citizens. This is, no doubt, an attitude quite different from the ethical one, but all the same internal. (c) Law is considered a heteronomous rule or imperative, namely, a rule imposed from the outside, which therefore can never fully satisfy the requirements of man's conscience. On the contrary, not only the moral but also the political imperative—insofar as this is the imperative of solidarity, of civic friendship—can arise only from the inside, and they are therefore autonomous.

III

Yet, in my opinion, this traditional view of the limits of the law is highly questionable. The behavioral examples and the theories I have quoted—which at first sight look highly conclusive—could be reversed, to demonstrate just the opposite, or refuted with other examples and opinions. Antigone, Socrates, and the Christian martyrs, by their serene and conscious acceptance of the legal sentence, showed that they considered the law just as sacred and inviolable as the imperative of conscience. Moreover, just because it is an ethical minimum, which makes it possible for everybody to lead a morally good life, law cannot be transgressed without offending ethics itself. Last, even the fundamental liberties cannot be called absolute, i.e., *legibus solutae*. Freedom of thought does not justify insults or instigation to commit a crime, just as liberty of religion does not legitimate ipso facto any behavior whatever that is peculiar to a certain creed: e.g., polygamy or human sacrifice. In such cases, is it not the law which sets limits to ethics?

No different is the case with politics. Common good can indeed be identified with legal institutions and procedures, statutes and judicial traditions—in short, with that legal order which keeps together the political group. The doctrines of the rule of law or of the *Rechtsstaat*, however different from one another they may be,[6] express exactly this conception. In this line, it can be held that a political community dissolves, or loses its identity, when it does not respect the laws, and the legal procedures for changing the laws, which the same community has given itself. So politics itself requires that law be obeyed: *fiat iustitia ne pereat civitas* (let there be justice lest the state perish). Likewise, as far as international relations are concerned, one might say: *fiat iustitia ne pereat mundus* (let there be justice lest the world perish). In spite of the theory of the full sovereignty of states, recent trends in international law run in the sense of an increasing legal limitation of national autonomy. One could then rightly maintain that, in these cases at least, it is law which limits politics.

In short, one would seem justified in stating that law represents that very hard core of ethics and politics which is withdrawn from subjective views and from immediate and particular interests in order to secure for everyone a peaceful and human coexistence. Can one then still speak of law as of a heteronomous rule? Law appears rather as that rule which goes beyond what *I* believe to be right and expresses what *we* believe to be right. In this sense law is neither autonomous nor heteronomous, but socionomous, if I may venture a neologism.

Last, the picture of the legalitarian man as a mere formalist, well satisfied with his, and his fellow men's, merely external behavior, looks rather questionable. Law requires more than a purely external or contrived obedience, such obedience being always precarious and very often fragile, not to say fraudulent. Let us think of what so often happens in the field of traffic norms. In reality, the full obser-vance of law implies an internal effort which may require a full human involvement. Therefore, to identify the legalitarian man with the Pharisee is quite unfair. In theory, indeed, the former identifies himself with the righteous man, who *neminem laedit, suum cuique tribuit, honeste vivit* (harms no one, gives everyone his due, lives honestly), according to a common rule overriding strictly personal opinions and interests.

With the foregoing reflections I did not aim to reverse the traditional opinion into its opposite. I only intended to show that that view lacks a solid foundation and fails to offer a satisfying solution to the theoretical problem of the limits of the law. We have seen, in fact, that it is impossible to establish an uncontroversial hierarchy between law, ethics, and politics on the basis of such criteria as autonomy/heteronomy, interiority/exteriority, means/end. Each of the activities we are analyzing may be held as socionomous, more than autonomous or heteronomous—two very ambiguous terms from a realistic point of view, as sociology of knowledge and cultural anthropology can show. To be fairly fulfilled, each requires an interior adhesion and assent. Each claims to be an end *in se* and not a mere instrument.

No more satisfactory are two other criteria widely used today to distinguish moral from nonmoral oughts. In Professor Alan Gewirth's clear summarizing formulation,[7] ethics is the ought-system whose rules, imperatives, or reasons: (1) are considered paramount as regards any other ought-system ("formal" criterion), (2) do not concern strictly the individual but the social welfare ("material" criterion). These criteria of distinction ipso facto put ethics at the top of the ought-system hierarchy. But are they really valid criteria? Law and politics too concern the social, and not only the individual, welfare. And I think it is difficult to deny, after what we have been saying, that they too have a reasonable claim, at least in some cases, to the primacy of their rules.

IV

       The usual arguments or criteria failing, in my opinion, to establish an uncontroversial hierarchy between ethics, politics, and law, a new approach seems to me necessary to solve our problem. To begin with, we must drop the usual distinction between moral and nonmoral oughts. From a purely formal point of view, ethics, politics, and law, as well as economy or aestheticism,[8] are all ought-systems alike. All are action-guiding activities; all are provided with sanctions, empirically and phenomenologically but not formally distinguishable from one another,[9] all claim, and have effectively claimed in the course of history, to exhaust the human oughtness, and therefore to be paramount.

Let us recall some examples. What Hegel calls ethics *(Sittlichkeit)* is nothing else than politics: a communitarian life lived in the full common consciousness of the supreme unifying and totalizing value of the state. An analogous meaning, for all its peculiarities, is the Bergsonian *morale close*.[10] On the contrary, the Old Testament ethics (not its religion, which has a larger scope) is clearly of a jural nature, centered as it is on the notions of law and covenant. If we are permitted historical generalizations, in spite of their approximate nature and ambiguity, we could say that the paramount and totalizing ought-system of the Greek city-states was a political one, as the Roman supreme ought-system was a legal one. The classical definitions of *jurisprudentia* as *ars boni et aequi*, and *humanarum atque divinarum rerum notitia* (known of human and divine things), are not merely emphatic statements but clearly sum up the Roman law-centered *Weltanschauung*.

In a certain sense, all our ought-systems might then be called moral. But differences emerge if we consider their phenomenological essence.[11] From this point of view, each of them appears as an activity (and a system) clearly defined and steadily consistent in itself, as each expresses itself in a different existential attitude and is inspired by peculiar principles or values. In this phenomenological perspective, I think a more satisfying solution to the problem of their relational limits might be given.

Yet it must be first pointed out that at the root of ethical, political, and jural ought-systems (to which the present analysis is limited) is a common human need, namely, that of responding to the challenge of the uncertainty and insecurity, typical of the human condition. Why this insecurity and uncertainty? No doubt man structurally is "a being-in-relation," as no individual can live and develop, both materially and intellectually, without communicating with other people. But man is always threatened by the possible changing of this basic interhuman relation from a peaceful and favorable relation of friendship into a menacing relation of enmity. This seems to me an adequate existential (or "ontic," in Heidegger's terminology) explanation of every ought-system, even if human oughtness may find a more profound explanation on the structural (or ontological) level.

Now, politics is in my opinion the activity aiming to remove insecurity and hostility by grouping or maintaining men in a solid and lasting community (be it a tribe, a city in the classical sense, or a nation), characterized by a general homogeneity of culture, interests, and ends. Belonging to the same political community gives to its members the consciousness of a common destiny, and, even more, of a common identity arising from a sort of consanguinity. It is not without reason that we speak of fatherland or motherland—and in romance languages the same idea is even more strongly expressed, through a repetition of the parental image, in such words as *mèrepatrie* or *madrepatria*.

Politics, then, expresses itself in a centripetal unitive trend (*e pluribus unum!*), which gives birth to a public or social friendship—as Aristotle states in the *Nicomachean Ethics*—which has its source and its end (its *causa finalis*, to adopt Aristotelian language) in what is rightly called *bonum commune* or common wealth. Let us remember that the Romans called the state *res publica* (to which term Cicero gave, in his *De republica*, the meaning of *res populi*), and the British call it commonwealth or body politic, which is another highly significant symbolic image of unity. As the *bonum commune* (whatever its historical or empirical contents) represents the link giving cohesion, security, and identity to those who in it are called fellow citizens, politics is the ought-system whose inspiring value is civic solidarity.

Law aims, on the contrary, at the removal of hostility from human relations—whether interindividual, intergroup, international, or other—evoking no more the idea of a common belonging to the same "body" or community but rather that of a common dependence from the same measure or rule. Under the authority of the same rule, human relations can be peacefully ordered so as to remove what is wrong or harmful. What is distinctive in the idea of measure, or of rule, is that of not being limited *in se* by territorial bounds or by group centripetal allegiances; rule extends itself universally, since from every point of the human horizon can arise a threatening danger.

That is why the result of jural activity is not a (political) sodality—necessarily circumscribed—but a partnership open to anyone who recognizes his dependence upon a common rule, whether this is held immanent in things (as natural law), established by common consent, or enforced by a recognized common authority. Law then expresses itself not in a centripetal but in a diffusive unitive trend. Now, the condition for the universal spreading and recognition of the rule is that it establishes a universally satisfactory order. This is no other than the definition of justice. Law is therefore the ought-system centered in the principle or value of justice.

Before considering our third ought-system, we must underline again that, in the phenomenological line we are following here, both politics and law appear as ethical activities, the former as the ethics of (civic) solidarity, and the latter as the ethics of (universal) justice. In the same way, economic activity may be called the ethics of utility and aestheticism the ethics of beauty. This does not mean that every empirical—or historical, political, legal, etc.—system is, or must be, ethically approved, but only that in the truth of their concept—as Hegel would have said—both politics and law, considered as human activities carrying a phenomenological sense, are different forms of the ethical level of existence, each commanding full obedience or allegiance.

Let us come now to our third activity—the one which is usually called ethics. It seems to me that it cannot be connected with such principles as solidarity, justice, utility, or beauty, which are, as we have seen, the immanent inspiring values of other specific activities. Therefore, I can see no other principle, historically and phenome-nologically documented, better suited to this activity than love. Under the name of *agape*, or charity, it has attained its theoretical and practical fullness in Christian ethics. But that cannot make us forget its active and central presence in many ancient and modern doctrines and *Weltanschauungen*. We find it in ancient Greece under the name, and in the phenomenology, of *eros* (e.g., in Plato's *Banquet*) or of *philia* (e.g., in Epicurism or Stoicism). In our times, we may recall the Bergsonian *morale ouverte* (open morality), clearly centered on love—and sharply opposed to the political *morale close*—or the ideal of philanthropy, a secularized version of Christian charity. Different as they are from each other, all these doctrines bear convincing witness for what may rightly be called the ethics of love.

Love-inspired activity does not follow, as politics does, a centripetal but universally diffusive trend, such as that followed by law. Yet it differs from the latter as it gives rise to a relation, not of mere partnership, but of inner brotherhood. Love does not establish a balanced relation by giving equal reward to equals and, proportionally, unequal reward to unequals; nor does it require an exact appreciation and regulation of the partners' positions so as to award the *suum* to everyone. It expresses itself in the fullness and the superabundant gratuity of gift and forgiveness,[12] in a unifying empathy which transcends calculation, equal balance, personal rights, etc. It does not take account of utility, positions, merits, equality, or the very notion of *suum*. Under its rule, enmity is ignored—as everyone must be everyone else's neighbor—or is an occasion for a superabundance of love.

Phenomenology, then, shows to us three (or more) moral activities giving rise to three (or more) moral ought-systems, which are quite different in principle and in action. And as all of them have solid roots and justifications in the existential ground, so each of them may rightly pretend to an exclusive or totalizing allegiance.

V

It would seem that the only way to get out of this impasse is by making a personal (or communitarian) choice, subjectively and freely attributing primacy to one of the ought-systems. In this case, their relational limits would be merely de facto, lacking a general, or universally recognized, foundation. We should then be obliged to accept conflicts among ought-systems, which de facto are so frequent and so difficult to solve—e.g., love versus justice, common good versus law, and so on.

And yet, from a strictly phenomenological point of view, it is possible to go beyond this "give-it-up" (as Dean Pound would have said) position. It may, in fact, be noted that the activities we have analyzed can find place in a hierarchical scale according to their objective structural characteristics.

As Bergson has shown definitively, civic solidarity cannot be universalized. Therefore, beyond the fatherland frontiers, remains always—both for individuals and for groups—the possibility of hostility. It is the very establishment of a political community that gives birth to an objectively menacing division among men.

Not being restricted to territorial and existential boundaries, but having a universal character and scope, law appears on the contrary as a wider and more reassuring response to the challenge of hostility. But owing to the fact that law, for its very nature, cannot renounce the balanced measure of justice, it fails to transcend the calculating mind. Now this latter, while on the one hand giving stability to the partners' relations and on the other hardening their differences, gives rise to a controversial attitude in the very name of justice and sometimes even to quarrelsome feelings. This more subtle form of enmity is fought and won only by love. The latter then appears as the most broadly ranging, and the most deeply penetrating, action-guiding principle. It is therefore rightly entitled, owing to its structural qualities, to supremacy and to the right of setting limits to other activities.

Yet it must be observed that, in the hierarchy now suggested, the superior principle (and activity), far from abolishing the inferior one, brings it to its perfection by drawing it into a wider and transcendent horizon. This is the idea clearly expressed in the famous words of St. Paul (Romans 13:10): "charity is the fullness of law." As justice does not eliminate solidarity but gives it a broader scope, so love does not eliminate justice but redeems it from all its stiffness and severity. Instead of a hierarchical scale, one could therefore speak of concentric circles, the larger enclosing the smaller and thus setting limits on it but, at the same time, giving it a more powerful inspiration.

REFERENCES

[1] See especially G. Dietze, "The Limited Rationality of Law," in C. J. Friedrich, ed., *Nomos VII, Rational Decision* (New York: Atherton Press, 1967), pp. 67-88.

[2] *Esprit des lois*, XIX, xiv.

[3] *Esprit des lois*, XIX, xiii.

[4] On this theory, see W. Friedmann, "Fenomenologia e scienza del diritto," *Rivista internazionale di Filosofia del diritto*, XLVIII (1971), 334-348.(This article will be published in English in M. Natanson, ed., *Phenomenology and the Social Sciences*, by Northwestern University Press.)

[5] See *Nicomachean Ethics*, VIII, ix-xii, where the different kinds of civic friendship are analyzed. For our times, see B. de Jouvenel, *De la souveraineté* (Paris, 1955), pp. 163-182.

[6] For a penetrating analysis of this subject see B. Leoni, *Freedom and the Law* (Princeton, N.J.: Van Nostrand, 1961), chap. 3.

[7] See his "Obligation: Political, Legal, Moral" in J. R. Pennock and J. Chapman, eds., *Nomos XII, Political and Legal Obligation* (New York: Atherton Press, 1970), p. 64.

[8] A good example of which is the romantic ought-system so sharply criticized by Kierkegaard in his *Enter-Ellen*.

[9] For instance, the feeling of dereliction that the mystic endures when failing in his effort to achieve an ecstatic union with God is sensed by him as a sanction for his guiltiness just as happens in the case of any legal punishment.

[10] *Les deux sources de la morale et de la religion*, chap. I. See my paper "La signification de la politique chez Hegel et chez Bergson," presented at the Hegelian symposium held in Heidelberg in September 1971, to be published in the *Annales de philosophie politique*.

[11] I have discussed this subject more widely in "Sul rapporto tra Filosofia della politica e Filosofia del diritto," *Rivista internazionale di Filosofia del diritto*, XLVIII (1971), 8-25.

[12] The strict link that relates forgiveness to gift is even more evident in romance languages: *dono-perdono*, in Italian; *don-pardon*, in French.

7

A BINARY THEORY OF
THE LIMITS OF LAW

Michael A. Weinstein

W. Friedmann has argued that the structure of legal theory is antinomic: "Legal theory stands between philosophy and political theory. It therefore is dominated by the same antinomies."[1] The dualisms within legal theory are expressions of the binary structure of Western civilization as a whole: "So persistently has the pendulum swung backwards and forwards between certain antinomic values that we cannot but register a tension which perpetually produces new efforts and a search for harmony."[2] Taking Friedmann's observations as a guide, this essay will explore the functions of law in social life, with the aim of developing a theory of the limits of law. The essay will begin by situating law as an aspect of social control, present three ideas of the function of law in social control, show how these functions impinge upon each other creating internal limits of law, interpret these internal limits as a series of binary relations, and sketch a view of the external limits of law based on an existential frame of reference. The goal is a binary theory of the limits of law.

In the present discussion law will be viewed as an aspect of social control. Social control is defined as human activity having as its aim or consequence the direction of human action to some ends rather than others. Under this definition three functions of social control can be identified. First, social control can be exploitative by allocating values to particular individuals and groups at the expense of other sections of the public. Second, social control can be regulative by maintaining a system of roles and thereby bringing a measure of predictability into human existence. Third, social control can be creative by opening up new opportunities for human activity. This creative function includes both facilitation of individual projects (e.g., laws standardizing contractual relations) and facilitation of collective projects (e.g., laws setting up public authorities to provide new services). Theories of law as an aspect of social control have grown up around these ideas of the functions of social control. Three theories have dominated the discussion of law in recent social science. Conflict theories have emphasized the exploitative functions of law, structural-functional theories have stressed the regulative functions of law, and existential theories have highlighted the creative functions of law.

Instead of attempting to define law, this study will sketch the major binary relations in legal theory. First, there is the relation between exploitation and regulation. Second, there is the relation between regulation and creation. Third, there is the relation between exploitation and creation. Analysis of these binary relations reveals the internal limits of law. However, this analysis depends upon a description of conflict, structural-functional, and existential theories of the social functions of law.

CONFLICT THEORY

In *The Greening of America* Charles A. Reich has developed a conflict theory of law to support his case for the necessity and desirability of a cultural revolution in America. A consideration of Reich's reflections on law will show the structure and limitations of conflict theories of law as an aspect of social control.

Reich begins his discussion by leveling an attack on those who hold that law is rational: "lawyers talk about the rationality and equality of the law, but they simply do not get outside the accepted assumptions to think about how the law operates as an instrument of one class in society against another."[3] For Reich, the exploitative function of law is most important. He recognizes the regulative function of law by stating that law is "supposed to be a codification of those lasting human values which a people agree upon."[4] However, in the contemporary United States "law has increasingly become the medium in which private maneuver for power, status, and financial gain could take place."[5] Law is a reflection of the distribution of power: "The real issue in any society is the degree of power. Is that power divided or massed? Is it controlled?"[6] Thus, legal change cannot bring significant social change: "for one interested in basic change, law and political institutions are virtually irrelevant (except as theaters in which to stage exemplary battles of consciousness)."[7]

Within this framework of conflict theory, Reich makes several specific observations about law in the United States. He notes that law has become specialized according to social class and argues that if law is a general rule then America is a lawless society. This argument seems to beg the question because even the most general legal rules make distinctions among situations and actions. The more important question is whether or not the distinctions made are relevant to the attainment of the good life. Reich has confused specialization and particularism.

Following his line of argument, Reich makes the further point that the very proliferation of legal rules has led to a greater amount of discretionary power for officials. The growth of discretion corrupts the rule of law and contributes to the "lawless society." This argument also appears to rest on a mistake. The number of laws bears no necessary direct relation to discretionary power. The specialization of law may actually lead to less discretion. There is maximum discretion when laws are vague and contradictory, not necessarily where laws are many.

The arguments that specialized and numerous laws creat lawlessness rest on the more basic assertion that law is an instrument of interest groups. Reich is most concerned that the highly specialized legal system is a front for privilege and inhumanity: "law can be given any form at all; it is capable of being made the servant of interests wholly indifferent to man."[8] However, there is a problem with this extreme version of conflict theory. If law in America is becoming the servant of interests wholly indifferent to man, why do so many men use it and obey it? Reich answers this question, and his response entails a rejection of the extreme version of conflict theory. He argues: "Diabolically, law can teach that what is wrong is right, that what is false is true. It does this by supplying the sole normative standard in a society become so complex, so confused, so divided, where people know so little about each other, that they can have no other standard."[9] Thus, in the highly specialized American society of today, law performs not only the social function of exploitation but also the social function of regulation. Paradoxically, in Reich's "lawless society" law is the only mechanism binding society together. Reich's observations lead to the conclusion that for law to perform an exploitative function it must also perform a regulative function. Thus, a simple conflict theory is not an adequate view of law as an aspect of social control.

STRUCTURAL-FUNCTIONAL THEORY

Charles Reich is a legal scholar who has applied sociological conflict theory to the analysis of law as an aspect of social control. Kenneth S. Carlston is a legal scholar who has applied structural-functional theory to the same problem. The starting point for Carlston's discussion is at the opposite pole from Reich's beginning. Carlston defines law in terms of the regulation of human conduct: "Law thus has a dual aspect. It may, on the one hand, be conduct which has become so institutionalized (i.e., established) within the group and so clearly related to and necessary for reaching group goals that the group regards it as obligatory. It may, on the other hand, be conduct which is the group response to deviant behaviour and which is designed to control such behaviour."[10] Thus, for Carlston law performs the social function of regulating human activity in accordance with institutionalized norms.

Carlston's notion of law is based upon the idea that social groups have an equilibrium which is subject to disturbance by deviants acting at variance with the established normative order: "deviant behaviour disturbs the equilibrium of the elements which go to make up the group, namely, the institutionalized or repeated sequences of human behaviour which characterize the group action."[11] Deviance is dangerous to the group because it frustrates effective role performance by members and thereby impedes the group in its efforts to attain common goals efficiently. Efficiency is lost because coping with deviant behavior involves diverting a portion of group energies to restoring the original equilibrium. This consideration leads Carlston to the conclusion that in the legal process "the standard or value is essentially one of maintenance of the relevant social system."[12]

Reich's discussion of the exploitative function of law ended in an implicit recognition of the regulative function of law. Carlston described that regulative function in the language of structural-functional sociology. However, there is a problem with defining law solely in terms of its regulative function, and in Carlston's work this problem becomes obvious. The idea that law performs a regulative function must be supplemented by both the notion that law performs an exploitative function and the idea that it performs a creative function.

Carlston is led to implicit recognition of the exploitative function of law when he discusses the application of the standard of maintaining the "relevant social system" in concrete cases. He notes that "no abstract formulas or values" will solve most actual disputes. When "the question concerns such a concrete issue as certain recent antitrust legislation" the outcome is a product of "group actions and interactions."[13] Thus, some groups win and others lose, and the law ratifies the results of the contest. Differential benefits are a by-product of law as a regulative process. Of course, for the conflict theorist, regulation is a by-product of law as an exploitative process.

In a similar argument, Carlston is led to an implicit recognition of the creative function of law. While the exploitative function of law was brought out by the impossibility of using only the standard of system maintenance in resolving concrete disputes, the creative function of law is revealed by the impossibility of using only the standard of system maintenance for deciding upon public policies. Carlston argues that the emphasis placed on "particular values or goals at a particular time in the history of a society will determine the extent to which human conduct is channelled into particular ways of behaviour."[14] Problems of policy involve planning and allocating resources for the whole society. When a course of action has been chosen "the commands of the legislature may establish new rules of law, new organisations or new institutions to accomplish the desired objectives."[15] Thus, law creates an experiment in living grounded in an idea of the good life. Friedmann has remarked: " 'What is the purpose of life?' is the fundamental question to be answered by legal theory as by philosophy, political theory, ethics, religion."[16] In his own argument Carlston has implied that the standard of system maintenance is not an adequate answer to this question, in the sense that this standard can be applied indifferently to all systems.

EXISTENTIAL THEORY

The American philosopher William Ernest Hocking developed an existential theory of law as an aspect of social control. Hocking's approach to law stresses the creative function of law rather than the exploitative or regulative functions. In his "Problems of World Order" Hocking defined law as a creative experiment: "Every actual legal community thus represents a decision, a law-pattern that might have been otherwise: but this means that *every positive law-system is experimental,* a way of living subject to revision by the results of experience."[17] Thus, for Hocking, law is an experiment in attaining the good life.

Hocking's notion of law is grounded in an existential analysis of the human condition. He argues that the human being is driven "not merely to become a fair specimen of the human type, but to achieve a destiny unique to himself."[18] While the ultimate "horizon" of this destiny is cosmic, the will to create in the face of apparent nothingness and suffering has political implications. The human being in search of meaning (an answer to Friedmann's question of purpose) is "not interested in enjoying forever, he is interested in doing something that will *last.*"[19] His contribution must find a place within the community: "If it is the mark of the individual to have a unique purpose, it must also be his mark to bring his idea into the current of community life; he must have a non-competitive will to power."[20] Thus, law which creates an experiment in living provides the human being with a way of making a distinctive contribution.

Like conflict and structural-functional theories, existential theory is not adequate as a description of law as an aspect of social control. Hocking described the creative function of law in terms of an existential analysis of the human condition. However, there is a problem with defining law solely in terms of its creative function, and Hocking is led to the recognition that law has a regulative function.

Hocking's recognition of the regulative function of law is a result of carrying out the implications of his analysis of the human condition. If the human being demands meaning and an opportunity for creation, rather than transient enjoyment, he can only satisfy his demand by seeing his work "embedded in a continuing current of life, the life of an historic community."[21] Thus, the very demand for permanence, contribution, and the opportunity to create implies recognition that law has a regulative function: "Unless, then, the community is political, in the sense of having its own individuality of legal decision, no human being can achieve the individuality of having his own 'task.' "[22] Just as discussion of the regulative function led to the necessity of recognizing the creative function, discussion of the creative function leads to recognition of regulation.

THE INTERNAL LIMITS OF LAW

The internal limits of law are revealed in the way that the various social functions of law impinge upon one another. Law cannot serve an exploitative function without also serving a regulative function, a creative function, or both. Law cannot serve a regulative function without serving an exploitative function, a creative function, or both. Law cannot serve a creative function without serving an exploitative function, a regulative function, or both. These limits of law can be clarified by arranging the social functions of law in binary relations. The binary relations take the form of W. H. Sheldon's polarity relation. For Sheldon, the principle of polarity includes "one or another phase, aspect, relation, event or entity and its counterpart, . . . the two opposite as it were in direction, in way of acting, yet each capable of fruitful cooperation with the other, also of opposing, denying or frustrating it, having thus a degree of independence and a being of its own, and between the two a trend or lure to cooperation in which one of the partners takes the initiative and the other responds, yet each freely; the relation has a certain asymmetry."[23] Thus, a polarity relation is characterized by terms opposite in direction, capable of being reconciled, independent and asymmetrical. The relations between exploitation and regulation, and creation and regulation, and creation and exploitation will be interpreted as polarities.

EXPLOITATION-REGULATION

There is no reason why exploitation must logically involve regulation. At the limit of exploitation is that form of slavery where the slave has no projects of his own. His future is willed by his master. This situation does not characterize contemporary complex societies, and in such societies, where law serves an exploitative function it also provides regulation. Compliance to laws which benefit one or more groups at the expense of others is gained by providing ways for all people to pursue some of their projects. This is the meaning of Reich's statement that when societies are complex, law is the most important standard for coordinating human activities and relations. Thus, approached from the viewpoint of exploitation, law is limited phenomenologically and empirically by the necessity of providing regulation.

Exploitation-regulation is the polarity relation of conflict theory. The terms are opposite in direction in the sense that exploitation involves taking advantage of another while regulation involves coordination of projects. They are independent in the sense that there is no logical necessity for exploitation to be paired with regulation. They are asymmetrical in this polarity relation because the aim is to minimize regulation consistent with maximizing exploitation. There is possible cooperation between the functions because in a complex society the most effective exploitation is accompanied by efficient regulation of activities.

REGULATION-EXPLOITATION

This polarity relation approaches the problem from the viewpoint of structural-functional theory. The exploitation-regulation relation is a description of the strategy an elite might use to maintain dominance. The rational elite provides sufficient regulation to maintain and extend its dominance. The regulation-exploitation relation is a description of the strategy for maintaining a social system in the face of demands of powerful interest groups for exploitative laws. Some of these demands must be met if the very system of social regulation, the rules for resolving disputes peacefully and providing coordination of complex activities, is to be maintained. Again, it is not logically necessary for regulation to involve exploitation. A social order in which no one took advantage of anyone else is imaginable. However, a second internal limit of law is the phenomenological and empirical need to satisfy some demands for exploitation in order to maintain a system of regulation.

In the regulation-exploitation relation the terms are opposite in direction and independent. They are asymmetrical because the aim is to minimize exploitation consistent with maximizing regulation. Conflict theory takes the viewpoint of the interest group or elite aiming at dominance. Structural-functional theory takes the viewpoint of systems maintenance. Perhaps the strategies of elite domination and systems maintenance ultimately amount to the same thing. If so, it is clear that the functions may be in a cooperative relation because meeting the demands of powerful groups will likely strengthen the support of these groups for the system of regulation.

REGULATION-CREATION

This polarity is also associated with structural-functional theory. While in the regulation-exploitation relation the social function of coordination was limited by the need to satisfy demands for wealth, power, and influence, in the regulation-creation polarity pattern maintenance is limited by the need to plan for a future. In the regulation-creation polarity planning new collective projects is undertaken with the aim of securing efficient adaptation of the social system to unplanned changes. When human activities have indirect consequences which threaten to disrupt the existing system of role expectations (e.g., when industrial pollution interferes with ongoing producer and consumer activities), laws may be put into effect with the aim of eliminating these unwelcome consequences. Here the strategy is to minimize the creation of new collective experiments consistent with maximum stability. Thus, a third internal limit of the law is the phenomenological and empirical need to resort to planning and experimentation as a result of unwelcome indirect consequences of human activity.

In the regulation-creation polarity the terms are opposite in direction, in the sense that new experiments are likely to disrupt pre-existing patterns of coordination. They are independent in the sense that there is no logical necessity that external changes will inevitably place strains upon the system of regulation. They are asymmetrical because the strategy involves using the creative function of law as a means to perform the regulative function more efficiently, in the sense that planning is primarily a means to stablize an existing role network. There is possible cooperation between the functions because planning is done to secure adaptation of the system to new challenges.

CREATION-REGULATION

This polarity relation approaches the problem from the viewpoint of existential theory. Here planning is not undertaken for the sake of adaptation, but is done to realize some vision of the good life. The strategy is to maximize control over the future consistent with the measure of regulation necessary to secure cooperation in the plan. Thus, a fourth internal limit of the law is the need to maintain a continuous system of regulation throughout the process of making and executing social experiments.

In the creation-regulation polarity the terms are opposite in direction and independent. They are asymmetrical because regulation is a means to experimentation. There is a possible cooperation between the functions because maintenance of a system of regulation is a way to secure cooperation in fulfilling the plan.

EXPLOITATION-CREATION

Exploitation and creation are logically independent, and their relations are not discussed by either Reich or Hocking. These writers seem to imply that the exploitative and creative functions are mutually exclusive, in the sense that they cannot both be performed in the same situation. However, logical independence is no guarantee of mutual exclusivity.

The exploitation-creation polarity approaches the problem from the viewpoint of conflict theory. It refers to the fact that in contemporary complex societies elites must engage in planning if they expect to gain benefits at the expense of other groups. The strategy here is to create those public authorities and allocate resources to those collective projects which will enhance the elite's share of the social product. For example, elites may create opportunities for automobile travel and work against opportunities for mass transportation because they will profit from the first and not the second. Yet unless they create some opportunities for mass transportation, the social product and their share of it will be diminished. Thus, a fifth internal limit of the law is the need of elites to open up opportunities for action if they are to maintain and extend their domination.

In the exploitation-creation polarity the terms are opposite in direction in the sense that new experiments may have the consequence of endangering traditional privileges. They are independent because they do not logically imply one another. They are asymmetrical because the strategy involves using the creative function of law as a means to gain greater benefits at the expense of other groups. There is possible cooperation between the functions because planning can be an aid to exploitation.

CREATION-EXPLOITATION

In this polarity the problem is viewed from the standpoint of existential theory. The exploitation-creation polarity describes the strategy of a rational elite which acts to create those opportunities which will maintain and extend its domination. The creation-exploitation relation is a description of the strategy for creating new opportunities in the face of demands of powerful interest groups for projects beneficial to them. Some of these projects must be undertaken to gain support for extending the opportunities of all. It is not logically necessary for creation to involve exploitation, since a situation of equal opportunity is imaginable. However, a sixth internal limit of law is the need to satisfy some exploitative demands in order to create new opportunities for individual and collective action.

In the creation-exploitation polarity the terms are opposite in direction and independent. They are asymmetrical because the strategy is to minimize exploitation consistent with maximizing creation of new opportunities. The functions may be in a cooperative relation because meeting the demands of powerful groups is likely to strengthen support of these groups for the facilitative agencies.

REVIEW

There are six major internal limits of law, derived from the ways in which the three chief social functions of law impinge upon one another. First, the exploitative function of law is limited by the need of elites to secure cooperation. This means that elites must perform to some extent the social function of regulation and do it through the means of law. Second, the regulative function of law is limited by the need to satisfy exploitative demands of powerful groups. Unless such demands are satisfied the system of regulation will not be accepted. Third, the regulative function of law is limited by the need to adapt human relations to new conditions. The system of regulation will not be accepted if it impedes people from coping with changes that disrupt their lives. Fourth, the creative function of law is limited by the need to maintain a continuous system of coordination as plans are devised and executed. Plans which ignore and conflict with existing patterns of cooperation are not likely to be followed. Fifth, the exploitative function of law is limited by the need to provide aids to the realization of individual and collective projects. This means that elites must perform the creative function. Sixth, the creative function of law is limited by the need to satisfy exploitative demands of powerful groups. Unless such demands are satisfied there will be insufficient support for authorities providing opportunities.

EXTERNAL LIMITS OF LAW

The preceding discussion of the social functions of law can be placed in the context of a view of the external limits of law. Following Florian Znaniecki, human actions can be creative, reactive, or habitual. In creative actions, "the purpose continues to evolve until the action is completed."[24] Habitual actions are triggered by a stimulus and their purposes are not consciously entertained by the actor. In reactive actions, the purpose is known to the actor before he acts.

Within Znaniecki's scheme it is clear that law is relevant to reactive actions. Law disappears when human activity becomes unreflective behavior and it is not yet in being when human beings are creatively remaking their conditions. Reducing human activity to habit is the ultimate aim of law as exploitation. Habitual repetition of activities beneficial to an elite is far better for that elite than conscious obedience by subordinates. Expanding opportunities for creative actions is the ultimate aim of law as creation. This is the meaning of Hocking's ideal of each person having a unique and satisfying project. Another way of putting this is that the ultimate limit of law is the creative activity of human beings as they remake their situation and search for an answer to the question, "What is the purpose of life?"

REFERENCES

[1] W. Friedmann, *Legal Theory* (New York: Columbia Unviersity Press, 1967), p. 82.

[2] *Ibid.*

[3] Charles A. Reich, *The Greening of America* (New York: Random House, 1970), p. 73.

[4] *Ibid.*, p. 117.

[5] *Ibid.*, p. 121.

[6] *Ibid.*, p. 126.

[7] *Ibid.*, p. 306.

[8] *Ibid.*, p. 127.

[9] *Ibid.*

[10] Kenneth S. Carlston, *Law and Structures of Social Action* (London: Stevens and Sons, 1956), p. 6.

[11] *Ibid.*, pp. 6-7.

[12] *Ibid.*, p. 22.

[13] *Ibid.*, p. 24.

[14] *Ibid.*, p. 23.

[15] *Ibid.*

[16] Friedmann, *Legal Theory*, p. 82.

[17] William Ernest Hocking, "Problems of World Order in the Light of Recent Philosophical Discussion," *American Political Science Review*, 46 (December 1952), 1127.

[18] *Ibid.*, p. 1126.

[19] *Ibid.*, p. 1127.

[20] *Ibid.*, p. 1128.

[21] *Ibid.*, p. 1127.

[22] *Ibid.*

[23] Wilmon Henry Sheldon, *God and Polarity* (New Haven: Yale University Press, 1954), p. 674.

[24] Florian Znaniecki, *Cultural Sciences* (Urbana, Ill.: University of Illinois Press, 1952), p. 212.

8

SOCIAL JUSTICE AND THE COURTS

Graham Hughes

Courts may be most simply thought of as judgmental organs to decide disputes under rules, the nature and content of the rules being matters for legislative and executive creative discretion. In a country such as Britain, where entrenched constitutional clauses giving courts even a limited veto over legislative and executive action do not exist, such a concept of the judicial function is the received and established one. But even in such a setting, so narrow a view of the nature of judicial activity severely distorts reality.

It is elementary to assert that courts engage in interpretation which is authoritative in the double sense of binding the parties and (at the appellate level) in having precedential significance for the future. This interpretative role of the courts gives a continuing accretion of meaning to particular rules of the system, imbuing them

It should be noted that this chapter, prepared for delivery at the meetings of the Society in December, 1970, has not been revised to take account of the rapid developments of the law in this field since that date.

with clearer perceptions of policies, aims, and objectives. Such development is not, at least in the short run, necessarily connected with the pursuit of justice, for examples are legion of well-intentioned legislative enactments being diverted by courts to different or narrower channels which cannot accommodate the legislative purpose of removing a particular social injustice.

But, in a broader view, there may be aspects of the interpretative process which are intimately linked with the concerns of a justice seeking social order. The business of social regulation through rules involves a pursuit of values and interests more extensive than the simple reduction of violence and provision of minimal protections sufficient to guarantee the continuance of human existence. It involves an attempt to fulfill expectations in the sense that individuals and groups may plan and order their lives to pursue and achieve legitimate social objectives without unexpected and arbitrary frustration. Such underlying themes express themselves in fundamental features of a legal system. Professor Lon Fuller has pointed to some of these in his discussion of the "internal morality" of law—that rules must be, by and large, prospective and public, that judgments must be in terms of the rules and have a minimally rational connection with them, and so on.[1] Gross departures from these requirements would not only do great violence to elementary concepts of justice but would at the same time lead us away from ordinary understanding of what it is to have a legal system at all.

Perhaps this approach may be properly pushed further into a contention that the most commonly accepted, elementary demands of fairness in decision making have, if not a necessary, at least a more than adventitious connection with the concept of a legal system. The English courts, although not bound by an entrenched Bill of Rights, nevertheless apply in their scrutiny of administrative procedures maxims whose antiquity is witnessed by their language— *audi alteram partem* and *nemo judex in causa sua.* These notions, that both sides should be heard and that no man should be a judge in his own cause, are certainly not logically necessary in order to construct any model of a rule system, but it might be said that they are necessary if we are interested in getting the best out of rules. For, if both sides are not heard, the judge will be unable to make the most informed judgment under the rules; and, if a man is judge in his own cause, our knowledge of human nature informs us of the risk that he may pay more attention to his own interests than to the promptings of the rules. Here there is relevance in the old saw about a government of laws and not men; not that we can eliminate human discretion from rule application but that the common subscription to basic notions of procedural fairness steers discretion away from the arbitrary and capricious and nudges it firmly into a posture of careful attention to rules.

Even, then, in a system lacking the constitutional mandates of the American one, the shared craft of judges and lawyers has a historical tendency to drive toward the best and finest expression of their own calling, by evolving principles which enable rules to operate with the least possible distortion from bias and error. The very basic understanding that judgments are only reached after argument and should commonly be supported by a reasoned opinion is a most powerful impulse in this direction. We could conceive of a functioning rule system where disputes under the rules were investigated by state officials who would gather evidence and submit it to a judge who would then render a summary decision unsupported by any opinion. But such a system would not only be most offensive to the traditions of the legal profession (that in itself might not be so important) but would also violate established conventions of justice. And the injury to principles of justice surely resides in the absence of public reasons which visibly link the judgments to the rules. Once the demand for reasoned opinions to support judgments is established, the other elements of fairness in process are natural corollary demands in order to give the greatest possible appearance of purity to the judgments and opinions that ensue. When it is the professional business of a class of people to argue about rules and make decisions under them, an articulated structure of fair procedures is likely to evolve, though bias and corruption may still be lively forces beneath the surface.

This tendency in a legal system to press toward the realization of at least procedural justice appears to be immeasurably fortified by the inclusion of basic norms in the system which, in the interests of liberty and justice, seek to limit the rule-making powers of legislature and executive. So the courts in the United States do not have to rely only on judicially evolved interpretative principles which embody concepts of natural justice, but may much more emphatically point to a basic constitutional document which imposes direct prohibitions on government with respect to "denying equal protection of the laws" or "depriving" people of liberty or property without "due process of law" and so on.

In the first place we may take note of the obvious ways in which such fundamentally controlling constitutional clauses enhance the powers of the American courts when compared, with, say, the British courts.

1. Often the rejection of an unjust practice found in a statute or earlier judicial decision may apparently be accomplished with as much ease in Britain through recourse to general principles of interpretation as in the United States through reliance on constitutional clauses. The Supreme Court of the United States decided in 1962 in *Robinson* v. *California*[2] that a statute which made it a criminal offense for a person to be addicted to narcotics violated the Eighth Amendment prohibition on cruel and unusual punishments, which was applicable to the states through the due process clause of the Fourteenth Amendment. The decision rested on the argument that it would always be cruel and unusual to punish a person for a status which did not necessarily involve any proof of his having done any voluntary act.

This decision is eminently right and would no doubt have been reached by a British court by much the same reasoning. But the British court, instead of referring to a constitutional doctrine of cruel and unusual punishment, would simply have cited an underlying general requirement for criminal liability, that the accused be shown to have voluntarily done some prohibited act. This doctrine is not in Britain propounded in any statute but is a part of the general body of principles, defining the scope and boundaries of the criminal law, which has been developed by the judges through centuries of decisions.

But the American court is patently wielding a mightier weapon, for it is immune from any legislative response. The British court, if pushed into a corner by a stubborn legislature bent on creating status offenses, would presumably have to yield in the face of a quite unmistakable expression of Parliamentary intent. While any obscurity was detectable, while any ambiguity remained, while any room was left for discretion, the British courts would undoubtedly go to great lengths to avoid any interpretation which created a status offense. But a doctrine of unconstitutionality has greater weight and stronger teeth than a principle of statutory interpretation.

2. The converse situation also deserves attention. Courts in the United States also exercise an affirmative role, which is not shared by the British judiciary, when they find a piece of legislation or official practice not to conflict with the demands of the Constitution.

To find that government action does not conflict with the Constitution is not of course to characterize it as in every respect

wise, prudent, and just, but it does exempt it from one important
kind of criticism. It is true that the criticism of unconstitutionality
in this sense is one that could not be made in Britain, so that
government there does not need this kind of judicial protection in
the first place. But arguments to the effect that a statute or a
government practice is unconstitutional are usually arguments raising
complaints of a kind of injustice. When an American court rejects
such arguments and affirms the constitutionality of government
action, it is therefore exonerating government from a certain category
of allegations of injustice in a much more affirmative way than is
open to a British court.

A striking and controversial recent example of this is the decision
of the Supreme Court in *James* v. *Valtierra.*[3] In that case the plaintiffs
had challenged a California state constitutional provision which required that low income housing be approved by a majority of
qualified electors in a referendum procedure. The plaintiffs argued
that such a procedure effectively enabled more affluent districts
perpetually to exclude the possibility that persons of low income
might live in their localities and that this constituted a violation of
the equal protection clause. Finding that California had a history of
reliance on the referendum procedure and holding that the procedure
in this instance could not be viewed as racial discrimination, the
Court rejected the claim and upheld the California constitutional
provision.

3. When an American court strikes down a governmental practice
as unconstitutional, the nature of the decree may amount principally
to an order to desist from certain conduct, such as the attempt to
enforce a statute or a police mode of interrogation. But in some
instances the decree will have a much more positive impact in the
sense of directing governmental agencies to embark on conduct or
even to initiate programs.

An example of the first kind would be *Lankford* v. *Gelston,*[4]
where a federal court found that the Baltimore police were in the
habit of conducting illegal and unconstitutional searches in the form
of late night "raids" on private homes of black citizens and enjoined
them from conducting searches which were not properly based on a
warrant or other justifying foundation.

In the second category we find many of the school desegregation
decisions, where school boards may be required to submit plans for
integration which must then be scrutinized by the courts. If the
plans are not satisfactory or are not implemented properly, they

may be supplemented by express directives from the court. Such deep interference in executive processes and such supervision over a field of government administration would be quite outside the realm of possibility for a British court.

It must then be abundantly evident that the discharge of judicial responsibility is often in the United States an infinitely more sensitive and complex task than in a system which lacks the American context of constitutional norms. Before considering some more subtle aspects of this responsibility, we might begin by pointing out two fairly obvious dangers to which the American system is exposed. There is, in the first place, a continuous possibility that the mandate of constitutional obligation may be stretched too far to include the promptings of more ephemeral considerations of prudence or tactical preference. Much of the criticism of the actions of the Supreme Court in the 1960s in the expansion of the rights of suspects and defendants alleges this kind of overkill.

Some would hold that the *Escobedo* and *Miranda* decisions are examples of this type of error.[5] These cases hold that, once the police take a suspect into custody, he has a right to the presence of counsel, a right which must be protected by reading to him a statement to the effect that he is not obliged to say anything, that he may have counsel present, and that one will be provided for him if he does not have the means to engage one. This setting up of a right to have counsel present at an interrogation is thought by many to be a dangerous remedy for a social injustice admittedly engendered by dubious police practices. Out of the many procedures which might be devised for the detection and prosecution of crime, a requirement that counsel must be present at an interrogation (unless the right is waived), is one about which many things might be said on both sides from the standpoints both of justice and efficiency. Even in the short-term context of a felt need to curb undesirable police practices it is only one among many possible procedures which might be designed to cure the abuse. But this procedure has now been plucked out of the many choices in this area and dressed in the armor of a constitutional assertion.

A second snare that threatens the court in the American setting is the possibility of coming into harsh confrontation with the legislative or executive branch of government. Traditionally the general supervisory role of the court has been acquiesced in by the other branches of government so long as that power has been exercised sparingly and within limits. When a court begins to step into fields where it had earlier not intruded or to press harder than before in traditional areas, protests from other organs of government begin to be heard.

In recent years the Supreme Court has hoisted itself with some boldness into territory which perhaps was earlier thought to be a legislative preserve. An example would be the reapportionment cases stemming from *Baker* v. *Carr*,[6] and the ruling on the powers of Congress to exclude its own members in the case of *Powell* v. *McCormick*.[7] In both these instances there has been much legislative grumbling and some muttered threats at what some see as unwarranted interference by the Court, but the Court's decrees have always secured compliance.

In one instance the Court itself has held its hand and abstained even from adjudication. This has happened where attempts have been made to raise the constitutionality of government actions arising out of the war in Indo-China. The Court has (usually) evaded these questions by invoking the "political-question doctrine," a theory of uncertain foundation and scope which permits the Court to characterize a question as either being reserved for decision by another branch of government or at least not timely for decision by the Court.[8]

What is surely apparent is that in the American system there is a breadth and sweep to the actual and conceivable activity of the courts which make continued harmonious relations between them and other branches of government depend on reciprocal restraint and at least a modicum of goodwill and mutual respect. In some ultimate sense this must be true of all legal systems, even those which do not include a power of judicial veto. For in all legal systems the courts are engaged in the business of discussing what is law and therefore what procedures and stamps of authority they must identify before accepting a putative enactment as valid. Even in England one could conceive of a constitutional crisis in which perhaps a government of the day might attempt to pass off as law a bill which had gone through only two, as opposed to the generally required three, readings in Parliament. Courts always live under the possibility of a government that will shortcircuit established procedures and try to pass off as law decrees which lack the conventionally accepted criteria. Conversely, legislatures and executives may be faced with courts who find specious or circuitous or seemingly highly complex and technical reasons for denying efficacy to putative laws and actual executive practices which appear to meet the formal tests for validity and also to embody the popular will. Such a possibility is enormously enhanced by the formal recognition of veto power in a court based on the controlling norms of a Bill of Rights.

Tranquil government and the avoidance of constitutional crises thus always rest on prudential principles, sensible observance of which cannot be replaced by any constitutional formula. Tranquillity and the absence of constitutional crises are not, of course, always the most important values to be pursued. In a community of rank injustice and widespread corruption or oppression, we might willingly sacrifice tranquillity in the interests of reasonable prospects of reforming change. If the situation is bad enough, constitutional crises might be embraced even though it raised the possibility of a revolutionary change in the form of government, including a breach of the basic norms of the legal system. But the special nature of the judicial office and the judicial task must at the least dictate a strong measure of respect for values of cooperation and harmony between branches of government, thus preserving the constitutional structure unshattered. The judge who is committed to revolution and uses his judicial decision making as a tactic to further revolution may be in the circumstances pursuing a more worthy ideal than that of supporting the constitution which carried him to his judicial office, but it is certainly an inconsistent ideal.

The foregoing was not meant to suggest that the judge who is properly troubled about injustice in his society must in his judicial activity make a stark choice between fomenting revolution and passive subservience to an ideal of not rocking the boat. There is a indeed a middle way between these unattractive alternatives, but, like most middle ways, the outlines of its trail are often faint and hard to follow.

A brief examination of the history and present standing of judicial, constitutional intervention in precollege education in the United States may be helpful in endeavoring to assess both the limits of judicial capacity to achieve social justice and the dangers inherent in strenuous thrusts in that direction. Perhaps, too, it may assist in trying to proffer some principles which may be of some help to the judge who is searching for the middle way.

In 1896 a majority decision of the Supreme Court in *Plessy* v. *Ferguson*[9] held that a Louisiana statute which enforced segregation of the races in public transport did not offend the Constitution as long as equal facilities were supplied for all races. This "separate but equal" doctrine was held in many cases, though not in the Supreme Court, to be controlling in the field of public education, and for many decades the thrust of black plaintiffs and petitioners was to prove that the particular facilities afforded by state or municipal authorities were not in fact equal to those enjoyed by whites. The proceedings, sub nomine *Brown* v. *Board of Education*,[10] which came before the Supreme Court in 1954 were a consolidation of cases from Kansas, South Carolina, Virginia, and Delaware. In the courts below there had been findings that the black and white schools involved had been equalized, or were being equalized, so that the facts presented the Court with a plain opportunity to examine the validity of the "separate but equal" doctrine. The Court itself posed the question, "Does segregation of children in public schools solely on the basis of race, even though the physical facilities and other 'tangible' factors may be equal, deprive the children of the minority group of equal educational opportunities?" They answered, "We believe that it does," and so struck down the laws requiring or permitting school segregation as offending against the Fourteenth Amendment's requirement of equal protection.

In a well-known aphorism the Court said in the Brown case: "Separate educational facilities are inherently unequal." This state-ment can be given a broad interpretation and taken to mean that distinctions based on race are simply impermissible, quite apart from the nature of the sociological testimony as to their effects. More narrowly, it can be taken to mean that racial segregation in education cannot be defended by an assertion of a "separate but equal" response, since racial segregation in this setting inherently leads, on the basis of the sociological evidence, to unequal education. Curiously, in the area of education it is the narrower understanding of the Court's statement which may point to more radical developments, for it is the narrower interpretation which speaks most directly to the recent concern with the problems of *de facto* school segregation.

De facto school segregation is of course the product of the combination of the neighborhood school concept with the actual concentration of blacks and other minority groups in the inner city ghettos of American conurbations. It is a phenomenon as much or more of the North and West as of the South. The result is that many northern states, which have never or not for decades permitted *de jure* segregation in their schools, have in their great cities racial separation or imbalance in the schools as markedly as and sometimes worse than in parts of the South. This segregation of students in neighborhood schools may often be exacerbated by a clustering of black teachers in black schools and white teachers in white schools and by allegations of inadequate expenditures by school boards on ghetto and slum schools, as compared with the sums spent on other schools which contain a high proportion of white children. The difference in expenditures is often to be located in the salary budgets and is accounted for by the high proportion in the ghetto schools of black teachers whose qualifications are often not as high as those of white teachers and who consequently receive smaller salaries. Many education authorities, in an attempt to ameliorate these conditions, have mounted special programs in ghetto schools involving special expenditures and efforts at "enrichment." These programs have often not been significantly successful. Studies in this area suggest that the most potent depressant in ghetto and slum schools is the exclusive concentration of children from the same social low income group and that the most potent stimulant is to place these children in schools where there is a majority or a substantial number of children from more advantaged backgrounds. In the absence of such a commingling, remedial programs in the ghetto and slum schools may not have much impact.[11]

Put in these terms, the problem is not so much one of race as one of poverty and cultural disadvantage. In the large cities, where the great majority of the inner city poor are members of minority groups, the problem nevertheless presents itself as a racial one. Some states and cities have endeavored to meet the dilemma by modifying the neighborhood school principle and providing for the redrawing of school districts, or even the transportation of children to schools some distance away from their homes, in order to achieve a greater racial and social mix.

These measures have themselves been subjected to constitutional challenge on the ground that they required race to be considered as a factor in pupil assignments and thus themselves violate the equal protection clause. Such arguments may seem to have a tinge of perversity. It is difficult to imagine how positive, therapeutic steps may be taken to combat segregation without explicit reference to race. The courts certainly have not been much impressed by such challenges and have consistently taken the view that classifications in terms of race are permissible when the acknowledged purpose is to combat an existing situation of school segregation. This apparently holds good whether the existing situation of segregation was produced *de jure* or *de facto*.[12]

The Supreme Court decision in *Swann* v. *Charlotte Mecklenburg Board of Education* now confirms that, where there is existing *de jure* segregation in defiance of the Constitution, mandatory judicial order-ing of limited busing or rezoning, etc., may be justified to combat such a situation.[13] But the Court was careful to point out expressly that its ruling did not extend to an approval of mandatory judicial orders of this kind in a situation of *de facto* segregation.

Where the problem is more clearly seen as a *de facto* one, the constitutional issue is unresolved. We must distinguish here between the role of the courts in passing on the permissibility of legislative or executive action to remedy *de facto* segregation and, on the other hand, the power of the courts to order remedial measures. The former case would of course involve only the question of the consti-tutionality of the remedial measures themselves, while the latter case would involve a confrontation with the basic question of the unconstitutionality of the maintenance of a situation of *de facto* segregation.

A number of lower court decisions have held that revision of attendance units and other measures designed to alleviate *de facto* segregation do not offend against the equal protection clause, even though such measures may involve explicit reference to race, provided that they are not arbitrary and have a rational connection with the therapeutic aim of curbing racial imbalance. Understandably, the courts have been much more reluctant to look upon *de facto* segregation as a constitutional violation leading to mandatory decrees. A few lower court decisions have been premised on holdings that *de facto* segregation may amount to a violation of equal protection, but the majority trend has been to regard segregation which does not result from the action of school authorities as being free from constitutional taint, even though it may result from housing patterns which may historically be in part the product of public discriminatory practices. The Supreme Court has not as yet spoken expressly on this issue.

The present position may then be summarized as follows. *De jure* segregation (that which results from the official actions of school authorities) offends constitutionally and must be abated by judicial decrees which for that purpose may properly make orders which require express notice of race. As far as *de facto* segregation (that which does not result from the official action of school authorities) is concerned, legislative and executive bodies may at their discretion construct remedial schemes which will be immune from constitutional attack, even though they involve express reference to race, but the majority opinion is that such *de facto* segregation is not a constitutional offense which would permit courts to impose remedial decrees.

Starting with the constitutional precept that no state may deny any person the equal protection of the laws, it can be seen that we have already made something of a journey. The destination has not yet been reached and may indeed constantly recede. Nor should we expect that any particular point along the path will be obviously connected with our starting point. But, since the development of law through decisions ought not to be a series of leaps across chasms, we are entitled to expect that a retracing of the path will exhibit the chain of steps that has led us incrementally and persuasively to our present position.

It is surely of little relevance that the founding fathers (or rather here the framers of the Fourteenth Amendment) never had *de facto* school segregation in their minds. In evaluating the spreading ambit of a rule or principle, it is not the presence of the latest application in the contemplation of the framers of the rule that should be controlling as much as the reasonableness of the extensions in the light of accumulated experience with the rule's operation in seeking to fulfill broad purposes. This is because a rule in a legal system (and most especially in a constitution), is not like an order given in a more personal relationship. If there is uncertainty about the scope of a personal order, it is often possible to go back to the person who is the source of the command and seek clarification. Statutes and constitutions do not ordinarily include the possibility of referring to the makers for clarification or interpretation. Then again, orders are usually of narrower compass both in terms of duration (extension into the future) and in terms of application. Certainly, of course, orders may sometimes be ambiguous and there may often be doubts about tacit or implied exceptions or qualifications which must be resolved by the recipient if he cannot consult the commander. A military superior may order an officer to storm a position and, having lost contact with his superior, the officer may indeed be responsibly undecided whether he should carry out the command when it now seems that its execution would involve taking eighty percent casualties. But in such a situation, where obedience is the prime value, the task of the subordinate is simply to make the best informed guess that he can about the commander's intent and wish with respect to the situation now confronting him.

We cannot so appropriately see ourselves as bound to carry out the commands of those who frame constitutions and statutes. The position would be better described by saying that we regard rules and principles which have been established in a certain way as being authoritative, and we acknowledge, therefore, an obligation to make decisions under them and in the light of them. The concerns which prompted the original framers of the Bill of Rights are of course eminently relevant in making decisions and settling interpretations today, for they give us a platform of history and tradition on which to stand. But the relevance is in the broad sense of charting principles for guidance rather than in the narrower sense of being pregnant with correct answers for problems which could not have occurred to the draftsmen.

The equal protection clause of the fourteenth amendment was born out of a desire to throw a special mantle of protection around racial minorities who had, in the history of the United States, never before been accorded even the most rudimentary legal shelter. *Brown* v. *Board of Education* now seems solidly placed in the mainstream of such an endeavor. But there are, at the least, two aspects of the current *de facto* school segregation problem which serve to point out differences from the *Brown* model.

In the first place, *de facto* segregation is not so obviously the product of state action as the segregation struck down in *Brown.* The hand of the state may indeed sometimes be traced in *de facto* segregation; it can be argued that it sometimes proceeds from discriminatory patterns in housing which have historically, at least, been tolerated by the state or that the general pattern of the division of a state into educational subdivisions demonstrates an intent to perpetuate segregation. But such connections are by no means always to be found and, even where they are, they constitute a less direct instance of state action than was present in the *Brown* cases.

Second, in the light of the assertion of a right to equal educational opportunity, it must be said that educational disadvantage probably arises most directly from socioeconomic differentiation of school populations and the resulting difference in ambiance between schools in different districts. Such differences in the United States overlap considerably with racial distinctions but they are by no means coterminous. That the imbalance is not necessarily connected with race at all can readily be seen by noting its presence in other countries. Britain, for example, has long had an educational system in which a very small percentage of young people from working class homes go on to higher education. Until recently this disproportion has been supported and, indeed, ensured by consigning a very large majority of children, at the tender age of eleven or twelve, to schools whose professed aim is to prepare them for an artisan role in life, schools from which it is extremely difficult to enter college. The family backgrounds of working class children, coupled with their natural *de facto* segregation in neighborhood schools, combined to make it certain that few of them would be able to display certain rather artificial skills sufficiently well at the age of eleven to qualify for an academic education.

If, in the United States, a serious attack were to be made on educational inequality of opportunity it would be predestined to failure if it were made only in terms of racial separation, since that simply is not the root of the problem. For courts to move only against *de facto* racial segregation would at one and the same time be lacking in logic and also in prospects of success in the wider sense. If there is a right to equal educational opportunity in the United States, it would be a sad disappointment to discover that it meant no more than that blacks and whites might be educated together, important as that is. The inevitable outcome would be that most blacks and some whites would be educated together and poorly, while many whites and a few blacks would be educated together and well.

One of the few cases which has expressly recognized the validity of such an analysis is the judgment of Judge Skelly Wright, sitting in the District Court for the District of Columbia, in *Hobson* v. *Hansen*.[14]

In that case suit was brought on behalf of black children and poor children in the District of Columbia, alleging that the District's Board of Education had unconstitutionally deprived black and poor public school children of their right to equal educational opportunity. Among its findings of fact the court found that (a) "racially and socially homogeneous schools damage the minds and spirits of all children who attend them"; (b) "the scholastic achievement of the disadvantaged child . . . is strongly related to the racial and socio-economic composition of the student body of his school"; (c) "adherence to the neighborhood school policy by the School Board effectively segregates the Negro and poor children from the white and the more affluent children"; (d) "the teachers and principals in the public schools are assigned so that generally the race of the faculty is the same as the race of the children"; (e) "median annual per pupil expenditure . . . in the predominantly . . . Negro elementary schools . . . has been a flat $100 below the median annual per pupil expenditure for its predominantly white schools"; (f) "generally the 'white' schools are under-populated while the 'Negro' schools are generally overcrowded"; (g) "as they proceed through the Washington school system, the reading scores primarily of the Negro and the poor children, but not the white and middle class, fall increasingly behind the national norm"; (h) "the 'track' system as used in the District's public schools is a form of ability grouping in which students are divided in separate, self-contained curricula or tracks ranging from 'Basic' for the slow student to 'Honors' for the gifted. The aptitude tests used to assign children to the various tracks are standardized primarily on white middle class children. Since these tests do not relate to the Negro and disadvantaged child, track assignment based on such tests relegates Negro and disadvantaged children to the lower tracks from which, because of the reduced curricula and the absence of adequate remedial and compensatory education, as well as continued inappropriate testing, the chance of escape is remote. Education in the lower tracks is geared to . . . the 'blue collar' student. Thus such children . . . are denied equal opportunity to obtain the white collar education available to the white and more affluent children."

Judge Wright went on to hold that if *de facto* segregation and other features, such as the tracking system, led to a violation of the notion of equal educational opportunity, then the court in its equitable jurisdiction was empowered to make an order for the reform or abrogation of these practices. Accordingly the court issued a decree which, among other things, ordered (a) an injunction against racial and economic discrimination in the school system; (b) abolition of the track system; (c) transportation for volunteering children from overcrowded schools to underpopulated schools; (d) that the defendants file a plan for approval by the court providing for pupil assignment to integrate the teaching staffs.

Hobson v. *Hansen* may be one of the strongest examples of the intrusiveness of the judiciary into American life. Being the decision of a District Court the case is not of great weight in the doctrine of precedent,[15] but it is of considerable interest in pointing to the complexities of any serious-minded enforcement of the right to equal educational opportunity. Judge Wright, in his findings of fact as well as in the content of his decree, made it clear that racial separation alone was not the sum of the evils he was moving against. The separation of poor white children from children of more prosperous background was equally to the fore. As the earlier summary of the decree indicated, fashioning a remedy for such an injustice involved such judicial determinations as the sweeping away of the track system and a general directive to the school authorities to bring about a more even socioeconomic mix in their schools.

Interventions of this kind entail the court's assuming some of the tasks of educational policy makers and administrators. Judge Wright's opinion rested largely on his acceptance of certain expert testimony to the effect that lack of socioeconomic mix in school populations leads to unequal education. It is not easy to see where such a path stops. Suppose majority expert opinion among educationalists tomorrow agrees that one kind of curriculum is less well suited than another to prepare a child for entrance to college. Does that curriculum become an offense to the Constitution if used in some schools while others use the "better" one? The road that Judge Wright's opinion takes is one that leads to a conclusion that equal educational opportunity has a meaning which is to be derived from the best current opinion among educational experts. One commentator at least has expressly invited such an interpretation:

"Equal education has to be given concreteness, specificity and refinement as educational policy. The contours of equal education as a constitutional requirement and its design as educational policy, practice, or methodology should be virtually the same. Where educational policy concludes that equal education requires certain specific practices, the courts should make those practices a part of the constitutional dimensions of the equal education guarantee. Educators have simply failed to tell us what equal education connotes as educational policy, and the courts have been forced to rely on their own judgment concerning what the equal education guarantee requires or prohibits."[16]

This passage shows a touching faith in the wisdom of experts and great expectations that they could produce the right answers if only they weren't lazy or stubborn or something. It conjures up a future, which some may find frightening, in which the Supreme Court adjusts the content of the Constitution monthly to conform to the latest configuration of expert opinion and proceeds to do its best to outlaw any deviationist practices in our educational institutions. The position must indeed be approaching the desperate when such remedies can be strenously advocated.

There is of course nothing in the language of the equal protection clause, concise and infinitely expansible as it is, which precludes interpretations involving a grand judicial attack on every conceivable aspect of inequality in our educational systems. Neither is the present discussion in the least intended to favor a conservative position with respect to social change in general and education in particular. For the sake of the argument, we may be willing to admit that the United States is riddled with scarifying social injustices and that the educational scene exhibits gross examples. The most vigorous measures to effect change in this and other areas may be eminently desirable. The only question now being raised is what principles should govern a court in deciding how far to take up such a task.

The Supreme Court of the United States is indeed a very peculiar court. Its assumed mandate to override legislation and executive action which conflicts with the Bill of Rights thrusts it inescapably into an area of semipolitical judgments which would be alien to the judicial practice of most nations. Not much assistance can be derived from appeals to precedent in the technical lawyers' sense of *stare decisis.* As one writer has observed, "The difficulty with *stare decisis* is that, like Christianity, it never has been practised, and anyone who begins practising it will be at a distinct disadvantage."[17] But a court which has one foot in the field of political decision making will be properly attentive to a set of principles of mixed juridical-political origins to guide its steps. A partial, and probably by no means exhaustive, list of such principles might be the following.

1. The Court is not elected and not accountable in any usual political sense to anyone. As Professor Alexander Bickel has put it, it "has no earth to draw strength from."[18] This should encourage modesty about its policy making role for the nation.

2. Attention should be paid to the possibility that legislative and executive branches may regard a decision as an encroachment on their spheres of jurisdiction with the attendant tensions, strains, and possible constitutional crises that may be precipitated.

3. There may sometimes be a danger that a decision will outrage majority opinion in the population at large. The outrage may of course result from the irrational prejudices or bigotry of the people. Here a passage which Bentham addressed to legislators may be relevant also for the Court: "But when I say that antipathies and sympathies are no reason, I mean those of the legislator: for the antipathies and sympathies of the people may be reasons, and very powerful ones. However odd or pernicious a religion, a law, a custom may be, it is of no consequence, so long as the people are attached to it. The strength of their prejudice is the measure of the indulgence which should be granted to it. . . . The legislator ought to yield to

the violence of a current which carries away everything that obstructs."[19]

4. There may be a prospect that a decision will be largely ignored or defied by those to whom it is directed, in such circumstances that enforcement by the courts would be difficult.

5. The Court should be vigilant for the dangers which may ensue from dressing up ephemeral sociological and psychological opinions as constitutional propositions.

6. There may be dangers in making sudden doctrinal "leaps" for which a sufficient foundation has not been laid in professional discussion and argument.

7. Sometimes the fashioning of a remedy for the instant grievance before the Court may seem practicable and attractive but may contain implications that point compellingly to further intervention which may be much more complicated and difficult. It is not easy to take only one step into a bog.

8. Attention must be paid to the appropriateness of the question for judicial settlement. A question may be "inappropriate," for example, where a remedy could only be effective through a large remodeling of institutions which could only be envisaged through a regulatory code implemented by a bureaucracy of supervisors and enforcers.

The history of the Court has demonstrated different degrees of deference at different times to the above considerations. It may be that at some times the Court has been too deferential and at other times not attentive enough to such principles, for the list of guiding principles given above was certainly not meant to be exclusionary. Others of great importance may be readily seen which often must compete with those in the first group. Some of these would call for respectful attention to the following factors.

1. That the grievance presented amounts to a plain violation of the Bill of Rights within generally agreed current understanding of the scope of those rights.

2. The special historical position of the Court as the protector of minority groups.

3. The danger that the Bill of Rights may atrophy if there is no creative and imaginative application of its precepts to new situations.

4. The special role of the Court as the unifier of civil rights and liberties in a federal society.

Any court in any system of law must pay constant attention to competing principles of policy and prudence in fashioning its decisions. The special quality of federal courts in the United States is only that the principles to which they ought to be sensitive are more obviously and nakedly political than is elsewhere the case. America is consumed by anxieties about grave domestic problems to do with race, poverty in general, and urban ills in particular. Faced with what they feel to be legislative and executive inertia and imbued with deep moral feelings about the intensity of social injustice and with profound anxieties for the future progress of the United States, many Americans look to the courts as the most hopeful institution for achieving social progress.

But such great expectations are likely to be disappointed. There are limits to the reach of the courts in dealing with complaints of social injustice. These limits are not so much in the words of the Constitution, for these give enough purchase to scale most arguments for mandatory social change. The limits spring rather from the nature of the court as an institution, and they are both practical and principled. Lacking executive servants and an apparatus of coercion, courts simply do not have the equipment to do the elaborate planning, draft the complex regulations, and engage in the intricate implementation and supervision which fundamental social reform demands. At the same time, attempts to thrust too strenuously in this direction will result in an offense against the cautionary principles outlined earlier. Such offense is very likely to lead to constitutional crisis or at least to political and popular hostility against which the courts are peculiarly defenseless. Moral leadership without popular mandate, legislative technique, or executive power is a dangerous game which must be played with moderation and subtlety if it is not to prove ineffectual, divisive, and counterproductive.

REFERENCES

[1] Fuller, *The Morality of Law* (1964).
[2] 370 U.S. 660 (1962).
[3] 91 S. Ct. 1331 (1971).
[4] 364 F. 2d 197 (1966).
[5] *Escobedo* v. *Illinois* 378 U.S. 478 (1964); *Miranda* v. *Arizona* 384 U.S. 436 (1966).
[6] 369 U.S. 186 (1962).

[7] 395 U.S. 486 (1968).

[8] For a discussion of the political-question doctrine, see Hughes, "Civil Disobedience and the Political-Question Doctrine," in *Ethics and Social Justice,* ed. H. E. Kiefer and M. K. Munitz (1970), p. 207.

[9] 163 U.S. 537 (1896).

[10] 347 U.S. 483 (1954).

[11] See *Equality of Educational Opportunity* (1966), published by the United States Office of Education, and *Racial Isolation in the Public Schools* (1967), a report of the United States Commission on Civil Rights.

[12] See e.g., *Tometz* v. *Board of Education* 237 N.E. 2d 498 (1968).

[13] 91 S. Ct. 1267 (1971).

[14] 269 F. Supp. 401 (1967).

[15] *Hobson* v. *Hansen* was substantially affirmed on appeal *sub nomine Smuck* v. *Hobson* 408 F. 2d 157 (1969).

[16] Robert Carter, "The Right to Equal Educational Opportunity," in *The Rights of Americans,* ed. N. Dorsen (1971), p. 11.

[17] R. V. Denenberg, "The U.S. Supreme Court—An Introductory Note," *Cambridge Law Journal,* 29 (1971), 145.

[18] A. M. Bickel, *The Least Dangerous Branch* (1962), p. 184.

[19] Bentham, *Theory of Legislation* (Hildreth ed., 1876), pp. 76-77. It should be noted that Bentham went on to say, "It is to be observed, however, that too much deference for prejudices is a more common fault than the contrary excess."

PART II

9

TOWARD A JURISPRUDENCE OF "HARM" PREVENTION

Alan Dershowitz

INTRODUCTION

I am concerned about a silent but growing trend in this country toward confining people who have not committed crimes but who are thought to be dangerous—that is, likely to engage in harmful conduct at some future time. The issues raised by such preventive confinement of allegedly dangerous persons were perceptively captured in a dialogue between Lewis Carroll's Alice and the Queen. The Queen said:

> "There's the King's Messenger. He's in prison now, being punished; and the trial doesn't even begin till next Wednesday; and of course the crime comes last of all."
>
> "Suppose he never commits the crime?" asked Alice.
>
> "That would be all the better, wouldn't it?" the Queen responded. . . .

Alice felt there was no denying that. "Of course it would be all the better," she said; "but it wouldn't be all the better his being punished."

"You're wrong . . ." said the Queen. "Were you ever punished?

"Only for faults," said Alice.

"And you were all the better for it, I know!" the Queen said triumphantly.

"Yes, but then I had done the things I was punished for," said Alice, "That makes all the difference."

"But if you hadn't done them," the Queen said, "that would have been better still; better, and better, and better!" Her voice went higher with each "better," till it got quite to a squeak. . . .

Alice thought, "There's a mistake here somewhere. . . ."[1]

It is this mistake that I wish to explore today.

The twin questions posed by any system of criminal justice are: "Did he do it?" and "Will he do it?" These questions reflect different strategies toward a common goal: to reduce the frequency and severity of certain feared events. I will refer to the strategy reflected in the question "did he do it" as the punishment-deterrent strategy. Under this approach, the feared event is formally defined and proscribed. When someone brings it about he is punished, with the expectation that anyone contemplating similar conduct will be dissuaded by the unpleasurable response they now know awaits them. Thus, killing another under most circumstances is thought to be a harmful event whose frequency should be reduced. It is therefore defined as murder or manslaughter and formally proscribed. When such an event occurs, the perpetrator is imprisoned or executed, with the expectation that potential killers will have it brought home to them that if they kill they too may be imprisoned or executed.

The strategy embodied in the question "will he do it" may be called the prediction-prevention strategy. Under this approach the feared event may or may not be formally proscribed. Those persons who are thought likely to cause harm are sought out before they have had an opportunity to do so. They are then prevented from bringing about the feared action by some method of incapacitation. Thus, potential killers may be spotted by some predictive device or by the presence of some mental condition and incarcerated until the assumed danger no longer exists.

Throughout the ages, some societies have focused more directly on the punishment-deterrent strategy, others on prediction-prevention. No society has ever ignored either. A systematic, though imperfect, jurisprudence has emerged in response to the first strategy. Every schoolboy knows, for example, that our methods of determining whether he "did it" are limited by the maxim "better ten guilty men go free than one innocent may be wrongly imprisoned." Although more people are today confined under the prediction-prevention rationale than under the punitive-deterrent one, the former operates, for the most part, outside the confines of any jurisprudential framework. Even the most sophisticated jurists have given little thought to how many false positives—people who would not commit a predicted act—ought to be confined to prevent a true positive from bringing about a predicted harm. Indeed, when we look closely at what we are actually doing under the banner of prediction-prevention, we discover that our practices reflect a value judgment diametrically opposed to that which limits the punitive-deterrent strategy. The maxim seems to be "better to confine ten people who would not commit predicted harms than to release one who would." I do not mean by this to deny that an ounce of prevention may be worth a pound of cure. I do, however, question the assumption underlying that venerable adage, at least in the context of crime prevention. In law, it will often require a pound of prevention to replace an ounce of cure. And when these pounds and ounces measure human confinement, the issues raised are far more complex than the adage suggests.

It is the aim of this paper to propose a framework for analyzing the range of problems posed by our increasing reliance on the strategy of prediction and prevention of harmful conduct. My remarks are not intended as a brief in favor of this trend toward early intervention. Indeed, they will provide opponents of this development with much ammunition for attack. They may also provide proponents with some defensive ammunition as well. My thesis is that the strategy of preventive confinement, though widespread in this country, has not been accompanied by a systematic probing of its underlying empirical and normative assumptions, and that without this sort of careful analysis, no system of confinement based on prediction can be either accurate or just.

HISTORY

Although the punishment-deterrent strategy is the one most often associated with the Anglo-American criminal process, the prediction-prevention strategy has roots deep in our legal heritage. It was a source of great pride to Blackstone that preventive justice was part of the English tradition: "And really it is an honor," he said, "and almost a singular one, to our English laws, that they furnish a title of this sort, since preventive justice is upon every principle of reason, of humanity and of sound policy, preferable in all respects to punishing justice, the execution of which . . . is always attended with many harsh and disagreeable circumstances."[2] The "preventive justice" to which Blackstone was specifically referring consisted of requiring certain persons who had committed no crime, but about whom there was "a probable suspicion that some crime is intended or likely to happen," to find "pledges or securities for keeping peace, or for their good behavior."[3] Those unable to comply were incarcerated.

Now one could, of course, argue that this sort of preventive justice fits as well into the punishment-deterrent strategy as into the prediction-prevention one, since a predicted law breaker was not automatically confined but instead was threatened with an additional punishment—forfeiture of money—in the event he broke the law. This merely serves to point up the difficulty of dichotomizing complicated human processes into distinct categories. Blackstone himself saw the conceptual difficulty of separating the punishment-deterrent strategy (which he called "punishing justice") from the prediction-prevention one (which he called "preventive justice"). "If we consider all human punishments in a large and extended view," he observed, "we shall find them all rather calculated to prevent future crimes than to expiate the past. . . ."[4] And Blackstone's view is well taken. A convicted murderer is imprisoned or executed as much to prevent him, as to deter others, from committing further murders. All that my dichotomy is intended to suggest is that different assumptions and values are implicit in the decision to authorize state intervention at one point rather than another along the continuum of predicted danger to consummated harm.

PRESENT USE

Are both these strategies employed in the United States today? If one looked only to the pronouncements of our high courts for the answer, one would come away believing that the prediction-prevention approach has no place in our constitutional constellation. As Justice Jackson said in holding that bail must be set for defendants charged with violating the Smith Act:

> If I assume that defendants are disposed to commit every opportune disloyal act helpful to communist countries, it is still difficult to reconcile with traditional American law the jailing of persons by the courts because of anticipated but as yet uncommitted crimes. Imprisonment to protect society from predicted but unconsummated offenses is so unprecedented in this country and so fraught with danger of excess and injustice that I am loath to resort to it. . . .[5]

But if one looks carefully at our statute books, our court decisions, and, most important, our practices, there begins to emerge a much fuller picture of wide spread, though sometimes unarticulated, use of the prediction-prevention strategy in the United States. A justice of the Burma Supreme Court came closer than our own Justice Jackson when he observed: "Preventive justice which consists in restraining a man from committing a crime which he may commit but has not yet committed is common to all systems of jurisprudence. . . ."[6]

The prediction-prevention strategy is used widely throughout the world during times of war and emergency. During both world wars, Great Britain promulgated regulations explicitly authorizing the preventive detention of certain persons suspected of "hostile origin or association." During the Second World War the United States employed one of the grossest forms of preventive detention known to history: the mass transfer and internment of Americans of Japanese descent, allegedly on the basis of a prediction that otherwise they would sabotage our war effort on the West Coast and become victims of racial violence. The Supreme Court's approval of that device[7] laid the foundation for a statute recently removed from the books which had authorized the detention during a declared internal security emergency of any person "as to whom there is reasonable ground to believe that he probably will engage in or probably will conspire with others to engage in acts of espionage or of sabotage."[8]

During the recent riots in Detroit and other urban areas, thousands of persons were detained without bail, or with very high bail, on the pretense of awaiting trial for trivial offenses, but actually in order to prevent them from committing future crimes. As the Kerner Commission reported, "such high money bail has been indiscriminately set, often resulting in detention of everyone arrested during a riot without distinction as to the nature of the alleged crime or the likelihood of repeated offenses."[9]

Nor is our use of the prediction-prevention strategy limited to times of war or emergency. In this paper, I will simply catalogue some of the preventive devices currently employed in this country during peacetime and then focus on two of them in some detail.

Peace bonds—the Blackstonian technique of "preventive justice" —are still authorized in some parts of the United States. In a recent Pennsylvania case, a defendant was charged with assault and battery. He stood trial and was acquitted by a jury. Despite this, the judge required him to post a bond of $1,000 "to keep the peace for two years."[10] In its opinion vacating the bond as inconsistent with the right to trial by jury, the State Supreme Court cited data indicating that during ten previous years "478 men, after acquittal of criminal charges, were compelled to serve an aggregate of over 600 years in . . . prison in default of bonds aggregating $613,200."[11]

Juvenile statutes authorize confinement of young persons who have not yet committed criminal acts but who are thought likely to become criminals. Indeed, Mr. Justice Harlan cited figures in his separate opinion in the *Gault* case indicating that between 26 and 48 percent of the 600,000 children brought before juvenile courts "are not in any sense guilty of criminal misconduct."[12] Some sex psychopath laws also authorize detention of persons who have never been convicted of sex or other crimes but who are thought likely to engage in such acts. Many states permit the incarceration of so-called material witnesses—that is, persons not charged with crimes themselves but who may be important witnesses at the trial of someone charged with crime. Such witnesses may be required to post bond, and if unable, may be confined to prison until the trial, on the basis of a prediction that otherwise they might disregard the subpoena.[13] Another widespread American practice is the so-called preventive arrest, recently described in a government report as follows:

> A person trying front doors of stores, or peering into parked cars, in the early hours of the morning; a person "known" to the police as a pickpocket loitering at a crowded bus stop; a "known" Murphy game operator talking to a soldier or a sailor—such persons may be arrested . . . largely in order to eliminate at least temporarily the occasion for any possible criminal activity. The principle upon which arrests are made appears to be: if the individual is detained until 10 or 11 A.M. the following day, at least he will have committed no crime that night. . . .[14]

The courts are beginning to place limits on police discretion in some such situations. For example, the arrest of a person found wandering around toilets on the ground that there is probable cause to suspect that he is about to perform an act of homosexuality might not be sustained as a valid exercise of police discretion. But many legislatures have made it unnecessary for the police to justify such arrests by reference to as yet uncommitted crimes. They make the "suspicious" act itself a crime justifying arrest. Thus a number of states now make it a crime "to loiter in or about public toilets" or "to wander about the streets at late or unusual hours without any visible or lawful business."[15] The preventive aspect of such vagrancy statutes was recently recognized in a judicial decision condemning the District of Columbia statute.[16] Judge Green suggested that the real objection to the vagrancy law is that "its basic design is one of preventive conviction imposed upon those who, because of their background and behavior, are more likely than the general public to commit crimes, and that the statute contemplates such convictions even though no overt criminal act has been committed or can be proved."[17] Accordingly, he defined the real issue in the enforcement of vagrancy type statutes as "whether our system tolerates the concept of preventive conviction on suspicion."[18]

In addition to these and other purely preventive devices, there are a good many statutes which, though triggered by commission of a criminal act, rest primarily on a prediction-prevention rationale. Included in this mixed category are defective delinquency, habitual criminal, and addict or alcoholic commitment laws.

The two prediction-prevention devices employed most widely in the United States today are: (1) denial of pretrial release to persons charged with, but not yet convicted of, crimes; and (2) involuntary hospitalization of the mentally ill. Though different in rationale, focus, and duration, these devices raise sufficiently similar questions so that a comparative analysis may shed some light on the general issue of preventive confinement.

PREVENTIVE DETENTION OF PERSONS AWAITING TRIAL

When a person is charged with having committed a serious crime, he is generally arrested. Since his trial will not be held for a number of months, a decision must be made as to whether he will be detained or released during this hiatus. But this decision is not made by the judge, at least not directly. For the judge is required, in all but a small number of capital cases, to "set bail"—that is, to condition pretrial release on the posting of a certain amount of money as security for the defendant's appearance at trial. In setting the amount of the bail, the judge is supposed to consider the likelihood that the accused will not appear for trial. Even if that likelihood is high—that is, even if the judge predicts that the accused will probably flee—he must still set bail. But he will set it at a high amount, in the expectation that the accused either will not be able to post it, or, if he can, that the threat of forfeiting so much money will dissuade him from fleeing. Although in setting the amount of bail judges are supposed to consider only the likelihood that the accused will flee, it is clear that they also consider the likelihood that he will commit crimes, threaten witnesses, or bribe jurors while awaiting trial.

Thus, the present system of pretrial preventive detention seems to function in the following way: if the judge predicts that any of the feared occurrences is likely, he sets high bail; if he predicts that they are unlikely, he sets low bail. The imprecision of this indirect system of preventive detention is apparent. The access of the accused to money is a crucial variable which bears little relevance to the system's goal—detention of predicted wrongdoers. For if an accused can post high bail, he will be released even if he is thought to be dangerous. But if an accused person cannot post bail, he will be detained even if he is not thought to be dangerous. Thus the apparent goal of the system—the detention of all dangerous people —is distorted by the critical role played by an irrelevant variable: money.

This system has recently come under heavy attack, both because it effects the release of too many wealthy dangerous people and because it effects the detention of too many poor nondangerous people. In its place, there has been proposed a plan which would explicitly authorize the preventive detention pending trial of certain predicted law breakers. In other words, instead of pretrial release depending on the defendant's financial ability. it would turn explicitly on his predicted dangerousness. In cautiously suggesting this change, one thoughtful commentator has said:

> Our hostility towards the notion of preventive detention ought not lead us to continuing the game of making believe that the practice does not exist. It ought not blind us to the fact that the practice is indulged in by criminal courts every day through the often unfair and ineffective medium of excessive bail, without the candor that is needed to make it visible, controllable and susceptible to appellate review and constitutional testing.

It does not, of course, follow from the fact that preventive detention is surreptitiously "indulged in by criminal courts every day" that its continuation should be authorized. Its social benefits and costs should be articulated and balanced. If the former are thought to outweigh the latter, then perhaps some form of preventive detention should be authorized in appropriate situations. If not, then procedures should be devised to purge it from the system. If preventive detention is to be authorized, then surely it should be candid, visible, controllable, and subject to review. Moreover, it should not employ distorting variables—like money—which result in the detention of some people who are less dangerous than others who are released.

The conditions giving rise to the call for pretrial preventive detention are not difficult to understand. A person suspected of committing a crime cannot stand trial on the day of his arrest; he must be given time to consult with his lawyer and prepare a defense. Although this should rarely take more than a few days, the delay between arrest and trial has been growing, until it is now almost as long as two years in some cities and a year in most other cities, including the District of Columbia. This is the consequence primarily of our unwillingness to pay for needed increases in judicial machinery.

At the same time there has been a growing sensitivity to the plight of the indigent accused, who are unable to raise even modest bail; this is reflected in a 1966 bail reform law which authorizes federal judges to release most defendants without requiring money bail.[19] The net result of bail reform and increased delays in court has been that more criminal defendants spend more time out on the street awaiting their trials than ever before. This has led to an increase—or at least the appearance of an increase—in the number of crimes between ·arrest and trial. And so, in an effort to stem this tide of increasing crime, many political leaders have focused their attention on the defendant awaiting trial. The slogan "crime in the streets" has found its first political victim.

The resulting proposals for preventive detention vary: some are limited to the District of Columbia, while others apply to all federal courts; some would seem to authorize the confinement of a very large number of defendants, while others are narrower in their scope; some include methods of shortening the time interval between arrest and trial, while others seem satisfied to leave things pretty much as they are now. But they all have one point in common: they permit the imprisonment of a defendant who has not been convicted, and who is presumed innocent of the crime with which he stands charged, on the basis of a prediction that he may commit a crime at some future time. These predictions would be made by judges on the basis of their appraisal of the suspect's dangerousness, after study of his prior record and the crime for which he is being tried. The proponents of preventive detention hope thereby to identify and isolate those defendants awaiting trial who account for the apparently high incidence of serious crime. The opponents of preventive detention maintain that, under our system of criminal justice, which is characterized by "the presumption of innocence," conviction for a past crime is the only legitimate basis for confinement; they are fearful that acceptance of this "novel" approach to crime prevention might be an opening wedge leading to widespread confinement of persons suspected, on the basis of untested predictions, of dangerous propensities. And they reject the idea of confining anyone on the basis of statistical likelihood that he "may" be dangerous.

As I have shown, however, this preventive approach is not nearly as novel as the opponents of preventive detention suggest. Nor can

I reject—as necessarily unjust—a system which relies on statistical likelihood. Statistical likelihood—gross and impersonal as that sounds —is all we ever have, whether we are predicting the future or reconstructing the past. When we establish rules for convicting the guilty, we do not require certainty; we only require that guilt be proved "beyond a reasonable doubt." And that means that we are willing to tolerate the conviction of some innocent suspects in order to assure the confinement of a vastly larger number of guilty criminals. We insist that the statistical likelihood of guilt be very high: "better ten guilty men go free than one innocent man be wrongly condemned." But we do not—nor could we—insist on certainty; to do so would result in immobility.

What difference is there between imprisoning a man for past crimes on the basis of "statistical likelihood" and detaining him to prevent future crimes on the same kind of less-than-certain information? The important difference may not be so much one of principle; it may be more, as Justice Holmes said all legal issues are, one of degree. The available evidence suggests that our system of determining past guilt results in the erroneous conviction of relatively few innocent people.[20] We really do seem to practice what we preach about preferring the acquittal of guilty men to the conviction of innocent men.

But the indications are that any system of predicting future crimes would result in a vastly larger number of erroneous confinements—that is, confinements of persons predicted to engage in violent crime who would not, in fact, do so. Indeed, all the experience with predicting violent conduct suggests that in order to spot a significant proportion of future violent criminals, we would have to reverse the traditional maxim of the criminal law and adopt a philosophy that it is "better to confine ten people who would not commit predicted crimes than to release one who would."[21]

The reason why this is so can perhaps best be illustrated by turning to the preventive detention device most widely employed in this country: the involuntary hospitalization of the mentally ill.

PREVENTIVE DETENTION OF THE MENTALLY ILL

Tens of thousands of persons who have committed no criminal act are confined indefinitely without their consent on the basis of a diagnosis—that they are "mentally ill"—and a prediction —that unless confined they might cause harm to themselves or others.

It is often alleged that involuntary confinement of the mentally ill serves functions other than preventive detention, such as the treatment and cure of sick people. Yet, although some courts have articulated a general "right to treatment,"[22] no court, so far as I am aware, has ever actually ordered the release of a dangerous mentally ill person who is receiving no treatment or who is incurable or untreatable. Indeed, if courts were to order the release of inmates not receiving meaningful treatment, the population of many state mental hospitals would be reduced dramatically. This is not to suggest that the courts should issue such an order or that preventive detention of some mentally ill persons may not be justified. It is only to suggest that, as with preventive detention of persons awaiting trial, we should not continue "the game of making believe that the practice does not exist." Only if we recognize involuntary hospitalization for what it is can we begin to ask whether the criteria for such confinement promote or retard the legitimate goals of preventive detention.

The one universal criterion for involuntary hospitalization is the presence of mental illness. In some jurisdictions this is enough; in others, something else—such as danger to self or others—must also be established. In all jurisdictions, as a matter of practice, once mental illness is established, there is a presumption in favor of confinement. Thus, the critical criterion is "mental illness." But if the function of involuntary hospitalization is the preventive detention of dangerous people, then why should it matter whether such people are, or are not, "mentally ill"? Particularly since mental illness is not an accurate predictor of dangerous conduct. Recent studies suggest that the mentally ill do not, as a class, engage in more acts of violence than those not so diagnosed. If a "mentally healthy" person is sufficiently dangerous, why should he not be confined? If a "mentally ill" person is not sufficiently dangerous, why should he be confined? Consider a hypothetical case of two persons, one named Ira Ill and the other named Mike Mafia. Assume that a predictive device establishes a seventy percent likelihood that Ira Ill, who is diagnosed by a psychiatrist as "mentally ill," will commit homicide in the reasonable future, and an eighty percent likelihood that Mike Mafia, a mentally healthy gangster, will commit homicide in the reasonable future. Ira Ill's detention would be no more justified than Mike Mafia's unless it was designed to promote unarticulated values other than preventive detention. Just as in the bail area, where the preventive goal is distorted by the irrelevant variable of money, in the involuntary hospitalization area the preventive goal is distorted by the irrelevant criterion of mental illness.

The original legislative purpose underlying commitment laws seems clear: to isolate those persons who—for whatever reason—were regarded as intolerably obnoxious to the community. Medical testimony had little to offer in making this judgment; the people knew whom they regarded as obnoxious. By the middle of the nineteenth century, however, madness was becoming widely regarded as a disease which should be treated by physicians with little, or no, interference by courts. The present situation comes close to reflecting that view; the criteria for confinement are so vague that courts sit—when they sit at all—merely to review decisions made by doctors. Indeed, the typical criteria are so meaningless as even to preclude effective review. In some states, for example, the court is supposed to commit any person whom a doctor reasonably finds is "mentally ill and a fit subject for treatment in a hospital for mental illness, or that he ought to be confined."[23] This circularity is typical of the criteria—or lack thereof—in about half our states. Even in those jurisdictions with legal-sounding criteria—such as the District of Columbia, where the committed person must be mentally ill and likely to injure himself or others[24]—the operative phrases are so vague that courts rarely upset psychiatric determinations.

The distorting effect of this medical model of confinement may be illustrated by comparing two recent cases from the District of Columbia. One involved Bong Yol Yang, an American of Korean origin who appeared at the White House gate asking to see the President about people who were following him and "revealing his subconscious thoughts." He also wondered whether his talents as an artist could be put to use by the government. The gate officer had him committed to a mental hospital. Yang demanded a jury trial, at which a psychiatrist testified that he was mentally ill—a paranoid schizophrenic—and that although there was no "evidence of his ever attacking anyone so far," there is always a possibility that "if his frustrations . . . became great enough, he may potentially attack someone. . . ." On the basis of this diagnosis and prediction, the judge permitted a jury to commit Yang to a mental hospital until he was no longer mentally ill and likely to injure himself or others.

The other case involved a man named Dallas Williams, who at age 39 had spent half his life in jail for seven convictions of assault with a deadly weapon and one conviction of manslaughter. Just before his scheduled release from jail, the government petitioned for his civil commitment. Two psychiatrists testified that although "at the present time [he] shows no evidence of active mental illness . . . he is potentially dangerous to others and if released is likely to repeat his patterns of criminal behavior, and might commit homicide."[25] The judge, in denying the government's petition and ordering Williams' release, observed that: "The courts have no legal basis for ordering confinement on mere apprehension of future unlawful acts. They must wait until another crime is committed or the person is found insane."[26] Within months of his release, Williams lived up to the prediction of the psychiatrists and shot two men to death in an unprovoked attack.

Are there any distinctions between the Williams and Yang cases which justify the release of the former and the incarceration of the latter? There was no evidence that Yang was more dangerous, more amenable to treatment, or less competent than Williams. But Yang was diagnosed mentally ill and thus within the medical model, whereas Williams was not so diagnosed. Although there was nothing about Yang's mental illness which made him a more appropriate subject for involuntary confinement than Williams, the law attributed conclusive significance to the presence of mental illness. The outcomes in these cases—which make little sense when evaluated against any rational criteria for confinement—are typical under the present civil commitment process. And this will continue as long as the law continues to ask the dispositive questions in medical rather than legally functional terms, because a medical model does not ask the proper questions, or asks them in meaninglessly vague terms: Is the person mentally ill? Is he dangerous to himself or others? Is he in need of care or treatment?

Nor is this the only way to ask the questions to which the civil commitment process is responsive. It will be instructive to restate the problem of civil commitment without employing medical terms to see whether the answers suggested differ from those now given.

There are, in every society, people who cause trouble if not confined. The trouble may be serious (such as homocide), trivial (making of offensive remarks), or somewhere in between (forging checks). The trouble may be directed at others, at the person himself, or at both. It may be very likely that he will cause trouble, or fairly likely, or fairly unlikely. In some instances this likelihood may be considerably reduced by a relatively short period of involuntary confinement; in others, a longer period may be required with no assurances of reduced risk; in still others, the likelihood can never be significantly reduced. Some people will have fairly good insight into the risks they pose and the costs entailed by an effort to reduce those risks; others will have poor insight into these factors.

When the issues are put this way, there begins to emerge a series of meaningful questions capable of traditional legal analyses:

1. What sorts of anticipated harm warrant involuntary confinement?

2. How likely must it be that the harm will occur? Must there be a significant component of harm to others, or may the harm be to self alone?

3. If harm to self is sufficient, must the person also be incapable, because he lacks insight, of weighing the risks to himself against the costs of confinement?

4. Must the likelihood of the harm increase as its severity decreases? Or as the component of harm to others decreases? How long a period of involuntary confinement is justified to prevent which sorts of harms?

These questions are complex, but this is as it should be, for the business of balancing the liberty of the individual against the risks a free society must tolerate is very complex. That is the business of the law, and these are the questions which need asking and answering before liberty is denied, but they are obscured when the issue is phrased in medical terms which frighten—or bore—lawyers away. Nor have I simply manufactured these questions. They are the very questions which are being implicitly answered every day by psychiatrists, but they are not being openly asked, and many psychiatrists do not realize that they are, in fact, answering them.

Let us consider two of these questions and compare how they are being dealt with—or not dealt with—under the present system, with how they might be handled under functional, nonmedical, criteria.

The initial and fundamental question which must be asked by any system authorizing incarceration is: which harms are sufficiently serious to justify resort to this rather severe sanction? This question is asked and answered in the criminal law by the substantive definitions of crime. Thus, homicide is a harm which justifies the sanction of imprisonment; miscegenation does not; and adultery is a close case about which reasonable people may, and do, disagree. It is difficult to conceive of a criminal process which did not make some effort at articulating these distinctions. Imagine, for example, a penal code which simply made it an imprisonable crime to cause

injury to self or others, without defining injury. It is also difficult
to conceive of a criminal process—at least in jurisdictions with an
Anglo-American tradition—in which these distinctions were not drawn
by the legislature or courts. It would seem beyond dispute that the
question of which harms do, and which do not, justify incarceration
is a legal—indeed a political—decision, to be made not by experts
but by the constitutionally authorized agents of the people. Again,
imagine a penal code which authorized incarceration for anyone who
performed an act regarded as injurious by a designated expert, say
a psychiatrist or penologist.

It is argued, however, that there are differences between the
criminal and the civil commitment processes: the criminal law is
supposed to punish people for having committed harmful acts in
the past whereas civil commitment is supposed to prevent people
from committing harmful acts in the future. While this difference
may have important implications in some contexts, it would seem
entirely irrelevant in deciding which acts are sufficiently harmful to
justify incarceration, either as an after-the-fact punitive sanction or
as a before-the-fact preventive sanction. The considerations which
require clear definition of such harms in the criminal process would
seem to be fully applicable to civil commitment.

Yet the situation which I said would be hard to imagine in the
criminal law is precisely the one which prevails with civil commitment.
The statutes authorize preventive incarceration of mentally ill persons
who are likely to injure themselves or others. "Injure" is generally
not defined in the statutes or in the case law, and the critical decision
—whether a predicted pattern of behavior is sufficiently injurious to
warrant incarceration—is relegated to the unarticulated judgments of
the psychiatrist. And some psychiatrists are perfectly willing to provide
their own personal opinions—often falsely disguised as expert opinions
—about which harms are sufficiently serious. One psychiatrist recently
told a meeting of the American Psychiatric Association that "you"—
the psychiatrist—"have to define for yourself the word danger, and
then having decided that in your mind . . . look for it with every
conceivable means. . . ."

My own conversations with psychiatrists reveal wide differences
in opinion over what sorts of harms justify incarceration. As one
would expect, some psychiatrists are political conservatives while
others are liberals; some place a greater premium on safety, others
on liberty. Their opinions about which harms do, and which do not,
justify confinement probably cover the range of opinions one would

expect to encounter in any educated segment of the public. But they are judgments that each of us is as qualified to make as they are. Thus, this most fundamental decision—which harms justify confinement—is almost never made by the legislature or the courts; often it is never explicitly made by anyone, and when it is explicitly made, it is by an unelected and unappointed expert operating outside the area of his expertise.

Consider, for example, the age-old philosophical dispute about the government's authority to incarcerate someone for his own good. The classic statement denying such authority was made by John Stuart Mill in his treatise *On Liberty*. He deemed it fundamental: "That the only purpose for which power can be rightfully exercised against his will, is to prevent harm to others. He cannot rightfully be compelled to do or forbear because it will be better for him to do so, because it will make him happier, because . . . to do so would be wise or even right. . . ."

The most eloquent presentation of the other view was made by the poet John Donne in a famous stanza from his *Devotions:*

> No man is an island, entire of itself;
> Every man is a piece of the continent,
> A part of the main;
> If a clod be washed away from the sea,
> Europe is the less . . . ;
> Any man's death diminishes me, because I am
> involved in mankind;
> And therefore never send to know for whom the
> bell tolls;
> It tolls for thee.[27]

These statements—eloquent as they are—are far too polarized for useful discourse. In our complex and interdependent society, there is hardly a harm to one man which does not have radiations beyond the island of his person. But this observation does not, in itself, destroy the thrust of Mill's argument. Society may still have less justification for incarcerating a person to prevent a harm to himself which contains only a slight component of harm to others than if it contained a large component of such harm.

Compare, for example, a recent case which arose under the civil commitment process with a similar fact situation which produced no case at all. Mrs. Lake, a 62-year-old widow, suffers from arterio-

sclerosis which causes periods of confusion interspersed with periods
of relative rationality. One day she was found wandering around
downtown Washington looking confused but bothering no one,
whereupon she was committed to a mental hospital. She petitioned
for release and at her trial testified, during a period of apparent
rationality, that she was aware of her problem, that she knew that
her periods of confusion endangered her health and even her life,
but that she had experienced the mental hospital and preferred to
assume the risk of living—and perhaps dying—outside its walls. Her
petition was denied, and despite continued litigation,[28] she is still
involuntarily confined in the closed ward of the mental hospital
where she will probably spend her remaining days.

Compare Mrs. Lake's decision to one made by Supreme Court
Justice Jackson, who, at the same age of 62, suffered a severe
heart attack while serving on the Supreme Court. As Solicitor
General Sobeloff recalled in his memorial tribute, Jackson's "doctors
gave him the choice between years of comparative inactivity or a
continuation of his normal activity at the risk of death at any time."[29]
Characteristically, he chose the second alternative, and suffered a
fatal heart attack shortly thereafter. No court interfered with his
risky decision. A similar decision, though in a lighter vein, is described
in a limerick entitled "The Lament of a Coronary Patient":

> My doctor has made a prognosis
> That intercourse fosters thrombosis
> But I'd rather expire
> Fulfilling desire
> Than abstain, and develop neurosis.

Few courts, I suspect, would interfere with that decision. Indeed, a
number of courts, and at least one State Attorney General, have
recently gone so far as to apply Mill's restriction to the inconvenience
of wearing an unwanted item of apparel. The Attorney General of
New Mexico offered the following argument in support of his
conclusion that the state lacks constitutional power to compel an
adult motorcyclist to wear a protective helmet:

> It cannot be questioned that requiring a motorcycle rider
> to wear a helmet will render him less likely to be injured.
> However, if a motorcycle rider chooses to pursue his personal
> happiness by riding without a helmet it cannot be said that

his choice will injure his fellow man. Therefore, the adoption of the proposed ordinance would be an unconstitutional restriction upon a person's civil liberty, for the ordinance seeks to restrict his liberty when such restriction will not result in a benefit to the public at large or tend to preserve the safety of the community.

Why then do courts respond so differently to what appear to be essentially similar decisions by Mrs. Lake, Justice Jackson, the coronary patient, and the motorcyclist? The answer is because these similarities are obscured by the medical model imposed upon Mrs. Lake's case but not upon the others. Most courts would distinguish the cases simply by stating that Mrs. Lake is mentally ill, while Jackson, the coronary patient, and the cyclist are not, without pausing to ask whether there is anything about her "mental illness" which makes her case functionally different from the others. To be sure, there are some mentally ill people whose decisions are different from those made by Justice Jackson and the coronary patient. Some mentally ill people have little insight into their condition, the risks it poses, and the possibility of change. Their capacity for choosing between the risks of liberty and the security of incarceration may be substantially impaired. And in some cases, perhaps, the state ought to act in *parens patriae* and make the decision for them. But not all persons so diagnosed are incapable of weighing risks and making important decisions. This has been recognized by some of the very psychiatrists who advocate the medical model most forcefully. Dr. Jack Ewalt, Chairman of the Department of Psychiatry at Harvard, recently offered the following observation to a Senate Subcommittee:

> The mentally sick patient may be disoriented, but he is not a fool. He has read the newspapers about overcrowded and understaffed hospitals. He is alert to the tough time he will have getting a job when he gets out, if he does get out. He knows that there lurks in the minds of his former friends the suspicion that he is a dangerous fellow. He is sensitive that a mother may recoil in fright if he stops to give her child a pat on the head.

But Dr. Ewalt uses this sensitive observation not as an argument in favor of increased self-determination by the mentally ill but rather as showing the need for medical commitment without judicial interference.

The appropriateness and limitations of such benevolent complusion are in the forefront of our concerns in the criminal law. (Witness the wide attention received by the Hart-Devlin debate.) Although there is as much reason for concern about these issues in the civil commitment context, they are being ignored because the law has inadvertently relegated them to the unarticulated value judgments of the expert psychiatrist.

This is equally true of another important question which rarely gets asked in the civil commitment process: how likely should the predicted event have to be to justify preventive incarceration? Even if it is agreed, for example, that preventing a serious physical assault would justify incarceration, it still must be decided whether the occurrence of the predicted assault is sufficiently likely to justify this sanction. If the likelihood is very high—say ninety percent—then a strong argument can be made for some incarceration. If the likelihood is very small—say five percent—then it would be hard to justify confinement. Here, unlike the process of defining harm, little guidance can be obtained from the criminal law, for there are only a few occasions where the criminal law is explicitly predictive, and no judicial or legislative guidelines have been developed for determining the degree of likelihood required.

But someone is deciding what degree of likelihood should be required in every case. Today the psychiatrist makes that important decision: he is asked whether a given harm is likely, and he generally answers yes or no. He may—in his own mind—be defining likely to mean anything from virtual certainty to slightly above chance. And his definition will not be a reflection of any expertise, but again of his own personal preference for safety or liberty.

Not only do psychiatrists determine the degree of likelihood which should be required for incarceration; they are also the ones who decide whether that degree of likelihood exists in any particular case.

Now this, you may be thinking, is surely an appropriate role for the expert psychiatrist. But just how expert are psychiatrists in making the sorts of predictions upon which incarceration is presently based? Considering the heavy—indeed exclusive—reliance the law places on psychiatric predictions, one would expect that there would be numerous follow-up studies establishing their accuracy. Over this past few years I have conducted a thorough survey of all the published literature on the prediction of antisocial conduct. I have read and summarized many hundreds of articles, monographs, and books. Surprisingly enough, I was able to discover fewer than a dozen studies which followed up psychiatric predictions of antisocial conduct. And even more surprisingly, these few studies strongly suggest that psychiatrists are rather inaccurate predictors; inaccurate in an absolute sense, and even less accurate when compared with other professionals, such as psychologists, social workers, and correctional officials; and inaccurate when compared to actuarial devices, such as prediction or experience tables. Even more significant for legal purposes, it seems that psychiatrists are particularly prone to one type of error—overprediction. In other words, they tend to predict antisocial conduct in many instances where it would not, in fact occur. Indeed, my research suggests that for every correct psychiatric prediction of violence, there are numerous erroneous predictions. That is, among every group of inmates presently confined on the basis of psychiatric predictions of violence, there are only a few who would, and many more who would not, actually engage in such conduct if released.

One reason for this overprediction is inherent in the mathematics of the situation: violent conduct is extremely rare, even among the mentally ill, and any attempt to predict a rare event necessarily result in an undue number of false positives.

Another reason is that the psychiatrist almost never learns about his erroneous predictions of violence—for predicted assailants are generally incarcerated and have little opportunity to prove or disprove the prediction; but he always learns about his erroneous predictions of nonviolence—often from newspaper headlines announcing the crime. This higher visibility of erroneous predictions of nonviolence inclines him, whether consciously or unconsciously, to overpredict rather than underpredict violence behavior.

Moreover, the cardinal rule of medical and psychiatric diagnosis—that "judging a sick person well is more to be avoided than judging a well person sick"—suggests that overprediction as a modus operandi is built into the medical model under which the psychiatrist works.

What, then, have been the effects of virtually turning over to the psychiatrists the civil commitment process? We have accepted a legal policy—never approved by any authorized decision maker—which permits significant overprediction; in effect, a rule that it is better to confine ten men who would not assault than to let free one man who would. Or, in terms of the adage, a pound of prevention is worth an ounce of cure.

Now it may well be that if we substitute functional legal criteria for the medical model we would still accept many of the answers we accept today. Perhaps our society is willing to tolerate significant overprediction. Some of the proposals for pretrial preventive detention suggest that. Perhaps we do want incarceration to prevent minor social harms. Perhaps we do want to protect people from themselves as much as from others. But we will never learn the answers to these questions unless they are exposed and openly debated. And such open debate is discouraged—indeed made impossible—when the questions are disguised in medical jargon against which the lawyer—and the citizen—feel helpless.

The lesson of this experience is that no legal rule should ever be phrased in medical terms, that no legal decision should ever be turned over to the psychiatrist, that there is no such thing as a legal issue which cannot—and should not—be phrased in terms familiar to lawyers. And civil commitment of the mentally ill, like other mechanisms of preventive detention, is a legal issue; whenever compulsion is used or freedom denied—whether by the state, the church, the union, the university, or the psychiatrist—the issue becomes a legal one, and lawyers must be quick to immerse themselves in it.

If courts, legislatures, and psychiatrists continue to phrase the critical questions of preventive detention in the scientific-sounding jargon of psychiatry or any other discipline, then lawyers must become cryptographers; they must learn to break these codes. They must know exactly what the psychiatrist is saying; what is fact and what is fiction; what is theory and what is opinion; what is value judgment and what is bias. The testimony of the expert must be exposed to the glaring light of public understanding, so that the people, and not the pundits, may decide how much deprivation of individual liberty should be permitted to achieve a tolerable level of safety. So long as hundreds of thousands of our citizens remain confined by psychiatric prescription, lawyers and law students have an obligation to acquire an understanding of the tenets of this discipline because, in the words of Holmes, "When you get the dragon out of his cave on to the plain and into the daylight, you can count his teeth and claws, and see just what is his strength." Nor should we be diverted from this task by the seductive labels attached to confinement, labels such as therapy, treatment, help, and prevention. The words of Brandeis ring as true today as they did in 1927, and are even more applicable to the psychiatrist and the juvenile court judge than they were to the wiretapper: "Experience should teach us to be most on our guard when the Government's purposes are beneficent. Men born to freedom are naturally alert to repel invasion of their liberty by evil-minded rulers. The greatest dangers to liberty lurk in insidious encroachment by men of zeal, well-meaning but without understanding."[30]

REFERENCES

[1] C. Dodgson, *Through the Looking-Glass* (1902 ed.), p. 88.

[2] Blackstone, *Commentaries on the Laws of England* (Jones ed., 1916), Book IV, p. 2466.

[3] *Id.*

[4] *Id.*

[5] Williamson v. United States, 184 F. 2d 280, 282 (2d Cir. 1950).

[6] Maung Illa Gyaw v. Commissioner, 1948 Burma Law Reps. 764, 766.

[7] See Ilirabayashi v. United States, 320 U.S. 81 (1943). See also Dershowitz, "Stretch Points of Liberty," *The Nation,* March 15, 1971.

[8] 50 U.S.C. §813. Repealed in the fall of 1971.

[9] *Report of the National Advisory Commission on Civil Disorders* (U.S. Govt. Printing Office ed., 1968), p. 192.

[10] Commonwealth v. Franklin, 172 P. Super. 152, 92 A.2d 272, 273 (1952).

[11] *Id.,* p. 274.

[12] *In re* Gault, 387 U.S. 1, 76 (1967).

[13] See Comment, "Pretrial Detention of Witnesses," 117 *U.Pa.L.Rev.* 700 (1969).

[14] District of Columbia, Commissioners' Committee of Police Arrests for Investigation 18 (1962).

[15] Cal. Penal Code §647 (West 1955).

[16] D.C. Code §22-3302 (1967).

[17] District of Columbia v. Ricks, 94 Wash. L. Rptr. 1269 (1966), quoted in Ricks v. District of Columbia, 414 F.2d 1097 (D.C.Cir. 1968) at 1100, n. 15, and 1109.

[18] *Id.*

[19] 18 U.S.C. § §3146-52 (Supp. III, 1968).

[20] That there are occasional tragic convictions of innocent men was well documented many years ago in Borchard, *Convicting the Innocent* (1932), and more recently in Frank, *Not Guilty* (1957). But as Borchard observed on p. 407, there are still "about nine cases of unjust acquittal to one case of unjust conviction. . . ." And Frank warned (p. 38): "The horrors portrayed in this book, however, should induce no belief that most convicts are guiltless. On the whole our system works fairly and most men in prison are almost surely guilty."

[21] See Dershowitz, "Imprisonment by Judicial Hunch," *American Bar Association Journal* (June 1971), 560.

[22] Rouse v. Cameron, 373 F.2d 451, 456 (1966).

[23] Connecticut General Statutes Annotated §17-178 (1958). I believe that this statute was recently revised.

[24] D.C. Code §21-521 (1967).

[25] *In re* Williams, 157 F.Supp. 871, 872 (1958). Aff'd, Overholser *v.* Williams, 252 F.2d 629 (1958).

[26] *Id.,* p. 876.

[27] J. Donne, *Devotions* (1959 ed.), p. 108.

[28] See Lake *v.* Cameron, 364 F.2d 657 (1966).

[29] 349 U.S. xxix (1955).

[30] Olmstead *v.* United States, 277 U.S. 438, 479 (1928).

10

BEYOND DERSHOWITZ: LIMITS IN ATTEMPTING TO SECURE CHANGE

Stephen L. Wasby

Professor Dershowitz is engaged in arguing about the ethical limits of the law—How far should it go?—by examining the value judgments implicit in the prediction-prevention model. Speaking from the position that we should be extremely reluctant to deprive someone of his liberty, Dershowitz stresses the prediction-prevention model's reversal of the jurisprudential standard of "innocent until found guilty." He makes a thorough study of the effect of that reversal, showing how our practices reflect that model rather than the punishment-deterrent model and how the unarticulated assumptions of prediction-prevention pervade aspects of our criminal jurisprudence, e.g., in the granting of bail. He also notes how we have been seduced by criteria stated in medical language and indicates how we have turned over decision-making to psychiatrists who, because they have not been forced to decide cases in terms of well-defined criteria such as likelihood of occurrence, are quite inaccurate in their work. Dershowitz may have done more raising of questions than providing of answers, but his question-raising shows the inconsistencies in the use of prediction-prevention, as when he discusses how the use of the criterion "mental illness" in involuntary hospitalization leads us away from confronting the need to articulate standards and criteria for the incarceration of citizens, as well as away from confining those who might actually be dangerous.

While Professor McBride[1] notes the possibility of a decline in legal relationships, Dershowitz is asserting the need to treat more behavior in legal rather than medical terms. He concentrates on two particular devices, preventive detention and involuntary civil commitment, and it is to the latter that my comments are principally directed. Further utilizing David Danelski's distinction between ethical and empirical limits of the law,[2] I would suggest empirical limits to the acceptance of Dershowitz's argument.

Professor Dershowitz has done a thorough and forceful job of exposing the assumptions underlying the predictive-preventive model. One can add little to what he has said in this regard; we should listen closely to him. But if we are convinced that the model lacks a foundation and that the rationale for utilizing the punishment-deterrent model is more persuasive, we must still ask further questions. If our "systematic probing" of the "underlying empirical and normative assumptions" (p. 137) of the preventive confinement idea undercuts those assumptions, does it lead us any closer to a solution to the problem of dealing with people who make the community uneasy, those who, "in every society, . . . cause trouble if not confined" (p. 148)? There will be those whose "harms are [not] sufficiently serious to justify resort to [the] rather severe sanction" (p. 149) of incarceration who still bother the community. It may be not so much a matter that "our society is willing to tolerate significant overprediction" (p. 156) but that it wants people out of the way and will grasp at any devices which do the job. In a sense, it is simply American pragmatism operating, in this case nourished by awe of psychiatrists and others who wrap themselves in medical garb and use medical jargon.

I

If we cannot use mental illness as our myth, we will retreat to some myth, and the question becomes, "To what myth will we retreat?" That we need some myth is clear, as the reaction of President Nixon and a majority of the United States Senate to the

Report of the Commission on Obscenity and Pornography has shown. One can say, as Dershowitz says in another connection, "the people knew whom [read: what] they regarded as obnoxious" (p. 147). The underlying assumptions of legislation restricting the voluntary viewing by adults of sexually explicit material were laid bare—nay, stripped to the bone. The mask was yanked away. Thus, we find more people willing to reduce restrictions on such material than anyone had thought to be the case, and the negative reactions to sexual material are seldom if ever those of the person doing the viewing. And yet the Senate and the President, as well as some of the members of the Commission themselves, cry that this cannot be and that we cannot let smut loose upon the land. Without obscentiy, on what could we blame juvenile delinquency, rape, and the deterioration of the morals of the young? While matters sexual may touch very close to the heart of the emotional order, this reaction to challenged myths is not atypical and suggests the difficulty of getting acceptance of the thrust of Dershowitz's excellent analysis.

In addition, the attempts by Dershowitz and others raise the question of what we will do with those cases we eliminate from the predictive-preventive model. They will simply not go away. Herbert Packer has argued that punishment should be restricted to the offenses of "willful homicide, forcible rape, aggravated assault, and robbery"[3] but that doesn't tell us where other matters we now consider crimes will be handled. The problem is the same as Dershowitz's, except that, while Packer also poses objections to the "behavioral model," some of the items he excludes from punishment are likely to end up there. Thomas Szasz's forceful attacks on the uses of psychiatry also raise the same matter. If one accepts Szasz's argument, as stated in *Law, Liberty, and Psychiatry*, then far more would be removed from the predictive-preventive system. But this does not tell us where the cases might end up. Szasz suggests that "the aggressive paranoid person, who threatens violence, legally . . . should be treated like a person charged with an offense." A few pages later, he suggests that "if so-called mental patients commit violence, *or threaten to do so*, they should be treated for what they are—lawbreakers."[4] Szasz has also suggested that a deluded woman who tells someone that she intends to kill her children to protect them from someone she believes intends to kill them should be charged criminally, apparently even if she has not pointed a gun at them (or anyone else). This clearly expands the law of criminal

attempts, where courts have held that more than intention is necessary for a crime to have occurred; direct acts are also essential. And
the American Law Institute has noted, in its Model Penal Code, that
"law must be concerned with conduct, not with evil thoughts alone."
Perhaps society needs some way of dealing with someone like that
woman, but expanding the category of attempts that we will consider
criminal may produce as many problems as are reduced by taking
cases out of the mental health model. It is, in short, a lot easier to
kick cases out of one model than to find a model into which to fit
them—and society demands that they be placed somewhere. Society
will not let us leave the cases alone.

The desire of members of society to dispose of those who bother
them, to which I have referred, is one of the reasons that the lines
between the punitive and preventive models become in practice quite
blurred, however clearly we may distinguish them for purposes of
analysis, as well we should. Just as involuntary commitment of the
mentally ill and "preventive detention" of those awaiting trial begin
to blend into each other when pretrial mental capacity is raised as
an issue by the state to put someone away and avoid trial, so the
institutions established to operate under the prediction-prevention
model are used for punishment. As Szasz points out, "The motives
for restraining the mentally ill person are ostensibly therapeutic,
whereas for the criminal they are allegedly punitive. This distinction
. . . cannot be defended satisfactorily."[5] He is seconded by Packer
when the latter says: "Civil commitment is . . . a strategy for getting
resources more adequately allocated to the punishment of one group
of offenders than to other groups of offenders. *Under whatever name,
it is still punishment.* And it is punishment that does not have even
the minimal virtue of being labeled as what it is."[6] Thus, we should
look not only at society's stated intent in disposing of cases one way
rather than another but also at the effect such dispositions have and
the way they are viewed by the persons held. A person committed
to a mental hospital may perceive it as punishment, and those who
send him there may also do so. On this point, Szasz tellingly quotes
McGee, an attorney: "Quite a few people—maybe it is society's
desire—feel that a person who commits a crime, a criminal act,
should be punished. And they merely permit that punishment to
take place at St. Elizabeths Hospital."[7] On this basis, even someone
who quarrels with Packer's "objective" definition of punishment,
claiming "the actor's intent is as close as we are likely to get to a
working definition of punishment,"[8] would have to agree on an

empirical basis that punishment, not therapy, is going on, whatever the rhetoric involved.

II

If it is not possible to change the inclination of many individuals in society to "put people away," perhaps we can at least build some protections into the preventive model. This creates the risk that we will produce enough reforms so that the restructuring implied by Dershowitz will lose its force—or at least its chances for acceptance—but it may be a risk we have to take to protect those now affected by the despotic benevolence of those operating the system. Edmund Cahn's "consumer perspective" demands we do no less. And there have been a number of important protections announced by appellate courts within the last six years.

The most important case, which led the way for others, is *Baxstrom* v. *Herold*,[9] in which the U.S. Supreme Court held that a prisoner was denied equal protection of the laws when he was committed to a mental institution at the expiration of his criminal sentence without the jury review available to others civilly committed in New York State, and further that he was entitled to a separate judicial determination that he was dangerously mentally ill before he was committed to an institution maintained by the Department of Corrections. From *Baxstrom,* and *Specht* v. *Patterson,*[10] where a separate full hearing was required after conviction before commitment under a sex crimes act, flowed a series of cases in which the *Baxstrom* doctrine was refined and extended:

1. *Cameron* v. *Mullen:*[11] *Held* that mental hospital commitment after a finding of not guilty by reason of insanity was not authorized by a statute allowing such commitment before sentencing.
2. *Bolton* v. *Harris:*[12] *Held* that a hearing must occur before commitment after a defendant's plea of not guilty by reason of insanity.
3. *People ex rel. Goldfinger* v. *Johnston:*[13] *Held* that an inmate of a correctional school could not be transferred to an institution for defective delinquents without a hearing.
4. *People* v. *Lally:*[14] *Held* that a defendant was entitled to the same procedures for commitment to a special hospital for the

dangerously insane as available to those civilly committed.
5. *Shone* v. *Maine:*[15] *Held* that a transfer of a juvenile from a
boy's training center to a men's correctional center by an
administrative determination of incorrigibility without a judicial
hearing was invalid.
6. *U.S. ex rel. Schuster* v. *Herold:*[16] *Held* that commitment to
a state hospital for the criminally insane during a prison sentence
without a hearing was invalid.

These cases all point in the same direction: greater due process
protections. So do the *Kent*, *Gault*, and *Winship* cases,[17] which have
brought to juvenile proceedings a number of the protections common
in the adult criminal court, such as right to counsel, right to confrontation of witnesses, and the standard of "beyond a reasonable doubt."
Thus, another area characterized by aspects of prediction-prevention
has been "invaded" by standards from punishment-deterrence.

Even though courts may sit "merely to review decisions made by
doctors," as Dershowitz points out, the additional hearing provides
an opportunity for greater and continued challenge to the findings
of psychiatrists and others. (It is one of the ironies of the Nixon
administration's preventive detention proposal, roundly attacked by
liberals, that it would make more "candid, visible, controllable and
subject to review" a practice which has been in existence under
other names for quite some time, just as *Baxstrom*-type hearings
would do the same thing in other situations.) The lawyers who provide
the challenge to the intrusion of prediction-prevention into the
courtroom are increasingly well versed in the habits of psychiatrists
partly as the result of materials collected by law professors like
Dershowitz[18] and arguments by psychiatrists like Szasz. Szasz has
not only created waves inside the psychiatric profession with his
assertions about the "myth of mental illness" but has also attuned
those outside the profession to what was going on and has put them
on their guard. Dershowitz has been true to his own call that "lawyers
and law students have an obligation to acquire an understanding of
the tenets of [psychiatry]." It may be that as we become increasingly
aware of Dershowitz's arguments, we will find less and less acceptance
of prediction-prevention, providing an example of Danelski's suggest-
tion that the limits of the law are dynamic, affected by our socialization concerning legal norms.

Having mentioned cases which might lead to some optimism in
the area of due process, I must again become pessimistic. To some

extent, the protections promulgated in those decisions will be more available to some rather than others because of that constantly intervening variable, money, which as Dershowitz points out, distorts the bail process. Those who can afford attorneys will be better able to take advantage of new protections. And those with money may be able to avoid the matter of commitment altogether through obtaining private psychiatric services. Thus, "the rich man can have his pornography, or mental care at home, while the poor man is branded a deviate if he tries to have his pornography and the poor man is the one who must endure the worst abuses of the commitment process."[19]

At best, these cases are "leading cases," and but the beginning of a line which will expand the rights of those the state and its agents wish to put away. But if getting enforcement of even the modest protections we have now is such a continuing battle, will it be easy to enforce *Baxstrom*- and *Specht*-type protections? If a state trial judge presiding at a preliminary diagnostic hearing after commitment is unaware that his state's mental health code requires a full hearing within *five* days and that the patient should be so informed—certainly a simple requirement—how are we to obtain enforcement of more sophisticated and complex protections? And what of those institutionalized who do not have a civil liberties attorney accessible to point out to the incompetent judge the realities of present law?[20] Or, to take an example from Dershowitz, how will we reach the "preventive arrest" practice if we have the difficulty we now have in obtaining compliance by police with the Supreme Court's criminal procedure decisions of the 1960s? Studies have shown that while the rates at which policemen warned suspects of their rights increased after *Miranda* v. *Arizona*,[21] considerable noncompliance with the "*Miranda* rule" existed, even in large-city, supposedly professional police departments, or that when the warnings were given, they were offered perfunctorily or *after* interrogation had started, not before.[22] And the "*Miranda* rule" is one of the easier of the Court's doctrines to communicate. In the area of search-and-seizure, the "exclusionary rule" of *Mapp* v. *Ohio*[23] is regularly ignored, and the police frequently unreasonably search and seize—for example, in order to harass or to obtain informants—unless they have a major prosecution in mind.[24] And, to take an example closer to Dershowitz's concerns, avoidance of the thrust of the *Gault* ruling by judges in juvenile proceedings has been shown in a study of three major cities.[25]

The courts may try to place limits on police conduct or on the conduct of superintendents of hospitals for the criminally insane, but it may end up being little more than an attempt. At least with police, we are trying to talk to them in terms with which they are supposed to deal regularly—law terms. With the psychiatrist, our problem is getting them to work within a global framework, with which, at a minimum, they are unfamiliar, and which they often resist even when they understand it. Some of our problem with the custodians of the preventive-predictive model is their overweening benevolence, but part may be that they, like many of the rest of us, cannot think in the terms of another discipline, even if that discipline is law, on which our society, one of laws and not only men, is supposed to rest.

REFERENCES

[1] William McBride, chap. 2, pp. 28-38, this volume.

[2] David Danelski, chap. 1, pp. 8-27, this volume.

[3] Herbert Packer, *The Limits of the Criminal Sanction* (Stanford, Calif.: Stanford University Press, 1968), p. 297.

[4] Thomas Szasz, *Law, Liberty and Psychiatry* (New York: Collier Books, 1963 [paper 1968]), pp. 226, 229; emphasis supplied.

[5] *Ibid.*, p. 47

[6] Packer, *op. cit.*, p. 257; emphasis supplied.

[7] Szasz, *op. cit.*, p. 70. See also Szasz, *Psychiatric Justice* (New York: Macmillan, 1965), pp. 240-241, where McGee is cited to the effect that it is not illness but the seriousness of the offense which determines commitment to St. Elizabeths.

[8] Warren Lehman, "Notes on the Nature and Operation of Punishment," unpublished manuscript (1970), p. 5.

[9] 383 U.S. 188 (1966).

[10] 386 U.S. 605 (1967).

[11] 387 F. 2d 193 (C.A.D.C., 1967).

[12] 395 F. 2d 642 (C.A.D.C., 1968).

[13] 280 N.Y.S. 2d 304 (1967).

[14] 19 N.Y. 2d 27, 177 N.Y.S. 2d 654, 224 N.E. 2d 87 (1966).

[15] 406 F. 2d 866 (C.A. 1, 1969); vacated as moot, 396 U.S. 6 (1969).

[16] 410 F. 2d 1071 (C.A. 2, 1969). I am indebted to Howard Eisenberg for first calling this line of cases to my attention.

[17] *Kent* v. *United States* 383 U.S. 541 (1966); in *Re Gault*, 387 U.S. 1 (1967); in *Re Winship*, 397 U.S. 358 (1969).

[18] Jay Katz, Joseph Goldstein, and Alan M. Dershowitz, *Psychoanalysis, Psychiatry and Law* (New York: Free Press, 1967).

[19] The comment is that of William R. Johnson, Southern Illinois University, Carbondale.

[20] Szasz points out the drawbacks to the use of habeas corpus in *Law, Liberty and Psychiatry*, p. 66-69.

[21] 384 U.S. 436 (1966).

[22] See Stephen L. Wasby, *The Impact of the United States Supreme Court: Some Perspectives* (Homewood, Ill.: Dorsey Press, 1970), pp. 154-162, for a summary of those studies.

[23] 367 U.S. 643 (1961).

[24] See Jerome Skolnick, *Justice on Trial* (New York: John Wiley, 1966), p. 215.

[25] Norman Lefstein, Vaughn Stapleton, and Lee Teitelbaum, "In Search of Juvenile Justice: *Gault* and Its Implementation," *Law & Society Review,* III (1969), 491-562.

11

IS CIVIL COMMITMENT
A MISTAKE?

Martin P. Golding

One of the aims we pursue in the use of the social machinery
that is identified with law is the reduction of the frequency and
severity of feared or unwanted events. Professor Dershowitz's question
is: "At what point in the continuum from predicted danger to consummated harm ought this machinery intervene?" More specifically, he
is concerned to point out that the decision to intervene at one or the
other point reflects certain value judgments and empirical assumptions.
Dershowitz discerns a growing trend toward making that intervention
at the earlier rather than the later stages in the continuum, and he
views it with alarm because the assumptions that it entails have not
been subjected to careful analysis. This trend is also claimed by him
to rest upon a "mistake" of some sort. I should briefly like to
consider what this mistake is supposed to be.

This chapter consists of Golding's comments on Dershowitz's paper as
presented at the 1970 meeting of the American Society for Political and
Legal Philosophy.

Dershowitz begins with a discussion of two strategies, as he calls them, which are designed to decrease the incidence of feared or unwanted events: punitive-deterrent and prediction-prevention. Since he has explained these strategies, I need not go into details. But the main body of his paper is taken up with a discussion of two techniques employing involuntary incarceration, both of which are associated with the prediction-prevention strategy: (1) denial of pretrial release to persons charged with but not yet convicted of crimes, and (2) involuntary hospitalization of the mentally ill. Most of his paper, in fact, is devoted to an attack on the second.

The burden of this attack is that civil commitment of the mentally ill uses a "medical model." Two questions are asked, first, "Is the individual mentally ill?" and second, "Is he likely to cause harm to himself or others?" The characteristic fault that Dershowitz finds is "overprediction," which stems from the value orientation of the medical profession. The physician "plays it safe" in a manner that contrasts sharply with the traditional way of the law. Not taking chances, in an instance of doubt, is for the physician to regard the patient as ill rather than well. For the lawyer, it is to regard the accused as innocent rather than guilty. These presumptions, which reflect different value assumptions, run in opposite directions, and the law—by its adoption of one or the other presumption—will affect the individual in different ways, one toward incarceration and the other toward release.

What kind of "mistake" is involved when the criminal law adopts a presumption like that of the physician? Now I think it could be maintained that law and medicine as social institutions arise in societies to answer to very different needs, and they serve quite distinct functions. The lawman and the physician each play distinctive and distinguishable roles, and for each to answer to the needs that brought them into existence, they presuppose assumptions of very different sorts. It would be a "mistake," then, for one to adopt the presumptions of the other. But what kind of mistake? Is it like the mistake of the craftsman who uses a straight-edged screwdriver when only a Philips screwdriver will do the job right? Or is it something more fundamental, perhaps a "logical" or "intellectual" mistake of sorts, like the mistake, for example, of using a screwdriver to repair a faulty argument? In the latter case, one is using not just a bad instrument in place of a better one, but an instrument which of *necessity* couldn't do the job, for screwdrivers are made for a different *kind* of job. So one might say that the use of the presumptions of medicine in the law would be an intellectual confusion, for they are not only different institutions but are also different in kind.

It is rash, of course, to try to encapsulate the function of the criminal law in a single formula. But if a bit of foolhardiness should be permitted, I would put that formula as follows: the function of the criminal law is the protection of the *innocent* from harm. Societies may vary regarding the criteria of innocence and desert (and, also, harm), but the notions of innocence and desert (of the innocent and the guilty) are essentials of the criminal law. These notions apparently have no place in medicine, and the use in the law of such medical language as "pathology" and "cure" will be misleading in many contexts. The reason why the law employs both a strategy of punishment-deterrence and of prediction-prevention is that deterrence and prevention overlap in the task of protecting an innocent public from undeserved harm. Dershowitz is surely right in maintaining that the prediction-prevention strategy is a legitimate and inevitable feature of the criminal law. An innocent accused also deserves the protection of the law, of course. And at this point some compromise has to be made. But it is not obvious that any intellectual "mistake" of the sort mentioned above would be involved in the making of this compromise between protecting an innocent accused and an innocent public. The danger of the medical model here is that its adoption might lead to a greater sacrifice of the interests of the innocent accused than we should be willing to tolerate.

At any rate, I am not entirely clear on Professor Dershowitz's attack on civil commitment. Is he attacking the practice of civil commitment of the mentally ill as such, or is he attacking its current setup and operation, or is he merely attacking the extension of the medical model to other areas? It would seem that a good deal of what he has to say about civil commitment of the mentally ill could be detached from his general argument about the prediction-prevention strategy.

There is much to be attacked in the practice of civil commitment of the mentally ill. One could argue—and I am sure it has been argued—that it creates, in effect, a crime of status. Here the situation is analogous to narcotic addiction and chronic alcoholism. The "mistake" in this case would be neither a bad choice of instrument nor an intellectual confusion, but a moral error. For the mistake would be that involuntary hospitalization *is* punitive, and it is unjust to punish for what someone "can't help" being. If I understand Professor Dershowitz, he does maintain that civil commitment, if not directly punitive, is at least a technique of the criminal law, and might therefore be subject to this kind of attack. In addition, civil commitment might also be taken to violate the principle of *nulla poena sine lege,* because of the strong possibility of overly broad interpretation of the alleged crimes of being mentally ill or liable to cause injury.

But if one rejects the view that civil commitment is punitive—and I am not persuaded that it should be so regarded—and retains a dichotomy between criminal punishment and civil commitment, then the crucial issue apparently is whether current practices in civil commitment allow for sufficient safeguards against abuse and what improvements can be made. Since it seems that it captures individuals who should not be dealt with by hospitalization, the "mistake" in this case would be one that derives directly from overprediction. But there also could be another kind of "mistake" here, the mistake of using a defective instrument. Civil commitment of the mentally ill might be compared to the situation in which narcotic addicts are involuntarily required to undergo treatment. It has been argued that many current methods of "cure" are no cures at all, so that it is a mistake to require a course of treatment that is bound to be ineffective. A similar argument could be made in the case of the mentally ill. Does their incarceration in hospitals do them any good? Of course, this is a mistake we might well tolerate if those who are incarcerated really are mentally ill and dangerous.

The matter of safeguards deserves to be stressed. Just as Professor Dershowitz points out that there are those who say that we should honestly admit to the existing use of preventive devices before conviction, so also are there those who say that we should honestly admit that judicial admission to mental institutions is a rubber stamp operation. Therefore, they argue for an aboveboard system of medical admission. New York now has this under its Mental Hygiene Law as enacted in 1964. A typical argument in favor of medical admission was that psychiatrists found "infuriating" the requirement, under judicial admission, that "notice" had to be given to the patient. Psychiatrists claimed that a person in a depression might commit suicide on receiving this notice. This law also provides for summary admission. "Any person alleged to be in need of immediate observation, care, or treatment for mental illness" may be confined in a mental hospital for up to 30 days without further authorization. This is probably the case in many other jurisdictions as well. To deal with the matter of safeguards New York established the Mental

Health Information Service which oversees admissions. I do not know how well it works.

Medical admission raises a host of problems, to be sure. But if this represents the trend in civil commitment, then what we are likely to see is a contraction of the "medical model" rather than its expansion to other areas. The medical model asks two questions: "Is the individual mentally ill?" and "Is he likely to cause harm?" Dershowitz apparently finds fault with both. As he points out, however, it is the former which has become crucial. But if the latter gets jettisoned altogether, as seems increasingly to be the case, then the medical question *is* appropriate once one accepts the category of "mental illness" and the thesis that such illness can be cured. (I have some doubts about both.)

Whether it is proper to "cure" someone against his will is an issue that runs afoul of Mill's (unsuccessful in my opinion) attempt to set permanent limits to the law. Involuntary commitment perhaps should arguably turn on the likelihood that the individual will in any event become a ward of the state if not given psychiatric treatment. I am not sure how effectively this argument would handle the case of poor Mrs. Lake, which Dershowitz mentions. But I do think that something like it takes care of the addled-pated motorcyclist who refuses to wear a helmet. In our welfare state anyone who engages in a high-risk activity is likely to become a public charge if the hazard is realized, and there is therefore a social interest in reducing the risk. There is no reason to confine the state's action merely to conduct that is, as Mill says, "calculated to produce evil to someone else." The case of Justice Jackson, I think, is distinguishable from these others. He continued his normal activity at the risk of death. His activity, however, was enormously valuable to society. Society, in fact, depends on people who carry out tasks at great risk to their life or health.

Denial of pretrial release becomes more readily distinguishable from involuntary commitment of the mentally ill as the latter openly adopts medical admission. (I do not say this to applaud medical admission.) At least the application of pretrial detention is contemplated for persons who are charged with a specific crime. It occurs *within* the punitive-deterrent strategy. The problem in this case, again, is adequate safeguards. I don't know how to weigh up the ounces (or pounds) of prevention against the pounds (or ounces) of cure. If I understand Dershowitz correctly, he thinks that such a weighing can be done. The mere fact that an individual will be incarcerated although not convicted of a crime is not regarded by him as a "mistake." The issue of principle—that the person's "punishment" (if such detention be regarded as punitive) is undeserved because he is presumed to be innocent—is not held by Dershowitz as in itself determinative.

On this I think Professor Dershowitz is correct. As much as the accused's so-called punishment is undeserved, society also deserves protection. Though a principle is being sacrificed in part, and something is being lost, there is a good that is being promoted. Of course, whether this is so, namely, that a good really is being promoted, depends upon having adequate safeguards which ensure that as a class the detainees are actually likely to commit further crimes if released.

12

CRIMINAL PATERNALISM

Michael D. Bayles

Moral limits of law may concern the content, form, or method of legislation as well as procedures of enforcement. This paper concerns the rather narrow topic of one kind of content of criminal laws, namely, those designed for the welfare of the actor. John Stuart Mill asserted that an actor's "own good, either physical or moral, is not a sufficient warrant" for criminal legislation.[1] Despite the attempts of various authors to reject Mill's stricture against paternalism, there are no sound theoretical or practical reasons for doing so. Indeed, there are overwhelming reasons for agreeing with Mill. Paternalism may be an acceptable reason for non-criminal legislation; that question is not considered here. But it is not a morally acceptable reason for criminal legislation.

The attractiveness of criminal paternalism, that is, paternalism with respect to criminal legislation, stems from three failures of

I am indebted to Professor Alan Perreiah for numerous suggestions to improve the language of this paper.

analysis. First, it is not sufficiently distinguished from other reasons for criminal legislation, i.e., it is not adequately defined. Second, some attempts to justify paternalism only defend a broader concept of injury than the traditional one. Neither those using the broader concept of injury nor those using the narrower one have answered the objections to paternalism in criminal legislation. Third, some people falsely believe paternalism is necessary to justify retaining particular crimes of which they approve. But for most of these crimes other reasons suffice. When these three failures have been recognized and corrected, criminal paternalism loses its attractiveness.

DEFINITION

Most writers recognize a general presumption against criminal legislation. Criminal laws restrict freedom. People found guilty of violating criminal laws are deprived of liberty or property. Even law-abiding citizens have their freedom limited by the threat of fine or imprisonment if they break the law. Hence, criminal laws involve disvalues. Justifications of criminal legislation must show that positive values will result which outweigh the disvalues involved. For example, preventing murders is thought to be a value which outweighs the disvalues involved in criminal legislation. The burden of proof thus rests on those who favor criminal legislation; they must provide good reasons for overriding the presumption against it.

Reasons supporting criminal legislation may be stated as principles. A principle for criminal legislation presents a characteristic of actions which constitutes a reason, but neither a necessary nor sufficient one, for legally prohibiting or requiring them. The characteristic presented in a principle does not constitute a necessary reason because that of another principle might by itself justify legislation. It does not constitute a sufficient reason because it might not outweigh the presumption against criminal legislation. For example, that actions harm others is generally accepted as a good reason for making them crimes. But the harm caused to others by a kind of action may be so small that it does not outweigh the presumption against criminal legislation. There are also principles which present reasons against criminal legislation, e.g., that a law cannot be effectively enforced. When conflicting principles apply to a proposed law, they must be balanced against one another.[2] Collectively, all acceptable principles both for and against provide a standard of good criminal legislation.

Historically, many different principles have been advanced as good reasons for liberty-limiting legislation, including criminal legislation.[3] Three are relevant to this paper. (1) The (private) harm principle states that liberty may be restricted if actions cause injury to others. Some commentators interpret Mill (incorrectly, I think) as asserting this principle to be the only acceptable one for limiting liberty. (2) The legal moralist principle states that liberty may be restricted if actions are contrary to popular, or positive, morality. (3) The principle of paternalsim states that liberty may be restricted if actions will preserve or promote the welfare of actors.

The paternalist principle has two major versions, a positive and a negative one. Positive paternalism seeks to benefit or promote the welfare of an actor, for example, by requiring people to purchase retirement annuities through Social Security or to have blood transfusions. The point is that a person be better off after performing or omitting an action than he was before. Negative paternalism seeks to prevent injury to actors, for example, to prevent their committing suicide or becoming drug addicts. The purpose is not to increase the actor's well-being, but to prevent its diminution. Since criminal law is chiefly concerned to protect people, negative paternalism seems most pertinent to it. Most arguments about negative paternalism apply *mutatis mutandis* to positive paternalism. Hence, if the former is unacceptable, the latter probably is too.

The principle of paternalism is most apt to be confused with either the harm or legal moralist principles. The harm and paternalist principles are quite distinct. Although both seek to prevent injury, they seek to prevent it occurring to different people. The harm principle requires that A's action cause injury to B. On the other hand, paternalism requires that A's action cause injury to himself. That is, the harm principle logically involves two distinct persons, one whose actions are restricted and another who is injured, while the paternalist principle logically involves only one person.

Gerald Dworkin has argued against this distinction. He asserts that paternalism may involve restricting the actions of one person to protect the welfare of another. The manufacture of cigarettes might be banned in order to prevent people being injured by smoking them. Such a restriction differs from prohibiting a person from polluting the atmosphere, he claims, because individuals can, if they choose, avoid the injury from cigarette smoking but not that from pollution. "It would be mistaken theoretically and hypocritical in practice," he writes, "to assert that our interference in such cases is just like our interference in standard cases of protecting others from harm."[4]

However, Dworkin's argument fails because he has not recognized the relevance of the traditional maxim "*volenti non fit injuria.*" It has traditionally been held that what is done to a man with his voluntary consent cannot be injury.[5] The crucial point of the *volenti* maxim is that what happens to a person as a result of conduct in which he voluntarily participates cannot be injury; he cannot be wronged by it. By "voluntarily participates" is meant under no compulsion, psychological disturbance such as due to anger or alcohol, misrepresentation, or easily avoidable ignorance. This principle has traditionally been applied only to conduct in which a person engages with others. But it may also be applied to what, following Mill, may be called self-regarding actions, those which do not involve injury to others as specified by the harm principle. (Self-regarding actions so construed may affect others as long as they do not injure them.) Thus, a man who voluntarily goes skiing and breaks a leg suffers damage or harm, but he is not injured. Of course, the use of "injury" here is a technical one.

The harm principle has traditionally been used in conjunction with the *volenti* maxim. Thus, a person who voluntarily boxes another and is hurt has been held not to have been injured. But one need not use the harm principle in conjunction with the *volenti* maxim. Thus, one could claim that cigarette manufacturers injure smokers even though the users voluntarily participate in the activity. This case differs from air pollution, for most people do not voluntarily breathe polluted air.

Consequently, Dworkin is correct that a ban on cigarette manufacturing differs from one on polluting air. But the difference is not that in the former paternalism is the reason and in the latter the harm principle. Rather, the difference is that in the cigarette case the *volenti* maxim is not used with the harm principle but it is in the case of air pollution. One should also note that requiring warning labels on cigarette packages does not involve rejecting the *volenti* maxim but only ensuring that people smoke voluntarily, i.e., with full knowledge of the dangers.

From this discussion it is evident that there are strong and weak versions of negative paternalsim. The weak version uses the mediating maxim that actions cannot injure a man if he voluntarily chooses or performs them. The strong version does not accept that maxim and maintains that a person's own actions may injure him even if he does

them voluntarily. The great opponents of paternalism such as Mill
have been concerned to deny only the strong version. That is, they
have thought that even the liberty to perform self-regarding actions
may be limited if the actions are not voluntary.[6] Modern advocates
of paternalism have usually attempted to defend strong paternalism.

Patrick Devlin has argued that criminal paternalism leads to legal
moralism.[7] He claims that the injury or harm which paternalism
seeks to prevent must include moral as well as physical injury.
Parents, for example, are not merely concerned with the physical
well-being of their children; they also look out for their children's
moral welfare. So a reasonable paternalist principle would also concern
moral injury. But if one seeks to prevent moral injury to people, then
one must prevent their acting contrary to strongly held rules of
positive morality. So paternalism has the same practical results as
legal moralism.

Devlin's arguments to the contrary, one does not, logically, have
to move from physical to moral paternalism. First, that parents are
concerned with the moral and physical well-being of their children
does not imply that one cannot distinguish the two considerations.
Indeed, Devlin makes the distinction. Second, one may decide to
protect only the physical well-being of persons because judgments
of physical injury do not appear to involve controversial value judgments. Third, an attitude which is proper toward children need not
be proper toward adults. From a legal standpoint children are incapable of consent and, thus, of voluntary actions in the full
sense used here.

Even if criminal paternalism includes prevention of moral injury
to an actor, it remains logically distinct from legal moralism in two
respects. First, the moral injury which paternalism seeks to prevent
may be defined by either positive or rational critical morality. Thus,
paternalism may not prohibit actions because they are popularly
thought to be immoral, if moral injury is defined by rational, critical
morality. For example, homosexual relations may be immoral by
standards of positive morality but not by those of rational, critical
morality. Likewise, paternalism may prohibit as morally injurious
actions popularly thought permissible, e.g., drinking alcohol.

Second, even if moral injury is defined by positive morality,
criminal paternalism does not necessarily prohibit all the actions
which legal moralism does.[8] For legal moralism requires only that
actions be contrary to positive morality, not that an actor be morally
injured by them. It follows that paternalism and legal moralism will

not always prohibit the same actions. Moral injury may be the corruption of a person's moral beliefs. Hence, if a man does not believe his actions are immoral, he cannot be morally injured by them. Thus, moral paternalism does not prohibit homosexual conduct by an adult who does not think it immoral. If it be objected that moral injury may also consist in the development of a disposition to immoral conduct, then the argument moves back one step. For then paternalism will not justify prohibiting homosexual conduct by practicing homosexuals. The basic principle is this: Someone can be so evil in a certain respect that conduct of that sort cannot make him worse.

In sum, paternalism gives one reason for limiting a person's actions, namely, to promote or protect an actor's welfare. Positive paternalism restricts liberty in order to improve an actor's well-being, i.e., to benefit him. Negative paternalism restricts liberty only to protect a person. Weak negative paternalism restricts a person's actions only if they are involuntary and injurious. Strong negative paternalism restricts a person's actions even though they are voluntary. Mill and Feinberg accept the weak version; Dworkin and H. L. A. Hart appear to argue for the strong version.

JUSTIFICATION

In order to adopt the strong version of negative paternalism one must justify restricting an adult's voluntary action. To do that one must justify rejecting an adult's voluntary decision that on balance an action is not injurious to him. Some arguments presented for doing so only justify greater caution in deciding that a person chooses and acts voluntarily. In special situations one can be justified in so rejecting a person's voluntary decision. But one must still justify restricting the person's action to prevent him from injuring himself. Further, with strong or weak paternalism, to justify criminal legislation, it is also necessary to show that the use of criminal sanctions is a legitimate method of preventing a person from injuring himself. One must not only show that a person's action may be restricted and that criminal sanctions are an effective means but also that they are less "costly" than any other possible means of prevention. Discussions of paternalism have tended to ignore these last requirements.

H. L. A. Hart argues against weak paternalism and for the strong version. The mediating *volenti* maxim of weak paternalism, Hart claims, generally has been, and should be, abandoned. His reasons are a decline in the belief that a person knows his own interests best and a greater awareness of factors which prevent actions being fully voluntary. "Choices may be made or consent given," he writes, "without adequate reflection or appreciation of the consequences; or in pursuit of merely transitory desires; or in various predicaments when the judgment is likely to be clouded; or under inner psychological compulsion; or under pressure by others of a kind too subtle to be susceptible of proof in a court of law."[9] To these plain facts may be added the sheer complexity of the modern world, which makes it difficult for people to know all the circumstances and consequences of their choices and actions.

But the burden of this argument is not to ignore a man's voluntary choice. Rather, it is to observe that frequently men do not choose and act voluntarily. If a man's judgment is clouded or subject to subtle pressure or psychological compulsion, then he cannot choose or act voluntarily. The only conditions possibly compatible with voluntary choice and action in which Hart wishes to restrict liberty are when a person (1) does not adequately reflect or (2) pursues transitory desires. Dworkin argues for the justifiability of restricting liberty in similar situations.

Dworkin attempts to justify restricting a person's voluntary actions by invoking the future consent of fully rational persons. When children are made to do what they do not want to do, there is a moral limitation that when they grow up they should come to see the correctness of parental decisions. Similarly, it is sometimes wise to agree to let others coerce one at a future date. For example, Odysseus ordered his men to lash him to the mast and ignore his future orders to release him so he could not succumb to the enchantment of Sirens. Likewise, Dworkin argues, a government has a good reason for limiting liberty if the restrictions are such that fully rational persons would accept them as protections much as Odysseus did.[10]

This argument would justify restricting voluntary choices at the moment of action but insists on voluntary choice elsewhere. A person's voluntary actions may be restricted whenever it can reasonably be claimed that fully rational persons would choose the restrictions. This thesis with respect to negative paternalism implies that fully rational persons would view the prohibited actions as injurious. Since actions may be deemed injurious to an actor despite his voluntarily performing them, this argument defends strong negative paternalism.

When it comes to particular situations it is less clear that Dworkin would restrict voluntary actions. For he mentions as instances of such justifiable paternalism the prevention of (1) taking drugs which are "physically or psychologically addictive" and hinder reasoned choices and (2) attempting suicide "under extreme psychological and sociological pressures."[11] Neither of these cases seems to involve restricting a man's voluntary actions. Dworkin's main instances of paternalism involving anything approaching restrictions of voluntary actions are the prevention of actions due to (1) an incorrect weighting of values and (2) weakness of will.[12] These cases resemble Hart's cases of inadequate reflection and transitory desires.

These types of cases do seem to involve restricting voluntary actions. A person may believe he ought to stop smoking but lack the will power to do so; he pursues a transitory desire and sacrifices long-range to short-range interests. An ordinary man who values avoidance of injury may think he would rather not suffer the inconvenience of fastening a seat belt and thereby risk serious injury. His decision may involve either an incorrect weighting of values or inadequate reflections, both of which may fall under the general rubric of incorrect determination of interest. Both the cigarette and seat-belt cases involve, in one way or another, irrational choice. The *volenti* maxim's requirement of voluntary choice and action does not imply that a person choose rationally; it only sets necessary conditions for so doing. Hence, it is fair to assert that in these cases a person may be injured by his own voluntary actions.

The difficulty with restricting voluntary actions in these situations is that it assumes everyone has the same values. For both cases assume that a person has certain values, e.g., that he prefers a greater chance of a long life to the small inconvenience of fastening seat belts. In a pluralistic society with persons committed to various value schemes, many such persons may not be choosing irrationally. They may simply have different values. Hence, restricting such actions may involve coercing large numbers of persons who have not chosen irrationally. That is, fully rational persons with these different values would not think the consequences of the actions injurious or consent to the restrictions.

Dworkin is aware of this difficulty but does not meet it.[13] He does not solve the problem of the Christian Scientist who would rather die than have a blood transfusion. Instead, he shifts to the seat-belt case and assumes that the person has ordinary life plans.

In the end he simply places on legislators the burden of proof for showing consequences to be injurious.[14] But the values of legislators do not represent all those in society; they do not represent, say, the hippie subculture. The problem which remains is simply this: The voluntary actions of rational, strong-willed people with uncommon values would be prohibited in order to compel people with ordinary values to do what they would do voluntarily if they were not weak-willed or irrational.

Two ways out of this problem are (1) to deny that there are great differences in value schemes or (2) to claim that certain values are irrational. The first of these ways is simply false to the reality of modern pluralistic societies. The second way faces many difficulties too complex to be adequately discussed here. But it requires a generally acceptable method of determining which values are irrational. Needless to say, value theorists are quite divided as to whether or not there is such a method, let alone what it is.

Society can decide the rationality of personal values (i.e., goals pursued for oneself subject to moral limits to respect others) by a minority or a majority decision. If a minority is arbiter of the rationality of values, then a moral dictatorship becomes a distinct possibility. Democratic theory generally assumes a majority is more likely to be correct than a minority. Many different justifications of this assumption are possible. But it appears most reasonable when each person is judging matters which affect him, that is, social policies which affect his personal values (private interest) or social values (public interest) pertaining to him as a member of the community. But on this ground, members of a minority are the best judges of their own personal values unless their choices are involuntary or obviously not consistent with their values as exhibited in conduct.

Further, majority decisions of personal values do not answer the appropriate question. Each person decides which values are most rational for him given his circumstances, background, dispositions, and abilities. But the crucial question is what values are most rational for the members of the minority given their circumstances, backgrounds, dispositions, and abilities. And differences in these factors are most relevant to personal values and life styles. Hence, on the basis of the limited examination here there seems little reason to believe that majority opinions are more likely to be correct than minority ones concerning the rationality of personal values for the minority.

A third way out of the problem of forcing personal values on a minority would be to accept the principle that the liberty of some should be sacrificed to prevent injury to others. Even weak negative paternalism together with this principle could justify restricting some voluntary self-regarding actions. For example, slavery is a condition a person would not normally enter voluntarily. But it can be argued that a man might voluntarily contract into life-long slavery. However, the state may refuse to enforce such contracts. The difficulties of proof and consequent chance of mistake involved in ensuring that a person contracted voluntarily are too great. Hence, to prevent injury to those who would not voluntarily contract to be slaves but might mistakenly be determined to have done so, the state may refuse to recognize any such contracts.[15]

But there is a crucial difference between strong and weak negative paternalism with respect to the principle of sacrificing liberty to prevent injury. With the weak version the resulting injury occurs through no fault of the actor. Since his choice is involuntary, the injury is not his fault. It may not be anyone's fault. But with strong negative paternalism the resulting injury is the actor's fault. It results from his weakness of will or irrational determination of interest. While it seems reasonable to sacrifice the liberty of some to prevent injury to others when the injury is not their fault, it does not seem reasonable to do so when it is due to someone's own fault. Hence, only weak negative paternalism is an acceptable principle for liberty-limiting legislation.

Weak negative paternalism states that there is a good reason for legislation restricting involuntary self-regarding actions which are on balance injurious to an actor. But not even this version of paternalism is acceptable for criminal legislation. First, it is not obvious that the use of criminal laws is an effective method for preventing such actions. The actions will not be voluntary, so threats of punishment may not influence the actors. But the effectiveness of criminal laws as a deterrence is a complex topic. For purposes of argument it may be assumed they will deter. But even so, they will not always do so. Then sanctions will have to be imposed on those who violate laws. Of course many offenders may escape punishment if *mens rea* is required, for they will be in excusing conditions. But some offenders will have to be punished or the laws will cease to deter.

At this point criminal paternalism (weak or strong) is morally inconsistent. The motive behind criminal paternalism is benevolence, to avoid injury to actors. But if criminal laws justified by paternalism are to be enforced, offenders must be deprived of liberty or property; they must be fined or imprisoned. The result is injury to the actors, involuntary deprivations. From a motive of preventing injury to actors one inflicts injury on them. Kant would certainly reject this principle as involving a contradiction in the will. Of course the action is not logically inconsistent, for no action is. But there is a sort of inconsistency between the motive of avoiding injury to actors and intentionally inflicting injury on them. However, it may be claimed that the motive is to reform offenders and that the injury inflicted is the lesser of two evils.

But a utilitarian defense based on choosing the lesser of two evils is not feasible. First, such a justification must show that the injury inflicted by threat and actual imposition of punishment on offenders is less than that avoided by reform and deterrence. If it is not, one has increased, not decreased, suffering in the world. Second, as Dworkin recognizes, there must not be any less injurious method of preventing actors from injuring themselves.[16] But less injurious means of preventing those actions criminal paternalism would prohibit are almost always available. The government could undertake advertising to show the injury involved, e.g., campaigns against cigarette smoking by the American Cancer Society. The actions could be made less attractive by restricting the places and times in which they may occur, e.g., regulations concerning the sale of alcoholic beverages. Or advertising encouraging the actions could be prohibited, e.g., banning cigarette and liquor commercials from television. Such techniques may be as effective as criminal legislation. Even if they are less effective, they involve much less injury and are, therefore, preferable. So while weak negative paternalism may be a morally acceptable principle for noncriminal legislation, it is not acceptable for criminal legislation.

APPLICATION

The third main reason some philosophers have adopted criminal paternalism is that they believe it provides the only good reason for legislation which they believe is proper. Hart adopts paternalism as an alternative to legal moralism for justifying (1) denial of a victim's consent as a defense to assault or murder and (2) prohibitions on the use of narcotic drugs.[17] It has also been suggested as a reason for laws against euthanasia, dueling, marathon dances and other such "entertainments," suicide, jay-walking, cigarette smoking, and homosexual conduct, as well as for laws requiring motorcyclists to wear crash helmets and auto passengers seat belts. However, paternalism is not necessary to justify most of these laws. And those for which it does seem to be the only possible reason are absurd or cruel.

Hart and Dworkin to the contrary, paternalism is not relevant to the problem of consent as a defense. If A assaults B, denial of B's consent to the attack as a defense for A does not invoke paternalism. For A is punished for injuring B. B is not punished for injuring himself. Further, one need not even abandon the *volenti* maxim, only restrict the actions of those who would consent to protect those who would not. Protection rackets, for example, thrive on the threat of property damage and assault. If the law permitted consent as a defense, victims could be coerced by threat of further assaults into testifying that they consented to the original attack. Victims' statements of consent would frequently be false. But courts would have much trouble ascertaining that. It is better to restrict the liberty of those who would consent to assault than to permit injury to others who would not consent.

Criminal paternalism is also irrelevant to euthanasia and dueling because one person injures another. Again, one may still maintain that a person is only injured by conduct in which he involuntarily participates. Victims of both crimes may be subject to subtle pressures. Determinations as to whether people actually consented in such cases may be too fine for courts to make. In euthanasia, the victim may have been incapable of reasonable consent or may not have consented at all. So to protect those who prefer to live in agony, the law may prohibit euthanasia of those who would rather not. This argument is not to endorse laws against euthanasia, but merely to point out that one may reasonably fear its legalization without adopting criminal paternalism. Ultimately, these dangers can probably be sufficiently avoided to permit euthanasia in certain circumstances.

Criminal paternalism fares little better with drugs than with euthanasia. First, it is not always clear that a person takes them voluntarily. An addict is under psychological compulsion and, therefore, cannot take them voluntarily. A novice may be ignorant of the known effects of drugs. Still, some persons may voluntarily choose to use drugs. But to prevent their being sold to those who do not so choose, the law may have to prohibit all sales. Again, liberty is sacrificed to prevent injury. For nonaddictive drugs these considerations about voluntary choice are less clear. But there may be subtle social pressures to use drugs among the "in group." Second, one must distinguish between selling drugs and using them. Criminal paternalism is not relevant to the sale of drugs. Again, the seller, A, is being prevented from contributing to the injury of the buyer, B. Criminal paternalism only provides a reason for making drug use illegal, and it is becoming widely recognized that punishment of drug addicts is futile. Punishment neither cures nor deters them. Punishment may deter users of nonaddictive drugs, but they are more likely to have taken them voluntarily. Further, to claim that their use causes injury involves highly controversial value judgments.

With respect to marathon dances and the like, the value judgment about injury is less controversial. Almost everyone agrees that the physical suffering of participants is a disvalue. However, they do choose to participate. On the other hand, one may seriously question whether they do so voluntarily. During the Depression, the heyday of such "entertainment," participants were usually in dire economic circumstances. Had they not been in such need, they probably would not have participated. But one does not need criminal paternalism to justify making the promotion and operation of such "entertainment" illegal. For once again A is prohibited from injuring B. While it seems reasonable to punish those who run such "entertainment" and profit from human misery, it seems wantonly sadistic to fine or imprison those who endure it. But criminal paternalism only provides a reason for the latter.

Laws against suicide present a clear case of criminal paternalism, for a person injures himself. Further, the presumption against his so doing voluntarily is great. Nonetheless, a man may rationally decide that suicide is the best course of action; to prevent his suicide involves prohibiting his voluntary action. Since it may be rational, Dworkin does not advocate absolute prohibition of suicide.[18] Further, since a person who commits suicide cannot be punished, punishment for it is absurd. Only people who attempt suicide can be punished. Many persons who attempt suicide do not do so voluntarily. Often they are subject to none-too-subtle pressures or mental disturbances. Surely there are methods more humane than punishment for dealing with people who attempt suicide, e.g., counseling, financial aid, and social work. Perhaps in recognition of these points the Model Penal Code does not make attempted suicide a crime.[19]

But the Model Penal Code does make causing, aiding, or soliciting suicide or attempted suicide a crime. Once again, however, one is beyond criminal paternalism and concerned with the harm principle, for one person causes another to commit suicide. Nor does such a law necessarily involve rejecting the *volenti* maxim, for one must cause the other to act by force, duress, or deception. Soliciting may involve subtle psychological pressures, e.g., shouting "Jump!" to a man perched on a ledge. Moreover, since there is a strong presumption that the person does not act voluntarily, it should be assumed he will be injured until it is established that he has voluntarily chosen to kill himself. Hence, the harm principle can account for these crimes.

Finally, jay-walking, motorcyclists' crash helmets, auto seat belts, cigarette smoking, and homosexual conduct do not involve any injury recognized by weak paternalism. Hence, it does not give a reason for restricting liberty in these cases. It cannot be plausibly claimed that people who jay-walk or fail to wear crash helmets or seat belts do so involuntarily. People may indeed consider the risk worth taking. At worst weakness of will is involved. Dworkin does not wish to make the failure to wear seat belts criminal, only to assign all financial liability for their injuries to those who do not wear them.[20] A similar policy might be used for jay-walking and crash helmets. An argument for such a policy is that either the people are weak-willed and so partially at fault or they assumed the risk. Similar considerations apply to cigarette smokers. Of course, paternalism would only be involved in prohibiting cigarette smoking, not manufacturing and sales. Last, there are no reasons for believing that homosexual relations between consenting adults are injurious.

In conclusion, paternalism must be distinguished from legal moralism and the harm principle. It differs from legal moralism by requiring the occurrence of injury. It differs from the harm principle by concerning only one person. All arguments for criminally prohibiting classes of voluntary self-regarding actions fail. However, they do show that people may injure themselves even by voluntary actions if they choose them irrationally. People may also be injured by involuntary self-regarding actions. It may be justifiable to restrict a person's involuntary actions if they are injurious to him. But criminally prohibiting such actions involves an inconsistency inasmuch as it inflicts injury on those it seeks to protect. Nor is it justifiable on utilitarian grounds since less injurious methods are available for achieving the same goals. Nor is paternalism needed as a rationale for crimes most people wish to retain and for which it has been suggested. Its most clear application is with respect to suicide, attempted suicide, and drug use. In these instances its adoption is either absurd or cruel. The only justification for restricting any voluntary self-regarding actions is that most people may be presumed to perform actions of a certain type involuntarily and will suffer great injury. In such cases the liberty of some is sacrificed to prevent injury to others which would occur through no fault of their own.

REFERENCES

[1] *On Liberty*, ed. Currin V. Shields (Indianapolis: Library of Liberal Arts, 1956), p. 13. Mill held that it is insufficient for any liberty-limiting legislation, criminal or noncriminal.

[2] See my "Legal Principles, Rules and Standards," *Logique et Analyse*, 14:53-54 (1971), 223-228, for an account of principles and their relation to the standard of a good judicial decision. A similar account applies to criminal legislation, except that some of the principles are different. In the following, principles will frequently be said to justify prohibitions of actions or simply prohibit actions. Technically, what is meant is that they provide a reason for prohibiting them.

[3] See the list in Joel Feinberg, " 'Harmless Immoralities' and Offensive Nuisances," in *Issues in Law and Morality*, ed. Norman S. Care and Thomas K. Trelogan (Cleveland: Press of Case Western Reserve University, 1973).

[4] "Paternalism," in *Morality and the Law*, ed. Richard A. Wasserstrom (Belmont, Calif.: Wadsworth, 1971), p. 111.

[5] See the excellent discussion of the *volenti* maxim in Joel Feinberg, "Legal Paternalism," *Canadian Journal of Philosophy*, 1 (September 1971), sec, 1. His account of it and its application to self-regarding actions is generally followed here.

[6] Mill, *On Liberty*, p. 117; see p. 16 for his acceptance of something like the *volenti* maxim.

[7] *The Enforcement of Morals* (London: Oxford University Press, 1965), pp. 132-136.

[8] See Basil Mitchell, *Law, Morality, and Religion in a Secular Society* (London: Oxford University Press, 1967), pp. 71-72.

[9] *Law, Liberty and Morality* (Stanford, Calif.: Stanford University Press, 1963), pp. 32-33.

[10] Dworkin, "Paternalism," pp. 119-120.

[11] Dworkin, "Paternalism" pp. 122, 123.

[12] Dworkin, "Paternalism" pp. 121-122, 124.

[13] Dworkin, "Paternalism" pp. 120-121.

[14] Dworkin, "Paternalism" pp. 125-126.

[15] Feinberg, "Legal Paternalism," sec. 4.

[16] Dworkin, "Paternalism" p. 126.

[17] *Law, Liberty and Morality*, pp. 30-34.

[18] Dworkin, "Paternalism" p. 123.

[19] American Law Institute, *Model Penal Code*, Proposed Official Draft (Philadelphia: American Law Institute, 1962), Section 210.5.

[20] Dworkin, "Paternalism" p. 110.

13

JUSTIFICATIONS FOR PATERNALISM

Donald H. Regan

One of the most troublesome problems concerning the appropriate extent of government interference with individuals' activity is the problem of paternalism—that is, the problem of when, if ever, the state may compel an individual to do or to refrain from some act or activity "for his own good." One would hardly know this was a troublesome problem just from looking at the literature on political and legal philosophy. It is hard to think of an influential philosophical discussion of the matter more recent than John Stuart Mill's.[1] But paternalism is a problem which keeps coming up in discussions among philosophers as well as in discussions among people concerned with practical questions about the propriety of particular pieces of legislation, and it is a problem on which I think there is as yet no completely satisfactory view.

Possibly the reason there has been so little writing on the subject of paternalism is that the simplest and most natural approach to the problem—the straightforward hedonistic utilitarian approach—leads so quickly to what is apparently a dead end. My purpose in writing

this paper is to suggest two other possible justifications for paternalism, aside from pleasure-maximization, which are not, so far as
I know, part of the standard lore associated with the problem. It
may be that my suggestions are part of other people's standard lore
and that no one has ever seen fit to write them down. That is a risk
I shall have to take.

I

Before I present my "new" justifications of paternalism, I
should like to rehearse very briefly the main points of what I take
to be the standard dialectic of paternalism. In the context of a
hedonistic-utilitarian (which we shall hereafter abbreviate as simply
"utilitarian") approach to the problem of the justification of coercion
by the state, there is one necessary and sufficient condition for paternalistic coercion—namely, that the coercion will result in more pleasure
or happiness overall for the individual coerced.[2] If people will be
happier overall if they abstain from cigarettes, or from heroin, or if
they wear seat belts in cars or helmets when riding motorcycles, then
we should coerce them to do all of those things. That is all there is
to it.

The reason (perhaps I should say "one reason") why this single-
minded pleasure-maximizing approach is unsatisfactory is clear enough.
Anyone who suggests that we are always justified in compelling people
to do that which will make them happiest is ignoring another value
which is not the same as happiness, the value of freedom of choice.
It seems that individuals have a right to make bad choices, or choices
which sacrifice their own future happiness to their present whim, if
that's what they want.

Already we see why paternalism is a problem. It is a problem
precisely because in cases where paternalistic coercion would be
justified on pleasure-maximizing grounds, two important values, pleasure or happiness on the one hand and freedom on the other, seem to
be irreconcilably opposed. This is what I meant when I said that the
simple straightforward approach leads quickly to an apparent dead
end. We have reached a head-on conflict of very high-level values
before we have fairly begun our investigation.

To be sure, there are a few more standard moves. One such move
is to suggest that paternalism is justified when the individual coerced
lacks relevant information about the consequences of his acts.[3]

Presumably this justification for paternalism gets its force from a feeling that ignorance is a sort of unfreedom. Since the person who lacks information is unfree even if we do not intervene to constrain his choice, we are not really decreasing his freedom by intervening, and the conflict between freedom and happiness never arises. Just why being uninformed seems to be a way of being unfree is an interesting question. Certainly it smacks more of a lack of "positive" freedom than of a lack of "negative" freedom, but as an excuse for paternalism ignorance is in reasonably good repute even with advocates of negative freedom. The reason is no doubt to be found in an intimate connection between human freedom and rationality, but to say just what that connection is is beyond my present powers.[4]

Now if our justification of paternalism is simply people's ignorance, it might seem that we have a warrant not for coercing people but only for educating them. If the reason we feel justified in forbidding drugs is because we don't think users realize the danger to themselves, should we not concentrate on informing them of the danger, and then let them do as they please? In fact, there are a variety of possible claims we might put forth to justify coercion in particular cases. Sometimes there simply will not be time to educate the party coerced, as where an individual threatens to act in a way which will do him irreparable damage before we can convince him of what the facts are. In other cases, the party to be coerced may lack the expertise to understand or use the information he should have. Stretching the concept of information a bit, we might suggest that even where expertise is not in question, an individual might have all the facts within his cognitive grasp and still not really appreciate them. For example, someone might know all the medical facts about cigarettes and lung cancer and still fail to appreciate just how horrible it would be to die of cancer. In a similar vein, we might suggest that most people are simply incapable of taking very small probabilities properly into account, and this could be regarded as a sort of ignorance about consequences. With these arguments, and no doubt others like them, we can defend a good deal of paternalism with some persuasiveness on the ground that we are interfering only where people lack information.

Another move we might make, similar to the appeal to ignorance, is to claim that paternalism is justified when the subject of coercion is acting under an internal psychological compulsion. In this case also we might claim not to interfere with freedom, since the subject of coercion is already unfree, and we might nonetheless open up very considerable opportunities for benevolent intervention.

For some it may be that the arguments we have already sketched will suffice to construct a satisfying theory of when paternalism is appropriate and when it is not. For myself, I am not yet content. On the one hand, it is not clear that even after we limit utilitarian paternalism to cases of incomplete information or psychological compulsion (or only the first of these) we have given freedom of choice its due. We are so seldom fully informed of the consequences of our acts, and we are so seldom quite free of unconscious motivation, that our whole lives might be subject to paternalistic supervision if there were no other restrictions. It is always possible to make the rule-utilitarian move of saying that by and large government will do worse at arranging people's happiness than they would do themselves, but that seems to leave our claim to freedom too dependent on a contingency. A somewhat more appealing move, which can be made in either an act- or a rule-utilitarian framework, would be to claim that some considerable degree of freedom is a necessary condition of being happy. Unfortunately, this claim is not obviously true —witness the cases of nuns, soldiers, and others who manage to be happy inside total institutions—and even if it were true it would still seem to subordinate to happiness something which is in fact an independent value of equal stature.

I have just been suggesting that even a limited utilitarian paternalism may be too strong. I would also suggest that in other cases it may be too weak. I have a lingering feeling that it may be permissible to prevent cigarette smoking even by a smoker who has no family, who is clear-headed and as free of neuroses as a person can be, who is well informed about his chances of getting cancer and the general diminution of his life expectancy, and who just doesn't give a damn.[5]

My conclusion, after this rapid survey of the standard moves, is that there is still considerable room for new approaches to the problem of paternalism.

II

The first suggestion I would like to make is that we might regard paternalism as justified by a policy of coercing people in order to maximize human freedom. Whereas utility-maximizing paternalism coerces people "for their own good" in the sense of "for their own happiness," freedom-maximizing paternalism would coerce people "for their own good" in the sense of "for their own freedom."

The notion of freedom-maximizing paternalism is suggested by Mill's example of a contract for slavery. Mill says that although we generally enforce contracts, because they are made in the exercise of that liberty which we must respect, we should not enforce contracts for slavery. The reason is that slavery is the negation of liberty, and it would be absurd to give significance, in the name of protecting liberty, to an act by which the contracting party purports to destroy his liberty absolutely. In Mill's words: "[B]y selling himself for a slave, he abdicates his liberty; he foregoes any future use of it beyond that single act. He therefore defeats, in his own case, the very purpose which is the justification of allowing him to dispose of himself. He is no longer free; but is thenceforth in a position which has no longer the presumption in its favor, that would be afforded by his voluntarily remaining in it. The principle of freedom cannot require that he should be free not to be free. It is not freedom to be allowed to alienate his freedom."[6]

Now if Mill is right about this—if the principle of freedom does not require that a man should be free to destroy his freedom completely—it seems that the principle of freedom also does not require that a man should be free to destroy his freedom partially. In other words, if our general reason for letting people do as they please is that we value freedom, and if it is a countervailing reason in the slavery case that what the agent pleases will destroy his freedom, then it seems equally a countervailing reason in the cigarette-smoking case or the seat belt case that what the agent pleases will destroy his freedom to some extent.[7] When I say cigarette smoking or not wearing a seat belt will destroy his freedom to some extent, I refer to the fact that these forms of conduct will, at least statistically, shorten his life span and may also lead to debilitating disease or crippling injury.

It might be objected that there is a difference between the case of a contract for slavery and the case of smoking cigarettes, in that the former is *essentially* an act destroying freedom while the latter is only *incidentally* such an act. Now if what is meant by this is that the act of selling oneself to be a slave has no other consequence than the destruction of one's freedom, while the act of smoking a cigarette, whatever it does to one's freedom, may also be productive of pleasure, then I think the argument is misguided. Presumably no one would sell himself into slavery unless he hoped thereby to accomplish something very important to him. If we were trying to make up a plausible hypothetical case, we would posit a situation where selling himself into slavery was the only way some individual could secure the money for a very expensive operation which was necessary to save his child's life, or something similar. If this is the context in which the making of a contract for slavery is being considered, it is clear that the act of selling oneself into slavery does have consequences other than the mere extinction of one's freedom, and very important consequences at that.

Possibly what would be meant by saying that the act of selling oneself into slavery is essentially an act destroying freedom, while the act of cigarette smoking is only incidentally such an act, is not simply a matter of reckoning up the consequences, as the previous paragraph suggests. The claim may be rather that selling oneself into slavery is objectionable because the good consequences (saving the child) are obtained only through the mediation of the bad consequences (abdicating one's freedom), whereas in the cigarette-smoking case the good and bad consequences flow independently from the act, and the bad consequences are not a means to the good. If this is what is meant, we are dealing with something like the Doctrine of Double Effect, and a full discussion would take us far afield. Accordingly, I shall drop the matter, after observing that I see no convincing argument, at least along the lines so far considered, for treating the slavery case and the cigarette case differently.

A somewhat different objection might be raised. We were rather cavalier in the way we introduced the idea that cigarette smoking has as one of its consequences a diminution (statistically speaking, at least) of the smoker's freedom. It might be said that disease, injury, and death are not ordinarily regarded as causes of "unfreedom," but of disabilities or incapacities which are not strictly a matter of freedom at all. A long answer to this claim, involving a lengthy exposition of what we mean by "unfreedom," is possible. I shall content myself with a short answer, which seems adequate to this case. We are not trying to minimize unfreedom but to maximize freedom, and what we mean by "freedom" in this connection includes abilities, capacities, and in general whatever is a precondition for any human activity. What we desire is that the largest number of people should have the widest possible range of effective choice about what to do with themselves. From this point of view it is clear that death and injury and disease are all restrictions on freedom.[8]

An entirely different objection might be raised against the whole notion of freedom-maximizing paternalism, namely, that it is absurd to speak of coercing someone in order to promote his freedom. In fact, it is the objection which is, if not absurd, at least ill-considered. It would be self-contradictory in some sense to speak of coercing someone in order to increase his freedom at the point where he was being coerced, or in the act with respect to which he was being coerced.[9] But we are not speaking of that. We are speaking of coercing someone in order to increase his freedom at other times and in respect of other acts. In this there is no contradiction at all, just as there is no contradiction in the utilitarian paternalist program of promoting people's happiness by making them do things which make them unhappy at the moment where the coercion is effective.

We have left until last the most telling criticism of the freedom-maximizing approach, which is that it assumes freedom can be quantified and summed up, at least intrapersonally, and interpersonally as well if our freedom-paternalism is to be connected with a broader principle of freedom-maximization.[10] This criticism is plainly unanswerable, if in order to answer it we must provide anything like a full description of how freedom is measured and compared. But the parallel criticism of hedonistic utilitarianism is unanswerable in the same way, which has not prevented many people from being utilitarians and many more from believing that utility-maximization is *one* important moral consideration.

We can say a few things about how freedom is measured. First of all, it is clear that we do not determine the extent of a person's freedom just by counting up the actions available to him (or which will be available, at all relevant times) and saying that the greater the number of actions, the greater his freedom. For one thing, there is no obviously satisfactory criterion for individuating actions. More important, however, is the fact that freedom to do some things is much more important than freedom to do others, and any criterion based on mere counting would ignore such differences. In deciding how great a person's freedom is, we need to consider not merely how many different things he can do, but what the things he can do are. Freedom to do X will presumably count for more than freedom to do Y whenever X is more pleasurable to the particular individual than Y, or more highly valued by a rational individual than Y, or more essential to the individual's sense of his personal identity than Y, and so on. The considerations just listed do not exhaust the possibilities, and each must be taken as including the qualification "other things being equal," if only because the considerations we have listed might conflict for particular values of X and Y.

Now it may seem that in the last paragraph we replaced a nearly hopeless problem (how to count up actions) with an utterly impossible one (how to evaluate bundles of freedom in terms of the relative importance, according to various criteria, of the available actions). I do not think that is the case. We may be no closer to a well-defined procedure for ranking bundles of freedom (in fact, we may be further away from such a procedure), but the new problem is one that may be more amenable to acceptable intuitive judgments than the old one. If the criterion for ranking bundles of freedom is simply the number of available actions, my intuition says that almost all the bundles that arise in practice are going to contain the same infinite number of actions, and therefore be equally valuable. My intuition also says, however, that the conclusion that almost all bundles of freedom which arise in practice are equally valuable is ludicrous. Once the criterion is expanded to include reference to the importance of the actions, I find that I can make some rough intuitive judgments, just as I can make rough intuitive judgments about the relative happiness of various possible lives. What I am suggesting, then, is, first, that freedom-maximization may be no more susceptible than utility-maximization to the criticism of vagueness, and, second, that if the notion of freedom-maximization, like the notion of utility-maximization, strikes a responsive chord from somewhere among our moral intuitions, then we should perhaps struggle along with this vague notion just as we do with others equally vague.[11]

The most disconcerting part of any utilitarian argument is the part where the author waves his hands and produces out of nowhere conclusions about the morality of particular kinds of acts or particular practices. Still, having suggested freedom-maximization, and having suggested that I have some intuitions about when freedom is maximized, I feel obliged to apply the principle to a few examples of paternalism. Reluctantly, therefore, I shall now briefly assume the role of a moral clairvoyant.

Let us consider first the case of the man who wishes to sell himself into slavery in order to secure money for an operation for his otherwise doomed child. Although it was Mill's discussion of this case which suggested freedom-maximizing paternalism to us, it is not at all clear that, even if we accept the freedom-maximizing principle, we should prevent the enforcement of the contract. The first question is what is the net effect on the father's freedom of disallowing the contract? This is not an easy question, since saving his child may be more important to the man we are talking about than anything else he will ever do. Depending on whether it is his only child, and on his views about posterity, it may be important not merely in the sense that he badly wants to do it, but in the sense that it touches his deepest feelings about his own worth and identity. We should also remember that as a slave the man may have a degree of freedom which is not insignificant. He will have absolutely no *legal* freedom, but it is the freedom he is actually accorded by his master which is of primary importance, and that could be quite considerable. In sum, I think we might construct a plausible case in which, even considering the father's freedom alone, we would allow the contract. In general, however, I would expect it to be the case that, considering the father's freedom alone, the contract should not be allowed. At this point we need to re-member, though, that other considerations besides the father's free-dom are relevant. Our final decision must surely take into account not merely the father's freedom but also the child's freedom, or the child's happiness, or both. When we weigh these things, the father's decision to sell himself probably ought to stand.

I think our reluctance to allow the father to sell himself into slavery is based on two feelings which are not directly related to our freedom-maximizing principle. First, we refuse to accept the conditions of the problem, in particular that becoming a slave is really the only way to save the child. We feel that if a father ever found himself in such a position—and more generally if anyone ever found himself in a position where he was denied something so important that he might reasonably decide to sell himself as a slave in order to get what he was denied—there would be something drastically wrong with the broader social context, and we ought to focus on changing the social context instead of coolly allowing the contract for slavery to be enforced. The second reason we are not disposed to allow the father to sell himself is that we are concerned with unfreedom, and not just with freedom (here I qualify a bit what I said earlier in connection with death, injury, and disease as causes of unfreedom), at least in the following sense: Assume that the child, if allowed to die, and the father, if allowed to become a slave, would be losing exactly the same quantity of freedom. We would prefer the child to die than the father to become a slave because there is nothing positively offensive to our valuation of freedom in someone's being dead, whereas there is something very offensive in someone's being alive but totally unfree.

Consider now a related case, the case of suicide. Or rather, let us consider two cases of suicide. First, the man who is a terminal cancer patient, who is bed-ridden and in constant pain, but still sufficiently clear-headed so that we regard him as capable of rational choice, and who wants to end his life. Second, the man who is not suffering from any gross physical, psychological, or financial handicap, but who hasn't many friends or a job he likes, and who simply finds life a burden which he is convinced he would like to lay aside once and for all. I do not think either of these men should be prevented from committing suicide, but it might seem that freedom-maximizing paternalism would justify preventing the suicide in both cases, even though we assume that no one other than the described individuals is affected. After all, once either of them is dead, he has no freedom of any kind. So long as he is alive, he has some freedom, which we may maintain by coercion at the expense of a relatively minor limitation on the things he is allowed to do. The limitation looks very small if we describe the things the would-be suicide is not allowed to do as "shooting pistols into his head," "swallowing poison," and so on, by enumeration. The limitation may not look quite so small if we describe what the subject is not allowed to do more candidly as "committing suicide," since that is at least an act that is likely to be regarded by the person who wants to do it as fairly important. But we might still feel that the freedom to commit suicide is less than the freedom which is lost in being dead.

One counterargument is available which is peculiar to the case of the cancer patient. That is the argument that the cancer victim, once he reaches the agonizing final stages of that illness, will be incapable of rational activity and will be subhuman. He will be a positive offense to our value of freedom, like the man who becomes a slave, in a way in which the man who simply doesn't enjoy his life is not.

There is another argument, however, which applies equally to the cancer patient and the man who is merely tired of life and which sways me to believe we should allow the suicide even though we recognize the principle of freedom-maximization. When we prevent someone from committing suicide, we are not merely preventing that act. We are coercing the would-be suicide into every other act that he does. We are coercing him into getting up in the morning, dressing, eating, watching television—whatever he fills his time with. None of this is really done by choice. None of this is done freely.[12] We are assuming, of course, that the desire for an end to one's life persists. If the wish to commit suicide is only a passing fancy, then we are probably justified in preventing suicide by one in whom the desire to commit suicide is transitory. But if the desire to commit suicide does not pass, then preventing someone from committing suicide poisons everything else he does in a way in which preventing him from smoking cigarettes or compelling him to wear a motorcycle helmet if he rides a motorcycle does not. This is the reason why the freedom-maximization principle does not entail that suicide should always be prevented.

Finally, let us look at the case of forbidding someone to smoke cigarettes, or compelling him to wear a seat belt or a motorcycle helmet. As my comments made in passing in the previous paragraph suggest, these are cases where I have some feeling that coercion is justified. I have this feeling even in the face of assumptions which rule out the possibility of defending coercion by reference to the coercee's lack of information. And my feeling seems stronger than whatever feeling I have that it might possibly be all right to coerce people just to make them happier. I think the feeling may be accounted for by appeal to the principle that we may coerce people in order to protect their freedom. The restrictions involved in forbidding cigarettes or requiring a motorcyclist to wear a helmet appear as relatively slight incursions into the realm of individual freedom. The diminution of the individual's freedom which might result from a shorter life, cancer, emphysema, or an accident in which serious head injury was sustained is considerable. As I observed previously, forbidding cigarettes or requiring a helmet would not poison other activities, or cause other apparently free activity to be really unfree. In short, freedom-maximizing paternalism is made to order for the purpose of justifying coercion in such matters as these.

Of course, when I say that "forbidding cigarettes or requiring a helmet would not poison other activities," I am making an observation which I believe to be true in most cases and true contingently, not one which I believe is true universally or necessarily. It might be that if some particular individual were denied cigarettes, he would be so wracked by nervous tension which he could not otherwise assuage that he would be incapable of any meaningful activity.

Such an individual should be allowed cigarettes, even on a freedom-maximizing ground. Similarly, there might be individuals who, if they were only allowed to ride motorcycles wearing helmets, would prefer not to ride at all. Whether these individuals ought to be allowed to ride without helmets would depend on just how important riding was to them, but such individuals are already sufficiently unusual, I think, so that they might turn out to qualify for an exception as well.

We should also take note of a distinction between a prohibition against cigarettes or a requirement of motorcycle helmets and prohibitions against dangerous activities such as mountain climbing. It is plausible to suppose that there are some people for whom it is very important to engage in particular high-risk activities, or even to engage in just any high-risk activity, so long as it is sufficiently risky. Such people ought not necessarily to be restrained. The point about cigarette smoking and riding a motorcycle without a helmet is that these are activities which it would be difficult or impossible to build a life style around and which few people if any engage in because of the risk involved.

Before we leave the freedom-maximizing principle, one comment about the exact status of the principle is in order. I have written as if the freedom-maximizing principle might be taken as completely displacing the utility-maximizing principle. If we accepted freedom maximizing and ignored utility completely, we might find ourselves coercing individuals on paternalistic grounds when the result of coercion was to secure a small gain in freedom at the cost of a large loss of utility. Now there might be people to whom such a result would be acceptable, but I do not count myself among them. Perhaps we should coerce where a large gain in freedom can be secured at the cost of a small loss of utility, but freedom is not the only goal to be pursued any more than utility is. Where the freedom-maximization principle and the utility-maximization principle conflict, we may still have a difficult problem about how the conflict should be resolved. But we have not quite the same problem we started with—that is, we have not quite the same conflict between utility and freedom which we ran into at the beginning of the first section of this paper. Suggesting the freedom-maximizing principle, or, in other words, suggesting that our concern for freedom might be embodied in a teleological principle rather than a deontological one, reveals that there is a way of taking freedom into account while at the same reducing the number of cases in which utility and freedom conflict. The traditional way of looking at the paternalism problem seems to assume that any interference with free choice in any particular case is *prima facie* unjustifiable, with the result that every decision in favor of coercion must come as the resolution of a conflict between principles. Under the freedom-maximizing approach, any coercion is presumptively unjustifiable, but may turn out to be completely innocent, if it is shown that the overall effect on freedom is positive.[13] In such cases—and it is cases like cigarettes and heroin, seat belts and motorcycle helmets that I have in mind—there would then be no conflict of principles. The principle which reflects our concern for freedom and the principle which reflects our concern for utility would point in the same direction.[14]

III

So far we have looked at one "new" justification for paternalism. I should like now to make a second suggestion, which is considerably more radical, and to my mind considerably more interesting. That is the suggestion that we can bring much paternalistic legislation under the "harm principle," so that it presents no special problem at all. By the "harm principle" I mean any formulation of that central tenet of Mill's *On Liberty:* "That the only purpose for which power can be rightfully exercised over any member of a civilized community, against his will, is to prevent harm to others."[15] Plainly, the reason why paternalism is ordinarily thought to present a problem is that it appears to be a matter of exercising power over an individual, not to prevent harm to others, but to prevent harm to himself. If there were some good reason for regarding the harm done as done to a person other than the agent, the problem would disappear. I think there is a good reason for regarding the harm done by the agent as done to another, at least in many cases where paternalism seems justified. To bring out that reason, it will be useful to consider a specific case.

Let us consider statutes, of which there are a number, which make it an offense to ride a motorcycle without wearing a helmet. Such statutes are frequently attacked on the ground that they compel the cyclist to do something for nobody's good but his own and that if he wants to run the risk of serious injury, that is his own business.[16] From this point the defender of the helmet

statute might take the argument off into the question of completeness of information. That line we shall ignore. Another suggestion that the defender of the statute frequently makes goes as
follows: "Anyone who rides a motorcycle without a helmet is
risking serious injury. If he is seriously injured, then he is very
likely at some stage to become a public charge. He will be cared
for in a public hospital, or even if he can afford private care, he
will end up unemployed and drawing public compensation. Even
this may not happen in every case, but certainly in statistical terms
the helmetless cyclist is imposing a burden on public assistance
funds. Since public funds must be raised by taxation, the helmetless
cyclist is in fact hurting someone besides himself."

The argument just stated is not very satisfying. For one thing,
when we consider just what the statistical burden which the motorcyclist imposes on the public treasury comes to, it may well be that
the "harm" done by the motorcyclist to others by this route is
outweighed by the utility to him of riding without a helmet. Further,
the tenuousness of the connection between the conduct and the
"harm" gives the argument something of the false ring of rationalization. In any case, the opponent of the helmet statute, in order
apparently to avoid the force of the argument, has only to steel
himself and say something like the following: "You go too fast.
You say that the cyclist will be a burden on public assistance
funds, but the cyclist never asked for public assistance. The cyclist
I have in mind values his freedom, and he realizes that the price
of freedom is to suffer the consequences of his choices. If he suffers
a serious injury, leave him to manage as best he can. Leave him to
private charity, or let him die in the street. So long as you are prepared
to do that, his riding without a helmet doesn't hurt anyone but
himself."

At this stage the defender of the statute might say: "But we
can't leave him in the street. That would be inhuman. It would
cost us more in suffering to leave him in the street than it would
cost to care for him properly. So you see, he has harmed us, either
way." The obvious retort is: "If you value freedom at all, you must
admit that one person's mere emotional distress at another's behavior
is no justification for making that behavior a crime. If the cyclist
insists on dying in a public thoroughfare, let us remove him, as we
would any other offensive exhibitionist. But so long as he removes
himself from the public eye, he is as entitled to die as to read a
dirty book."

Now the defender of the statute, if he has not turned on his heel and stalked off, might say something like the following: "It's not simply a matter of squeamishness that makes me want to help the injured cyclist. I have a moral obligation to. Being denied assistance when one is injured is a punishment too great to visit on anyone's head just for making a foolish choice, even if the choice was precisely to risk that punishment. The cyclist may have made his original choice with full knowledge, but he must regret it now. I have a general duty to help people in need. My duty would be satisfied here only if the cyclist did not want help at the time he needed help. The fact that he decided he would do without help before he needed it is quite irrelevant." From here the defender of the statute would go on to say that being put in a position where one must undertake some burden or expense if one is to satisfy one's *moral* obligations (as opposed to reacting on the basis of one's feelings of pity or horror) is harm, so the cyclist has harmed someone after all.

At this point it seems the defender of the statute is in a strong position, and may have won the argument. What remains to be observed is that if he has won the argument, he has done so by hitting on a suggestion that makes most of the argument as we have described it superfluous. What the defender of the statute is really saying is that the cyclist at the time of deciding to ride without a helmet and the cyclist at the time of his turning up with a broken head are different people, and the choice of one doesn't bind the other. But if the cyclist is a different person at the later time from the person he was at the time of his original decision, then the cyclist at the time of his original decision has harmed another person, and the initial attack on the statute, to the effect that it violated the "harm principle," was mistaken.

Now it must be admitted that we would ordinarily speak of the cyclist as a single person throughout the events which befell him. And it must also be admitted that if we start regarding as separate persons what we would ordinarily regard as separate time-slices or time-segments of the same person, we will have opened a can of worms. Still, I think the suggestion that we should regard separate time-segments as separate persons, at least for some purposes, cannot be ignored. The argument we have just made about the cyclist hurting "another" may seem considerably more plausible if we think, say, about a man who smokes for twenty years, then quits for ten, and then turns up with lung cancer, of which his smoking was a causal antecedent. Here, it seems, nature has been distinctly unfair.

A similar sort of case may be suggested in connection with moral responsibility and the infliction of punishment. Even supposing we hold a retributivist view of punishment, I think we would be reluctant to punish an embezzler whom we find out ten years after his crime and nine-and-a-half years after he has squandered all his ill-gotton gains and returned to a life which has since been absolutely blameless. The reason is that although the criminal was (and perhaps timelessly "is") deserving of punishment, the criminal is no longer accessible to us. Inhabiting the criminal's body and social role, we find a new man.

The suggestion that for purposes of apportioning blame and punishment our ordinary criteria of personal identity may be inadequate is at least as old as Locke.[17] What I suggest in addition is that the problem of who should be allowed to suffer the natural (i.e., physical, psychological, and so on) consequences of a person's choices is much like the problem of who should be required to suffer the moral consequences of a person's choices. If different time-segments of one "person" may be distinguishable in the latter context, I think they may be in the former as well.[18]

The difficult question, of course, is still before us. If we adopt any such view as the one I have suggested, the crucial question is, just what makes different time-segments of what we would ordinarily regard as one person "different" people? Let us start with the case of punishment. I would say, roughly, that the embezzler is a different person when we discover him ten years later if he is no longer the sort of person who would embezzle, if placed in the same situation in which he did so originally (or a similar situation). What this means, of course, is far from clear. Many moralists, concerned about preserving freedom of the will, would probably want to hold that the question "Would Jones, if placed in the following situation, embezzle?" frequently does not have a well-defined answer. The theory of identity-of-persons-for-purposes-of-retribution which I have suggested seems to require, however, that the question "Is Jones the sort of person who, if placed in the following situation, would embezzle?" should have a well-defined answer. In that case, the second question, about what sort of person Jones is, cannot be just the same as the first question, about what Jones would do. Perhaps the second question is about what Jones would "probably" do, or what he would be strongly disposed to do, or what he might do without greatly surprising those who knew him intimately, or something along these lines.

If we press on, assuming that further reflection would provide us with a satisfactory sense of "the sort of person who . . .," the first thing we notice is the following. Our embezzler may, after ten years, be the same person for some purposes and at the same time be a different person for others. Thus, suppose the embezzler committed, at the same time he committed embezzlement, an unrelated aggravated assault. It is at least conceivable that after ten years the embezzler has grown much more conscious of duties of trust without becoming any more disposed to control a volatile temper which produces occasional physical aggression. In such a case, I think we might hold it inappropriate to punish the embezzler now for his embezzlement, but still appropriate to punish him for the assault (for which we assume he has not been previously punished).[19]

Returning to our main topic of paternalism, what, if anything, makes the motorcyclist a different person after his accident? The answer, I think, is that the motorcyclist is a different person, in the relevant respect, if he is no longer the sort of person who would ignore his future well-being for the sake of small increments of present utility. Of course, it is not certain that having the accident will produce any such change in the motorcyclist. But it seems likely to. In many cases, I should think, the cyclist will not merely wish he had behaved differently in the past, but will have a new appreciation of the virtue of prudence, and will alter his attitude toward risk in the future. Suppose the cyclist is not chastened and suffers no change in his dispositions toward risky behavior as a result of his experience. Does that mean we should not help him? Possibly, but only if we think the cyclist will not change in the relevant respect further in the future. After all, the cyclist who has been injured without being educated no more has the right to harm, by refusing help, any of *his* future selves who will have learned prudence than the cyclist who has not been injured has the right to harm, by not wearing a helmet, future selves who would be educated by an accident. In short, we are entitled to refuse help, and we should decline to coerce in the first place, only if the cyclist is incorrigible.[20]

It may occur to the reader to wonder why, if I am prepared to carry my unorthodox suggestion about personal identity as far as I have, I do not simply go the whole way and say that the cyclist is a different person at every moment in time. That would allow us to avoid the difficult questions we have wrestled with in the last few paragraphs about when people are the same at different times and when they are not. The reason for my reluctance to take this drastic step is that it would seem to undermine our whole concept of freedom. Freedom is concerned with making choices, especially, we like to think, with making rational choices. But rational choice requires deliberation and essentially involves time. If no one is ever the same person at successive instants, how can anyone ever make a rational choice, or a choice for himself? We might, of course, redefine rationality as an attribute, not of persons, but of series of persons which correspond to what we used to think of as persons. But no such radical reconstruction is required, at least in the present context. In connection with the justification of paternalism, all we need to recognize is that persons may, despite bodily continuity, become different persons *for some purposes* as they change over time. If we concentrate on consequences which are drastic, or which are considerably removed in time from the choices from which they flow, or preferably both, then what I have suggested about the attenuation over time of personal-identity-for-moral-purposes seems to help in understanding our paternalistic impulses, and may help in justifying them.

REFERENCES

[1] There is a brief exchange on the subject of paternalism between Devlin *(The Enforcement of Morals*, pp. 6-7, 132-137) and H. L. A. Hart *(Law, Liberty and Morality*, pp. 30-34), and passing mention is made of the problem in standard works such as Benn and Peters, *The Principles of Political Thought.* No doubt I would be aware of some full-scale discussions of paternalism if I were better informed about the literature of political philosophy outside the tradition which has come down to us from Bentham and Mill.

The one recent full-length essay on the subject which has come to my attention is "Paternalism," by Gerald Dworkin, in *Morality and the Law*, edited by Richard Wasserstrom. I discovered Dworkin's essay only after I had essentially completed this paper, but I doubt that having read his paper sooner would have much altered my own. Although his essay makes interesting reading, the conclusion seems to be approximately that paternalism is justified in those cases where a fully informed and rational individual in the position of the coercee would accept the coercion as justified. The question of what a rational individual would regard as justified remains. Some of Dworkin's remarks suggest the sort of "freedom-maximizing" paternalism I discuss in section II of this paper. On the whole, though, that does not seem to be a sufficiently strong thread in Dworkin's argument so that I am merely repeating what he has said, and there is nothing in Dworkin's essay that bears any resemblance to the view I suggest in section III.

2 It should be noted that throughout this paper I am adopting the viewpoint of an "ideal legislator," and even that in a very strong sense. I am considering when coercion would be justified from the point of view of an omniscient paternalist, who not only knows everything about the individual he is coercing and the consequences of various choices by that individual but who also has at his disposal means of coercion which can discriminate perfectly between different individuals and different acts. Thus, our paternalist need not frame general prohibitions and weigh the good consequences of such prohibitions as applied to some coercees against the bad consequences of the same prohibitions as applied to others. Nor need he take into account such problems, which may in practice be the most important connected with paternalism, as the effect of certain kinds of paternalistic legislation on the administration of the legal system generally. In other words, I am not speaking in this paper at a very practical level. It seems to me, however, that before we can decide what sorts of paternalistic prohibitions are justified in practice, we need to know, or at least to have an idea, what sort would be justified for my ideal paternalist. Hence my concern with what I recognize is a very abstract formulation of the problem.

3 Similarly, it is widely accepted that certain statuses, such as infancy or imbecility, justify paternalism. My present concern is not with the question of what statuses justify paternalism, but with the question of when, if ever, we are justified in coercing an individual who has a good general claim not to be coerced, in other words, who is, to the same extent as the rest of us, a mature and responsible adult.

4 I might have taken refuge in a more standard "beyond the scope of this essay," but if I knew what the connection between freedom and rationality was, I should be writing a different essay, and a more important one.

5 I have the same lingering feeling about the justifiability of prohibiting heroin, requiring the wearing of seat belts in cars and helmets on motorcycles, and so on. Generally when I mention one of these cases, I shall intend it as a stand-in for all cases of the same type. What counts as the "same type" the reader is left to infer from the discussion below.

6 *On Liberty* (Everyman ed., 1910), p. 158.

7 Of course, almost any choice will "destroy the agent's freedom to some extent" in the sense of reducing or eliminating his freedom to do some particular acts at various times in the future. But it is only a much smaller class of choices which will "destroy the agent's freedom to some extent" in the stronger sense of leaving him, on the whole, significantly less free after the choice than he would have been had he made a different choice. Obviously, a principle which goes under the name "freedom-maximization" is concerned with preventing choices of the second kind, not the first.

8 The inclusion of death along with injury and disease raises a question which proves troublesome for other "maximizing" theories as well. Are we really out to maximize human freedom to the extent that we might prohibit abortion or birth control so long as the totality of human freedom would be increased by increasing the number of people? I have no wish to undertake a discussion of that problem in this paper. I think we can distinguish between freedom, or happiness, or whatever, of people who actually exist, at some point in time, independently of our decision about coercion (or other moral decision), and of people who do not. If we can't make some such distinction, then the appeal of freedom-maximization is considerably lessened, along with the appeal of traditional utilitarianism.

[9] This sentence makes it clear that I have cast my lot generally with the "negative" rather than the "positive" sense of freedom. Even so, I have included the qualification "in some sense" to take care of peculiar cases, like the case of an individual who is under a psychological compulsion to do one particular act in some situation, but whom we can threaten with a sufficiently high sanction to override the compulsion, and who then finds himself free to choose among a wide variety of acts.

[10] Strictly, we would not need a cardinal measure of freedom if we were always concerned with only one person at a time. An ordinal scale ranking "bundles" of freedom for that person would suffice. If considerations of risk were introduced in the same way they may be introduced into utility theory, we might find ourselves with a cardinal measure, which was defined only up to a linear transformation. Even with more than one person, we might find ways of making decisions which took everyone's freedom into account without relying on interpersonal comparisons, such as a generalized Nash arbitration scheme. (See Luce & Raiffa, *Games and Decisions,* pp. 124-134, 349-350.) Such methods of making decisions affecting more than one person would fit uncomfortably, however, under the rubric of "freedom-maximization." What we say in the text is sufficiently fuzzy so that it probably doesn't matter much whether we regard ourselves as searching for ordinal or cardinal measures of freedom. The main object is to suggest that freedom-maximization may not be much vaguer in principle than utility-maximization, and utilitarian moral philosophers have, for the most part, managed to ignore the fascinating complications of modern decision theory.

[11] For the reader who would still claim to have *absolutely* no sense of when one bundle of freedom is "greater" than another which neither includes it nor is included in it, I would suggest that he consider whether he does not have some intuitions about when one *interference* with freedom is "greater" than another which is logically unrelated. Thus, is it not clear that a prohibition against traveling in any self-propelled vehicle would, in general, be a greater interference with personal freedom than a prohibition against wearing purple ties? I admit that examples like this don't get us very far. But they may shake the utter skeptic, to whom this footnote is addressed.

[12] Instead of claiming that we coerce the would-be suicide into "whatever he fills his time with," it might be somewhat more accurate to say we coerce him into the disjunction of all the things he might fill his time with, but the point is the same. For a person who would really rather be dead, one way of filling his time is much like another.

[13] I use *"prima facie* unjustifiable" and "presumptively unjustifiable" in what I take to be well-accepted senses, or at least senses parallel to well-accepted senses of *"prima facie* wrong" and "presumptively wrong." Very roughly, an act is *prima facie* wrong if it possesses some feature which is always wrong-making, and by virtue of which it will be wrong *sans phrase* except when it has some other right-making feature. An act is presumptively wrong if it has some feature which is generally indicative of wrongness.

[14] In view of this last paragraph, we may have strained unnecessarily to try to make plausible the conclusion that preventing suicide is not required by freedom-maximization. Perhaps preventing suicide would maximize freedom, but only at too great a cost in utility. Even if we defend allowing suicide in this way, however, the case is stronger, the less freedom is being sacrificed when the suicide is allowed. Our argument was not wasted, then, even if we may have overreached ourselves by stating the conclusion as strongly as we did.

15 *On Liberty* (Everyman ed., 1910), p. 73.

16 It is worth noting that it is almost always possible to find some way in which an apparently paternalistic piece of legislation could be held to prevent harm to others, even without resort to the "burden on public funds" argument discussed further on in the text. Thus, it has been pointed out to me by my colleague Vince Blasi that the requirement of motorcycle helmets might decrease the chance of injury to others when a motorcyclist has an accident, by making it less likely that he will be stunned and lose control of his vehicle completely. In the case of cigarettes it could be argued, as another colleague, Doug Kahn, has suggested, that the smoker harms impressionable children by setting them a bad example.

17 *An Essay Concerning Human Understanding*, Bk. II, ch. xxvii. This is not the place to argue about just what Locke's theory of personal identity is. In fact, I think that in the chapter cited he suggests at least two different theories, one of which is not unlike the theory I outline in the text below. Since I do not propose to indulge in exegesis, I will at least direct the doubtful reader's attention to the *Essay*, Bk. II, ch. xxvii, §§ 16-26.

18 Derek Parfit has argued convincingly that questions of personal identity are questions of degree, and Parfit, I am sure, would accept the general notion that the cyclist or the embezzler might be different persons at different times. See "Personal Identity," *Philosophical Review*, LXXX (1971), 3. Unfortunately, Parfit's discussion centers around hypothetical cases of fission and fusion of consciousness, and is aimed at establishing the possibility that what we ordinarily speak of as one person is a series of more or less closely connected ancestral and descendant selves. Parfit does not give any attention to the question of just where one self becomes another. He does point out that if we accept this view of personal identity, then the principle of prudence, rather than being at odds with the principle of concern for others, may be deducible from it—and may in fact have no other support! This observation of course exactly parallels our suggestion that paternalism may be justified by appeal to the "harm principle."

19 One untoward consequence of the theory I am suggesting might be that it would place a great strain on our adherence to another principle, the prohibition against punishing innocents even when good consequences would result. When the standard case of securing good consequences by punishing someone who is innocent is that of the sheriff framing somebody for a crime he didn't commit in order to avoid a riot, we may be able to say firmly "No—that would be an outrage" in part because of our belief that such cases wouldn't come up often, so the good consequences lost would not be significant. Our new principle, if taken seriously, might require nonpunishment of many persons for crimes which earlier inhabitants of the bodies they are attached to unquestionable did commit. To let too many such persons go unpunished might completely undermine the use of punishment as a deterrent. Of course, we aren't certain punishment has much deterrent effect anyway, but so far we haven't given up. Even aside from deterrence, the new theory might require us to discard any judicial system of punishment, even as retribution. Under the present judicial system and the ordinary view of personal identity, we know that some innocent persons are convicted, but we console ourselves with the thought that the number is small and that no one who is innocent is convicted "intentionally" despite knowledge of his innocence which is attributable to the judicial system. If we adopt the suggested view of personal identity, we might have to conclude that *any* system of judicial punishment would convict so many innocent persons that it would be insupportable.

[20] At this point a difficulty arises which is connected with the problem of "possible persons" (persons whose existence is prevented by abortion or birth control) which we encountered in section II. We have suggested that the cyclist may be coerced because of the possibility that he may develop into a person who is different in a relevant respect, such as attitude toward risk, or something of the sort. But we have also admitted that the cyclist may *not* develop into such a person. Are we not then interfering to protect merely *possible* future selves of the cyclist, and if we are prepared to protect these merely possible persons, why not the unborn? I think of two possible answers, or suggestions for answers, both of which have some plausibility. First, the possible persons we are protecting in the case of the cyclist might exist even without our intervention, even though they also might not (and might not ever exist even if we do intervene). Possible persons who are about to be prevented from existing by abortion or birth control quite certainly will not exist without our intervention. (Spelling this out might involve us in difficulties about the individuation of possible persons.) Second, it seems that we may be justified in treating differently possible persons who are not related by bodily or psychological continuity to any *actual* persons, and possible persons who are so related. (This requires a bit of spelling out too, to explain how a merely possible person could be related by bodily or psychological continuity to any actual person. I would suggest, however, that the reader who can't see approximately how this would go just isn't trying.)

PART III

14

LAW AND SOCIAL CONSEQUENCES: SOME CONCEPTUAL PROBLEMS AND ALTERNATIVES

Kenneth M. Dolbeare

I. INTRODUCTION

This essay is an attempt to suggest ways in which social science can contribute more fundamentally to understanding of the role of law in the contemporary United States.[1] The experience on which I draw is that of an empirical social scientist, much of whose research has explored the social consequences of "law" in some of its many manifestations. Others with similar experience have ably sought to inventory and synthesize the findings of the growing body of research in this area. At this stage, of course, their efforts are necessarily limited to the development of a number of hypotheses about the variables and relationships among variables that shape the actual effects of "law" within the society.[2] Their goal is clearly an important one. There would be much value in a catalog of findings which enabled us to say that particular forms of law, under given conditions, create certain specific effects and

give rise to identifiable problems or other unanticipated consequences, etc. From such a base, for example, it might be possible
to develop a clearer sense of the relative merits of alternative routes
toward particular goals—and more often to avoid unwanted consequences—in a purposeful manner. And it would be satisfying to
have a reliable explanation of these important sociopolitical phenomena.

But I shall focus in this essay on a quite different aspect of
empirical research: the problem of developing and applying conceptual frameworks that will enable us to look at researchable
aspects of important problems and to understand the meaning of
our findings in terms of such important questions. My view is
that the empirical study of the effects of "law" within the society
suffers less from incomplete harmonizing of scattered findings than
from a failure to ask sufficiently fundamental questions from the
most productive perspectives. In short, empirical research has been
for the most part narrow, isolated, and assumption-laden—and thus
unproductive of major insights into the basic dimensions of the
role of law in our society.

Let me be clear, however, that I do not reject the use of empirical
research for those kinds of questions for which it is suited. The
uses (or claims) of empirical research are sometimes misunderstood
by those unfamiliar with social science. No one would argue that
the collection of evidence about the "is" could answer questions
about the "ought." Normative questions or judgments require precise,
careful analysis of the nature of alternatives, choices, and values
involved—and a focus upon justification for any course chosen;
such issues cannot be resolved by the collection of purported facts
about current practices. The function of empirical research is to
establish an evidential base on which normative judgments can be
more confidently made. Just as we would not exclude any competent
evidence that helped to lay bare the issues in a trial, or in a choice
between policy alternatives, so should we welcome the findings of
empirical research when we seek to evaluate the performance of
our legal system. The potential contribution of empirical social
science lies in the focusing of those value questions that societies
must decide and in the preparation of the evidential base on which
those with normative expertise or responsibilities can rest their
judgments.

But these reflections serve only to point up the importance of
having confidence that our empirical research is not just an extension

of a particular set of values and assumptions, perhaps presented under another and more "scientifically neutral" guise. We must be sure that, to the (necessarily limited) extent possible, what is available in the way of description of how things work today does not contain eradicable biases. (I do not suggest the existence of a fact-value distinction, but only that there are relatively better and worse ways to gather and present what passes for evidence in our system of thought.) It is easy, even natural, for empirical research to suggest the pragmatic necessity, propriety, inevitability, or general justifiability of whatever set of conditions or processes is found to exist. This occurs unconsciously in most cases, through a variety of self-limiting approaches or methods accepted by researchers. Much of this can and should be eliminated.

I shall first discuss some general aspects of the conceptual task—the development of appropriately unbiased premises for, and clarification of the purposes of, empirical research. Then, in separate sections, I shall comment on some specific current problems of empirical research in this area, and then contrast these with some applicable principles for guidance of such research in the future. In final sections, I shall explore an illustrative alternative conceptual framework at some length, examine the range of empirical questions applicable within it, and then add some summary reflections.

II. THE GENERAL CONCEPTUAL TASK—AND GOALS

Research must be designed, and findings interpreted, through conceptual frameworks that are unstructured by parochial, culture-bound, or innocently ideological assumptions or premises. Such frameworks should offer ways to distinguish the important from the trivial, provide opportunities for integration of findings in separate subfields, inspire questions and hypotheses for further research, and suggest possible linkages between the law and other dynamic social processes. Much contemporary research is seriously flawed in these respects: it is often trivial, fragmented, and particularized; it is interpreted through a heavy fog of orthodoxy, and it therefore offers little of real significance to either society or scholarship. I do not propose to demonstrate this comprehensively, but rather to try to move toward improving the conceptual approaches of empirical research through identification of some key weaknesses in present efforts at defining and interpreting the consequences of law.

At the center of any meaningful discussion or research resides the task of definition. What is law? I shall not attempt to improve upon the efforts of centuries of scholarship and philosophy in this regard, and I have no wish to open this problem in all its depths. For purposes of empirical research, we are limited to some tangible manifestation of the law, such as a constitutional provision, a statute or regulation, a court decision, or a precisely defined and accepted official practice. What is crucial to these purposes is that definitions avoid normative assumptions about propriety or democraticness, that we recognize the multiplicity of levels and manifestations of the "law," and that we carefully examine the standards by which we propose to evaluate the role of law in society.

I do not mean to transcend the difficulties of shaping a sophisticated definition of law. Let me soberly acknowledge these difficulties, but then move to my major concern with the way in which we seek to understand the operation of the law in social settings.

Law is highly differentiated. Constitutions, statutes, court decisions, regulations, traditions, ethical norms, and sheer power—to say nothing of the distinction between substance and procedure—may be involved at different times and in different proportions as "law" becomes manifest. Nor are legal rules normally self-enforcing. Thus, they not only emerge from a social process involving interest, discretion, and power but they also promptly plunge back into a similar process in which application and response depend on many of the same factors. (The issue of the standard to be employed in assessing the role of law is rendered even more acute by this realization: beyond our own likes and dislikes, or those of some other person or group, what standards are there? Are they neutral, and should they be?) Next we recognize that law as such has no independent existence, and therefore cannot be taken as a given from which to begin analysis. Law is a means, a social instrument, designed to further some ends and inhibit others; it must be seen in a context of ideology, interest, power, and particular circumstances. Although it facilitates the organization of the society and the transaction of social affairs, it does so through a value bias reflecting the perceptions and interests of those who are currently dominant. And it also serves purposes of social control, education, and other society-managing functions. Finally, for all these reasons, law cannot possibly be neutral; it must always (sometimes unjustly) advantage some while burdening others, sometimes explicitly and sometimes implicitly because it simply furthers a particular status quo.

What we need is a conceptual framework which reaches behind assumptions about the propriety or neutrality of any given law, sees it in a context of social forces, and interprets its role in the society in the light of some independently definable and defensible standard. Law is a vehicle for the expression of norms, an instrument of social ordering—and law-applying institutions are subordinate bodies within the society. Our purpose in analyzing law and the empirical effects of legal processes is to see deeper, beyond manifestations of law, into the more fundamental questions of social order, or what I earlier termed the "important" problems: the questions of who holds power, what interests they serve and what values animate them, and the manner in which they achieve their goals. Only then will we understand the role of the law in the society and have the basis to evaluate its social consequences.

III. SOME SPECIFIC PROBLEMS OF EMPIRICAL RESEARCH

A major premise of this essay is that the study of the *consequences* of law can tell us much about the role of the law in society, and provide a base for evaluation of the operations of the legal system itself.[3] Thus I do not take up issues pertaining to the manner in which laws, decisions, or regulations are made, although much empirical research has been directed at the description of such processes. I should note, however, that much research which sets out to examine the "impact" or consequences of law does not proceed much further than the description of the processes by which the law was enacted or the decision made. But my attention is directed exclusively at that research which actually does define some aspects of the effects of law upon the surrounding society.

The specific problems of this growing body of research may be summarized by three basic characterizations. The first is *fragmentation*. Studies focus upon different levels, different stages of law implementing, different actors in the process, etc., almost at will, as if each existed in isolation or in a unique context of other forces. Much attention has been paid to courts' decision-making, for example, but little to the systematic linkage of their activities with features of their environments.[4] Thus, studies which focus on courts pay little attention to the effects of their decisions or to the reactions of relevant publics; those which concentrate on public attitudes do so without much regard for the substance of the actions to which reactions are solicited.[5] Studies of judges' or legislators' career lines and behavior do not ordinarily link such factors to patterns of impact of their decisions, nor do impact studies explore secondary consequences or resulting demand patterns.[6] Few studies of any kind are undertaken with any sense of the social, economic, political, and ideological context in which the action analyzed takes place. Small wonder then that what is produced is a set of disconnected findings, each dependent on a specialized version of "tunnel vision." Ignoring most of the surrounding reality, researchers have dealt with aspects of the law as if it could exist in a compartmentalized state. In part, this is inherent in the need to find "manageable" topics for research, but the effect is to leave analysts without capacity to interpret their findings in a meaningful way. Important questions of power and purpose cannot be reached. We are left in effect with a multitude of parts but no instructions concerning the manner in which they may be fitted together to make up the whole.

The second characteristic problem, perhaps ironically, is that of a *law/decision focus.* Studies take a statute or a court decision as the beginning point, and seek to trace the consequences thereof out into the society. For the most part, these studies ask whether or not there was "compliance," and what such processes looked like in various settings.[7] Such an approach greatly exaggerates the part played by any governmental intervention into an ongoing and dynamic social process. It tends to assume that the new law or decision was the beginning of an entirely new social process and that all actors at various levels related primarily to that particular government action. Overlooked are the many other forces shaping social problems and people's behavior, the many other higher priorities in the minds of various actors, and even the second- and third-stage effects of the law or decision itself. Once again, the scope and complexity of social life is reduced to stimulus-response correlations, and the subtlety of the role of law may be missed entirely.

Another potentially serious bias introduced by this approach is that of adopting the policymakers' or lawgivers' perspective on social relationships. By taking the law/decision as the focus, the researcher almost inevitably looks at the processes involved from a managerial viewpoint, e.g., through the eyes of the decisionmaker —and with the biases not only of middle class social science but also of perceived political feasibility, acceptance of the continuity of existing social structures and values, the need to maintain stability and order, and the propriety of existing values and goals in the order in which decisionmakers see them. When research is undertaken in this manner, it becomes very difficult to ask questions which challenge such assumptions.[8]

Third is the problem of *particularism*. By this characterization, I mean the acceptance of levels of empirical evidence-gathering that insist upon step-by-step demonstration of every logical stage in a process of cause and effect. Acceptance of such a requirement not only imposes a very high standard of proof upon one's research but also inhibits reaching findings in many cases. It also forces research into narrower and narrower boundaries, and as the researcher seeks to reach satisfactory levels of proof he loses touch with important problems and ends up with only trivial ones. Of course, he may not be able to obtain the evidence which scrupulous logic posits as necessary in any event, because decisionmakers frequently are unwilling to reveal their motives, the bases of action are anticipations or expectations, record keeping is insufficient, etc. And, in the absence of acceptable proof in these terms, the tendency often is to assert or accept the validity of ideological images of how things work. Orthodoxy, once established, may be supported not only by repetition and ignorance but also by inability to demonstrate its falsity. That inability, of course, is a function of the kind of proof that empirical social science establishes as necessary to validate conclusions.

I do not suggest that all problems of this body of research are subsumed within these three characterizations. Nor do I believe it possible to devise approaches that will enable us to avoid these difficulties completely. What I seek is merely the development of conceptual frameworks that will be relatively freer of both the general and specific problems described here.

IV. SOME GUIDELINES FOR A BETTER CONCEPTUAL FRAMEWORK

It should be possible to state some criteria for a better conceptual framework, if only in general terms. Of the many suggestions that might be made, I shall urge only three in such general terms, and then move on to explore some illustrative possibilities. These three points are interrelated and are jointly rather than independently responsive to the three characteristic problems just noted.

1. Law should be analyzed only in its total context. That is, manifestations of law emerging from authoritative political institutions should be seen in conjunction with the other dimensions of social reality which produced them and which give them meaning. Law neutral in its apparent substance is rendered nonneutral in its real character by the particular social reality that lies behind it. A highly stratified system of wealth, status, and power distribution, for example, belies egalitarian provisions in the law. We should attempt to understand the law, its effects and its social role, against a background of its effective integration with social, economic, and political systems and processes. It should not be enough to trace the direct consequences of a statute or decision; an appropriate analysis should define the beginning social reality, the secondary and tertiary consequences of the law's enactment, and then extend these patterns through time to see how the ongoing social system and process absorbed and was affected by such intervention.

2. Law should be analyzed not only from the perspective of the lawgiver but also from the perspective of the consumer. As a means of avoiding class and value biases, as well as those inherent in policy-makers' managerial purposes and goals earlier described, the individual should be taken as the focus for at least some of the analysis. By first setting the individual object of the law in his total context —by defining the relative weights of the various factors and forces shaping his (pre-enactment) life situation—the real impact of the law may be understood in a much more accurate fashion. There will be a much clearer sense of perspective on the relative importance of the legal intervention involved, and a better chance of realistic assessment of the consequences of the manifestation of law under analysis. A substantial correction for the perhaps inevitable class biases of social research will also be achieved. Conclusions drawn from research which takes such a bottom-up viewpoint, first establishing a "baseline" of the individual's routine life situation, might well be quite different from the more aggregative and social-engineering approach of most social science. A clearer sense of the dynamism and reality of social problems, of the limited scope of legal impact, and of the subjective reactions of people seems inevitable—as well as desirable. Moreover, this approach should serve

to emphasize the integration of social, economic, and political factors in setting the context; compartmentalization or a limited focus upon one or another set of factors should be more difficult when they are seen through the eyes of the individual consumer, who cannot help but receive the effects of all of them at one and the same time.

3. Law should be seen to have symbolic functions as well as tangible effects. It may be less important to note the patterns of tangible burden and benefit distribution in some instances than to understand the ways in which laws are perceived by people at various levels in the society, and the meaning of such enactments to such segmented publics. What is "real" is what is real in the eyes of the beholder, and we should in no instance be satisfied with only tangible or behavioral indices of the consequences of law. This dimension should be more readily emphasized by adherence to the consumer perspective above, and the shared goal would be to see the role of the law in its various forms as it is seen by the ordinary citizen. This requires that the "baseline construction" referred to above include definition of the ideology held at various levels within the society, of course, for there would be no other way to understand the symbolic appeals of law at various times.

These three criteria seek to locate the linkages that tie together the law-giving or policy-making level of authoritative action in a society with the law-receiving behavior and evaluative reactions that give meaning to the role of the law. They run up and down the scale from the enactment of a law to perception and reaction by the individual citizen, and potentially include mediating forces in between. What would be most desirable would be to find or develop an interpretive framework that would combine the "macro" and "micro" levels here identified, and relate them in some fashion. Ideally, such a framework would also include cues to an evaluative standard that would serve to give tentative meaning to the findings generated. In all probability, there are several such comprehensive frameworks *cum* evaluative standards available. Others might well be worked out, given time. But, for illustrative exploration only, one already at hand may lend itself well to our purposes. I refer to the general concept of legitimacy, or as it is now often stated, the "crisis of legitimacy" in the United States.

V. AN ILLUSTRATIVE FRAMEWORK:
THE "CRISIS OF LEGITIMACY" THESIS

In seeking a broad and inclusive framework that will serve the general goals set forth in section II above while avoiding the dangers described therein, and which will follow the guidelines just described, I have nominated something I call the "crisis of legitimacy" thesis. I do so not because I now assert the validity of the thesis (shortly to be described), but because I think it illustrates well several of the points I have tried to make more abstractly. It has, I believe, sufficient plausibility that it cannot be automatically dismissed by careful scholars. It is certainly unorthodox enough to avoid assumptions and premises stemming from established American ideology; it reaches from the objective and "macro" level of the actions of institutions to the subjective level of the reactions of individuals; it offers not only comprehensiveness but also evaluative standards; and, not least, it is articulated by others in sufficiently well-formed fashion that it can be picked up and examined here for these illustrative purposes. Once again, it is no part of my argument to assert the validity of the thesis at this time. I seek only to employ it as a means of illustrating the kind of reconceptualization requisite to useful empirical research in the future. After defining the substance of the thesis, I shall try to show how it would affect the nature of the questions to be asked in the course of research.

VI. THE "CRISIS OF LEGITIMACY" THESIS

There is no dearth of well-informed journalism, and considerable scholarly speculation, to the effect that the United States is undergoing a crisis of legitimacy of its political institutions and values—and, presumably, of its legal institutions, values, and practices as well. Conservatives have deplored for years a perceived trend toward ad hoc, result-oriented uses of the law. Lowi's *The End of Liberalism*[9] is a recent version of this argument, casting it in broader terms of steadily increasing failure to govern adequately. He calls for a return to "juridical democracy," which means essentially clearer and fuller specification of rules and purposes and reinvigorated adherence to them. More recently, Charles Reich's notorious *The Greening of America*[10] alleges a near-total disjunction between existing law and practice and the more desirable values of the young counter culture. He foresees comprehensive rejuvenation of dominant values and a restoration of legitimacy through the inevitable triumph of that new culture. A much more profound analysis, focused sharply on the problem of legitimacy, is John Schaar's lengthy article appropriately titled "Legitimacy in the Modern State."[11] He may be permitted to speak for all in summing up our current condition:

> What we mainly see are the eroded forms of once authoritative institutions and ideas. What we mainly hear are the hollow winds of once compelling ideologies, and the unnerving gusts of new moods and slogans. What we mainly feel in our hearts is the granite consolidation of the technological and bureaucratic order, which may bring physical comfort and great collective power, or sterility, but not political liberty and moral autonomy. All the modern states, with the United States in the vanguard, are well advanced along a path toward a crisis of legitimacy.[12]

Lowi, Reich, and Schaar all understand legitimacy partly in terms of the validity of the claim to moral authority on the part of values, institutions, and practices, and not merely as the sum of expectations and acquiescence on the part of people. Political scientist, law professor, and political theorist—all allege arbitrariness, discretionary and preference-oriented behavior, self-interested perpetration of injustice, the lack of remedies on behalf of a powerless and excluded population, growing alienation, and ultimately self-destructive motive forces within the "corporate state." Thus, the crisis of legitimacy is caused *both* by the failure of institutions, values, and practices to maintain a moral claim *and* by the associated rejection of such values, institutions, and practices by large segments of the population. (There are, of course, others who argue related positions. I make no effort at an inventory here, for these three seem to me to touch upon all essential dimensions of the thesis.)

Does this possibility offer a sufficiently comprehensive framework in which to understand the implications of our data? Granted that empirical research reaches no further than the immediate manifestations of law in statute, court decision, and responsive attitudes and behavior, it may be that meaning can nevertheless be found through this frame of reference. Moral authority is hardly measurable, but the specific acts of institutions, and the apparent values and tangible practices of officials and elites, clearly are. So are the attitudes and behavior of the general public, and legitimacy in the practical sense is certainly to be found principally in the minds and hearts and actions of citizens.

Let us imagine a crude and obvious continuum of declining legitimacy. At one pole, power is clothed with moral authority. The behavior of law-giving institutions is consistent with established traditions and principles, perceived as such by the population and accepted within the society as right and proper. Obedience follows, because one has a duty to comply with such justified acts. At the other, power is merely a reflection of resources and interests. Law is the product of the interplay of power and has no moral authority; obedience may nevertheless be extended, but simply as a result of a cost-benefit judgment in which advantages and the prospects of punishment are weighed against each other. Somewhere between these extremes, power enjoys some moral authority, chiefly in pragmatic terms. These institutions, and the policies produced by them, have by and large over the years satisfied the needs and preferences of most people. Moreover, many recognize that there have to be some rules governing behavior, and so are inclined to comply with reasonable accommodations even if they would not have been their first choices.

With such a continuum in mind, empirical findings might be organized and interpreted. Evidence of law-givers' arbitrariness, personalized use of opportunity for discretionary behavior, self-servingness, policy preference orientation; of the limited involvement of legal institutions and the absence of remedies for perceived injustice; and of failure of institutions to act in accordance with established standards—all would bear upon the claim of the legal system to moral authority. Evidence of elite and public rejection of law-based action for preference-grounded behavior, of ignorance and distrust for legal institutions and processes, and of obedience only because of the prospect of coercion—all would go to the question of public acceptance of that claim. Enough evidence would permit the positioning of a given political system on the legitimacy continuum. Analysis of shifts from one point to another on the continuum might identify leading causes of such movement. Comparison between systems, or between a single system at different points in time, would be possible. And so forth.

From what we have seen, legitimacy *might be* in a state of crisis. We would need comparative data to add the vital time dimension and broader inquiries into other legitimacy-related attitudes and behavior. Instead of merely noting certain isolated facts in some way related to the effects of law, we might then be able to see them in a far more profound light. Instead of noting that state and federal trial courts perform in interstitial, property-oriented ways, for example, we might go on to show that their claim to impartiality and justice is weak—that they aren't impartial, don't and can't do justice, solve problems, etc. Instead of merely noting that local and administrative elites exercise discretion and respond to their policy preferences, we might go on to show that over time the "rule of law" effectively reduces to "how do elites get what they want." I do not mean to suggest that all conclusions would or should be supportive of the "crisis of legitimacy" thesis, though I suspect that the balance would tend in that direction. This illustration is intended only to point out that the *question* of legitimacy as evidenced in the behavior of legal institutions and responses to their actions is an important, insightful way to organize and interpret that evidence. It has never been used in this way, however, as far as I know. Perhaps it is becuase of the limited state of empirical knowledge, or for some other good reason; I note only that legitimacy has not been used where it might have served important purposes.

The "crisis of legitimacy" scholars all share a useful and unfortunately distinctive approach to understanding the current dilemma of law and (or versus) order. They all attempt to interpret the role of law chiefly in terms of its social and political context. In particular, all stress the significance of the ideology which first gives rise to and then justifies particular legal forms and practices—and the crucial questions of the relationship of that ideology to problems and conditions within the society. Lowi suggests, for example, that the degradation of liberalism from a consistent public philosophy to a mere contest for advantage among interest groups is the root cause of contemporary inability to have clear and purposeful rules of law. Reich sees the forms and practices of law in two distinct stages. The first found its origin and justification in the role of the state as impartial arbiter of individual striving. The second (and current) role of law is as the managerial tool of the administrative or "corporate" state. Schaar employs the concept of ideology instead of Reich's "consciousness I and II," but makes much the same point. As technology and bureaucracy advance, he argues, the state seems to become a mindless machine with neither controls nor purpose; it has only those motive forces inherent in its own productive needs, but these are so powerful and so destructive that a decent life has

become impossible. Law then is no more than a tool of state management, to be used, circumvented, or resisted as one's goals and
opportunities may suggest.

A different range of empirical questions would have to be asked,
if this framework were employed, and a considerably broader approach
taken to the nature and contextual setting of the law—both of which
I would think highly desirable. I have gently criticized empirical
research here, for obvious reasons principally my own, for being overparticularized, overdescriptive, and insufficiently linked to larger problems with important (and normative) payoffs. But others who formulate questions for research, or who help to establish the parameters
within which the role of law is conceptualized, may be equally guilty
of thinking small or conducting their analyses within unconsciously
and undesirably narrow ranges. If we were seriously to examine the
values, attitudes, principles, and practices that make up law-in-action
in the United States today—seeking to understand the state of legitimacy, the purposes of the law as revealed in its consequences, or
the evolving functions of law in a technocratic society—what questions should we ask? Where should we look and for what?

VII. ILLUSTRATIVE ADDITIONAL DIRECTIONS
FOR EMPIRICAL INQUIRY

I shall continue to use legitimacy as the organizing framework, for two reasons. It is not only topical nationally and central
to the concerns of the American Society for Political and Legal
Philosophy but also is seldom employed in empirical studies of law-
related activity. I shall begin with what existing studies suggest are
vital areas for analysis and move on to consider some of the suggestions implied in the "crisis of legitimacy" thesis.

If we study law-related activity to understand delegitimization
(or relegitimization) as a short-term process, the evidence suggests
that a focus on local and administrative elites will be most rewarding.[13] The words of national elites are too often mere rhetoric,
their actions too often merely ritualistic. The general public is
almost too heavily engaged in the problems of everyday living to
generate independent responses. The real meaning of the law, and
the extent of legitimacy reflected by it, is determined at the law-
implementing level of the middle ranges of elites—local judges and
mayors and police chiefs, rising corporate and government bureau-

crats, lawyers and other key professionals, managers of the media, etc. Here is where affluence and status and aspiration converge to make for the greatest unwillingness to rock the boat, and yet the greatest actual and potential resistance to social and political change. Moreover, these elites control the uses and applications of the law; they may not act, act only self-interestedly or inconsistently with the standards and expectations of the law itself—or the reverse. Public response to law, the evidence suggests, is highly dependent on the actions and the positions taken by these opinion-leading elites.[14] If there is repeated arbitrariness and self-serving at this level, it cannot help but reduce legitimacy, perhaps faster than the agents of socialization can restore it. But if resistance amounting to denial of legitimacy manifests itself at this level, it seems clear that the process has gone so far the restoration will be time-consuming and difficult. There must be a limit to the number of times that any group of elites can go to the well of available legitimacy and draw popular support for institutions and practices to which they themselves do not give loyalty and fidelity of behavior.

The more interesting problems of legitimacy arise when long-term considerations are involved. If we are, as some say, in the early stages of social disintegration—or just in the midst of a "crisis of legitimacy"—the study of law-related activity should expand in several major directions, two of which may be described for pusposes of illustration. One is to seek to understand the impact of counter-ideologies upon perceptions of law and associated behavior within the society. We are in a period in which regime-challenging ideologies deny validity to our current concepts and uses of law. Simultaneously, the reactions of governing elites to the movements associated with these counterideologies often amount to a denial of the validity of those same concepts and uses of law. The impact of the latter may well be far more extensive than that of the former. In any event, we should seek to understand the extent to which holders of such counterideologies are detached from the values and expectations that support the established legal order, the extent to which they have generated a substitute sense of legitimacy for other institutions and practices, the extent to which objective conditions in the society contribute reinforcing effects to the strength and viability of the new ideologies, and, finally, how the attitudes and behavior of adherents and opponents are affected by elite repression, manipulation, or rationalization. I do not suggest that these inquiries be undertaken for the purpose of managing or otherwise responding to such counterideologies or their adherents, but rather for the purpose of gaining new insight into the state of law and legitimacy—and their relationship to the values, needs, and context of our society today.

A second major direction in which inquiry might expand is toward the process of value change among youth—particularly the so-called counterculture. Again, the purpose would not be social management and "rehabilitation," but to understand how the current usage of the law looks from this perspective and for what we may gain in the way of insight from such apparent transcending of our existing conceptual assumptions. Reich alleges that the coming value change among youth will automatically reverse the directionless machine and create new opportunities for human life and happiness:

> The crucial fact to realize about all the powerful machinery of the Corporate State—its laws, structure, political system—is that it possesses no mind. All that is needed to bring about change is to capture its controls—and they are held by nobody. It is not a case for revolution. It is a case for filling a void, for supplying a mind where none exists. No political revolution is possible in the United States right now, but no such revolution is needed.[15]

It sounds highly romanticized and quite unlikely, but we might be well advised to examine the nature and thrust of spreading value change. Continued recession/depression, frequent incidents of mass violence, or exacerbated racial tensions may well contribute to social unpredictability and combine with value change to produce a new generation with fewer inhibitions against regime-challenging violence. Similarly, repeated uses of violence against groups of dissident or unorthodox persons may lead to value change in the direction of accepting calculated official brutality as the real standard of rulership instead of what used to be known as "law." In either event, of course, we would be on our way to the naked power end of the continuum of declining legitimacy.

VIII. CONCLUSIONS

I have been operating with the premise that contemporary empirical approaches to the effects of law have not employed sufficiently inclusive frames of reference. In short, they have aimed at description rather than interpretation. Accordingly, they have not sought to address the major problems of the times, nor to provide cues to understanding or evaluation. The fault, if there be some to be assigned, lies not merely with empirical researchers, however. It may equally be assigned to those who formulate definitions of the problems surrounding the rule of law in the society and to those who set the parameters within which law is conceptualized. The latter have not indicated the ways in which the law and law-related activity could be examined so as to provide substantive grounding for speculation about the important questions. Nor have they been sensitive to the evolving role of the law within a rapidly changing society.

Notably absent from my sketchy catalog of possible improvements in the way in which empirical studies of law-related activity are undertaken are studies aimed at making the existing approaches to law work better. This is no coincidence, as may now be recognized. Efforts to make the law "work better" (i.e., to have its consequences more fully approximate current intentions and expectations) would *necessarily* accept the current framework within which it is analyzed and understood. In effect, such studies would accept, perpetuate, and more fully effectuate whatever values actually animate such uses of the law. But the point is to get outside of existing frameworks and to see the law through the eyes of its objects as well as its sponsors. To conduct a truly objective analysis, we must employ a framework that is capable of asking questions about these very values and purposes that now animate our law and legal processes—a framework that is wide enough to see those values as possible causes of problems. In short, I have been seeking to find a way to view the law from outside the contemporary (liberal) conceptual framework. Until we get outside of established assumptions and concepts, I suggest, we shall be mired in trivial and purely descriptive efforts. A rewarding use of evidence gained through research is in store if the right questions could be formulated for a joint empirical and normative speculative inquiry.

228   KENNETH M. DOLBEARE

REFERENCES

[1] The paper began, under the title "The Limited Effectiveness of Law," as an effort to draw some implications from empirical research concerning the limits on the capacity of law to affect behavior and/or to serve as an instrument of social purpose. It became increasingly clear, however, that certain "limits" of the conceptual, perceptual, and interpretive approaches of researchers were a more important problem than such empirically defined limits to the effectiveness of substantive law that could now be described. The focus of the paper thus shifted toward the goal stated in this introductory sentence. This movement was no doubt hastened by the questions raised by the commentators, Professors Hall and Bedau, whose help is gratefully acknowledged; any lack of fit between their comments and the substance of this paper may be attributable to the continuing evolution of the focus of my paper rather than to any failures on their part. I am grateful to Professors Roland Pennock and John Chapman, whose comments on an earlier draft also helped to sharpen my focus. I am also indebted to my colleagues Trevor Chandler, Philip Meranto, Stuart Scheingold, and David Schuman, many of whose comments or other thoughts have found expression here.

[2] A large number of studies validate these generalizations. Stephen Wasby's *The Impact of the United States Supreme Court: Some Perspectives* (Homewood, Ill,: Dorsey Press, 1970) synthesizes these studies, generating 136 hypotheses concerning factors affecting impact in various specified ways.

[3] For a full statement of the uses of such an approach, see my "Public Policy Analysis and the Coming Struggle for the Soul of the Post-Behavioral Revolution," in Philip Green and Sanford Levinson, eds., *Power and Community: Dissenting Essays in Political Science* (New York: Pantheon Books, 1970).

[4] There seems little point in singling out particularly egregious examples of the problems of research approaches to be identified; nearly all contemporary empirical research evidences them to a considerable degree. Because my own investigations are essentially typical, and reveal these weaknesses as well as any, I shall cite them as examples of types of research that display the problems described. This characterization, for example, draws upon my *Trial Courts in Urban Politics: State Court Policy Impact and Functions in a Local Political System* (New York: John Wiley & Sons, 1967).

[5] See my "The Public Views the Supreme Court," in Herbert Jacob, ed., *Law, Politics and the Federal Courts* (Boston: Little, Brown & Co., 1967).

[6] See my "Federal District Courts and Urban Public Policy," in Joel Grossman and Joseph Tanenhaus, eds., *Frontiers of Judicial Research* (New Your: John Wiley & Sons, 1969), and Kenneth M. Dolbeare and Phillip E. Hammond, *The School Prayer Decisions: From Court Policy to Local Practice* (Chicago: University of Chicago Press, 1971).

[7] *Ibid.* For some promising movement, however, see Frederick M. Wirt, *Politics of Equality* (Chicago: Aldine, 1970).

[8] For a full-length demonstration of the difference between top-down and bottom-up frameworks, see William Ellis, *White Ethics and Black Power* (Chicago: Aldine, 1969).

[9] Theodore Lowi, *The End of Liberalism: Ideology, Policy, and the Crisis of Public Authority* (New York: W. W. Norton, 1969).

[10] Charles A. Reich, *The Greening of America: How the Youth Revolution Is Trying to Make America Livable* (New York: Random House, 1970).

11 John A. Schaar, "Legitimacy in the Modern State," in Philip Green and Sanford Levinson, eds., *Power and Community: Dissenting Essays in Political Science* (New York: Pantheon Books, 1970).

12 *Ibid.*, pp. 278-279.

13 For analysis leading to this conclusion, see Dolbeare and Hammond, *op. cit.*, note 6 above.

14 *Ibid.*

15 Reich, *op. cit.*, p. 305.

15

JURISPRUDENTIAL THEORIES AND THE EFFECTIVENESS OF LAW

Jerome Hall

The "limited effectiveness of law" suggests that law is effective only to certain degrees or within certain bounds. This calls to mind the limitations on the effectiveness of law of the maxim *de minimis*, the more subtle aspects of interpersonal relations, complex problems that require constant management, the assumption that law can establish or maintain only the minimum of morality necessary for survival, and such beliefs as that law is only one of many agencies of social control. One might also discuss the question whether law ought to be employed in areas where harm to other persons is vague or, possibly, nonexistent, e.g., homosexuality between consenting adults and the possession of obscene literature, and there is the related, long-standing question whether law by its very character (assuming that to be fixed) is limited to the control of external action and cannot be used to influence conscience. Philosophers, of course, are expected to elucidate the meaning of "effectiveness of law" and to show how this advances our knowledge of the above and other relevant questions.

Finally, many legal philosophers would make an affirmative submission in terms of a theory of law intended to illuminate the entire subject of the law's effectiveness.

I

Empirical Research

Our concern in this meeting is particularly with so-called interdisciplinary problems, and an important difference in approach from that indicated above is immediately apparent when one sees how many political scientists deal with the question under discussion. What is paramount in their view is empirical research, and this is the first question I shall discuss, it being granted, of course, that facts and factual knowledge are important. The pertinent question is, how useful is empirical research or, more particularly, what gains can reasonably be expected in empirical research on the effectiveness of law and similar problems?

In the paper presented by Professor Dolbeare,[1] who is a political scientist, the premise is that empirical research can solve those problems or, at least, that that is the best way to advance our knowledge of those problems, and the first half of his paper deals with "empirical findings about the effectiveness of law." He discusses certain courts and on the basis of those findings he concludes that they have little effect on policy-making; instead, as Holmes said long ago, without benefit of empirical research, their contribution in that regard is interstitial. The larger problems, says Professor Dolbeare, are handled through administrative processes and by bargaining or negotiation. But administrative processes are usually regarded as part of the legal process, and bargaining and negotiation are influenced by law. And besides administration, or much of it, and other functions of the executive, and besides the courts, there is legislation. The legislation sponsored by Bentham's disciples and the many far-ranging changes in 18th- and 19th-century England are widely regarded as abundant proof that law can be very effective. Any study based only or mostly on empirical research on what courts do (even all courts) hardly supplies an adequate basis for generalizing about the effectiveness of "the law."

As regards many other factual statements in the paper, e.g., that "The nature of the law and of court decision-making is such as to render the courts specially defensive of the status quo and highly subject to judges' discretionary preferences," that courts "are little used today with reference to major public questions," and that "The general picture that emerges is anything but a law-oriented society, whether we look at elites or public," it must be said that little or no empirical evidence in support of those generalizations was referred to in the paper and, more important, that it is doubtful whether such formulations can validly be derived from research on the effectiveness of law. Indeed, for various reasons to be discussed later, after some necessary distinctions are made regarding "the effectiveness of law," the assumption that empirical research on that question can greatly advance our knowledge of those problems must be doubted.

There is another specific observation to be made on Professor Dolbeare's paper before proceeding to a more general discussion, and that concerns his interpretation of "the facts." Having attended to the courts and after expressing the above and other negative estimates about the effectiveness of the law, Professor Dolbeare turns to what he thinks really counts in that regard, namely, the influence of "the elites," and he asks a simple question to which he gives a straightforward answer: "What do elites do? The short answer to this question is that elites do what they want to." The empirical proof relied upon is the alleged failure of the segregation and school prayer decisions; they failed, says Professor Dolbeare, because "the local elites did nothing to comply with the Courts' mandate." It seems to me (in all innocence of the relevant research) that a more probable explanation is that, as regards both segregation and school prayers, the dominant force has been not the desires or the power of the elites, but the desires and the power of the lower middle and working classes. Some years ago a distinguished jurist, a North Carolinian, told me that the opposition to integration of the schools in his state came not from the elite ("they," he said, "can send their children to private schools") but from the large classes of persons who lack the resources to do that. This was reinforced by my own observations during four years in a southern state where it was often the most prominent persons in the community who protected black people from mass animosity or discrimination and often went far out of their way to advance their interests. As regards evasion of the decisions on the school prayers, is it necessary to labor the fact that the so-called Bible belts in

this country, North and South, are not conspicuous for their inclusion of members of the elite?

What is important regarding the above matters is not that there
is a difference of opinion about the facts, but that one opinion,
which is at odds with ordinary observation, is based on findings
of empirical research (with its honorific connotation of "science"),
and this raises doubts about empirical research on problems related
to the effectiveness of law. I shall shortly discuss some problems
that must be dealt with by quite different methods and some aspects
of the effectiveness of law which require a very different kind of
empirical research than the rigorous type based on mechanical or
biological models.

By way of introduction to these problematic aspects of empirical
research, it may be noted that Professor Dolbeare's interpretation
of relevatn factual findings and even his selection of certain studies
become understandable in view of his acceptance of the "crisis of
legitimacy" thesis, which challenges the claim to moral authority
of present values and institutions; criticizes the law for its alleged
arbitrariness, injustice, and lack of remedies for the poor; and
emphasizes the alienation and the self-destructive forces of the
corporate state. How or why these alleged shortcomings of American
law are relevant to the effectiveness of law was not pointed out,
but it was argued that what is needed for fruitful research is something beyond or better than theories that reflect the attitudes of
liberalism.

That the current *Weltschmerz* and the "framework" beyond
liberalism might also impair the quality of research is not considered.
Indeed, any skepticism about the "crisis of legitimacy" thesis is
farthest from Professor Dolbeare's intention. He finds no particle
of irrationalism or salesmanship in the "crisis of legitimacy" literature, nor does he give any evidence of thinking that law is to some
extent inevitably imperfect, as did Plato in the *Statesman*. Instead,
and far from being pessimistic about the prospect of increasing
knowledge about the effectiveness of law, he is optimistic about
the discoveries of future empirical research if they are based on what
are called three "frameworks": first, that of legitimacy, to be measured in a continuum of degrees of legitimacy; second, the purposes
served by the law, which means, we are told, that we are to ask
who benefits from the law and in what ways. The answer, however,
as was seen, is given in advance of the indicated far-ranging research.
The answer is that the elites benefit, and the pertinent questions
that must guide the research is "how do elites get what they want?"[2]

The third "framework," which was very briefly discussed, is to ask what may be the *next* stage of the law? If empirical research is based on these frameworks, we are assured, great discoveries and important advances in our knowledge of the effectiveness of law will be made. It is the familiar song, resonant with hopes and promises, that has been sung ever since Hume suggested that it might be possible to build a moral, i.e., social, science, that would be as scientific as physics.

What can be said in the briefest possible terms about the troublesome problem of ultimate perspectives is both trite and necessary: unless some findings of facts and interpretations are sounder than others, i.e., unless, implicit in every scholar's inquiry, there is acceptance of "the truth," however imperfect anyone's grasp of it may be, all inquiry and discussion are futile; the "solution" of problems can only be a more or less disguised exercise of force. Second, all persons share certain physical, biological, and mental traits as well as the experience of a world ("reality") which, in significant degrees, has a similar impact on human actions and minds regardless of ideologies. This is plainly the case in natural science, as is shown by the failure to construct a racial physics or a Marxist biology, and it is also operative in social and political theory, e.g., in the Russian abandonment of the "withering away" of the state thesis in the face of hard facts. Third, there are many differences in the competence of researchers, and although opinions about that may vary, one fact is plain—sophistication in methodological techniques plays a minor role there. It must be concluded that any postulate or perspective is worth only what it produces or supports and that criticism of the product of competing perspectives is necessary and is sometimes, also, valid.

Without suggesting that all of this applies to Professor Dolbeare's paper and his book, *Trial Courts in Urban Politics* (1967), there is sufficient agreement with behavioral jurisprudence to warrant and require discussion of the wider implications of the above observations. When reading the current literature of that discipline, it must be difficult for many legal philosophers to avoid the impression that nothing has been learned from the jurisprudential debates of the thirties regarding legal realism and that the fallacies of the extremist versions of that mode of thought are repeated and compounded by an innocence of law and an obsession with methods of scientific research. Hoping that there would be some fire where there is so much smoke, I have driven my flagging spirit through reams of the dreariest possible prose to discover that being a Democrat or a Republican is and is not positively correlated with certain decisions and that the like opposed findings have been discovered as regards religion, economic class, and education. Sometimes, after a meticulous laboring with models, inputs, outputs, and the like, we are enlightened by such profundities as that judges are apt to be selected from lawyers who have been politically active, and so on and on. If this is an unwarranted stricture—if, in fact, important knowledge has been discovered in the current behavioral jurisprudence by the use of scientific methods—I very much hope it will be pointed out.

Without that information, it is submitted that behavioral jurisprudence suffers from two basic defects, each of which has large implications regarding the acquisition of knowledge of the effectiveness of law. In the first place, the perspective is exclusively scientific or deterministic, the assumption being that, given certain facts, e.g., regarding background, as "stimuli," there will be certain responses that are called "decisions." There is, accordingly, a concentration on differences among officials which, given the deterministic premise and a simple view of power (which rarely includes the power of ideas or the power of a sense of moral obligation), inevitably leads to different decisions.

What is wholly ignored in all of this is the paramount fact that despite differences in background, ideology, and so on, there is almost always an honest effort to reach sound decisions; and it is even more important to see that if the sound solution of problems is ignored, it is meaningless to point out that certain differences among judges are positively correlated with certain decisions. Yet valuations are usually avoided, apparently because such expressions would mar the scientific character of the research. Actually, many valuations are implied, such as that judges who decide in favor of defendants in cases involving criminals, women, and labor unions are "liberals" and that that has honorific meaning. But these judgments, even when selected facts are supported, hardly reflect a perceptive grasp of the complexity of sociolegal problems or an evaluation of judicial decisions as intended solutions. The solution of a problem is meaningful in the context of certain facts, values, and institutions, but if that is ignored because "solution" does not lend itself to scientific research, there is a consequent lack of criteria by reference to which facts are significant even if they escape the orbit of simplistic generalizations.

The other major defect in current behavioral jurisprudence results from the neglect of rules of law. For example, we are informed by a leading representative of that discipline that, instead of taking account of legal rules, "Inquiry has focused on what human beings . . . do in their interactions and transactions with each other. . . . We do not (and need not) speak of *legal* facts and *legal* values, thereby letting the adjective suggest a mystique which is beyond analysis—at least by non-experts (i.e., by non-lawyers). . . ."[3] What may be expected of empirical research on judicial behavior and the relevant effectiveness of law that is based on this tenet?

Many years ago a judge in France and one in North Dakota and, no doubt, others elsewhere, had the bright idea that rules and doctrines of law only cloud the solution of problems and confuse the voice of conscience; any intelligent person, providing, of course, he was pure of heart, could solve any problem directly and with the plenitude of justice. Unfortunately, there are many questions about which conscience is silent or divided. For example, should inadvertently negligent harmdoers be subjected to criminal sanctions? The scholars disagree. When property has been stolen and passes into the hands of an innocent purchaser, should he or the owner of the property be the loser? Should parents be liable, civilly or criminally, for the damage or injury done by their minor children? Should the acceptance of an offer have legal effect when it is received or when it is mailed or otherwise placed beyond the control of the offeror? On all these questions different legal systems, equally advanced and civilized, reach different conclusions. It seems not mystical but elementary that anyone who wanted to understand judicial decisions in those areas would need to take careful account of the relevant rules of law. And when that is not done, what results is apt to be misleading if not meaningless.

Although the rejection of 19th-century legalistic or formal political science was warranted, indeed necessary to advance the discipline, the leap of many social scientists from the aridity of legal positivism into an indiscriminate ocean of fact is regrettable. The quest should be for a subject matter that includes not only the factual data postulated in any social discipline but also the ideas of rules and doctrines of law and other norms which give those data their meaning and distinctiveness. I shall discuss this shortly, and it will then become quite clear, I trust, that the present issue is not the worth of empirical research—no one these days doubts the importance of factual knowledge. The question concerns the nature, direction, and guidelines of significant empirical research, especially as these are determined or suggested by an uninhibited view of the subject matter.

II

Analysis of the Terms

I turn now to what seems to me to be questions that very much need to be discussed if we are to elucidate the meaning of "effectiveness of law," not least for the purpose of deciding what empirical research, if any, can produce the desired knowledge. "Effectiveness" is obviously ambiguous. First, there is the question whether "effectiveness" is descriptive or normative or partly normative and partly descriptive. On an assumed level of pure descriptiveness, it is important to distinguish results from consequences.[4] Results are what are aimed at, and the connection between action and result is intrinsic, while consequences are external effects. A policy-maker may enact a minimum-wage law with the result that certain persons receive higher wages, but a consequence might be that other persons lose their jobs. Other social changes that were not foreseeable are bound to occur, and the very enforcement of a law changes the facts so that the situation keeps on becoming different from what it was when the law was enacted. Even if it is assumed that the end or purpose of a law is definitely known and "stays put," it is difficult to assess its effectiveness. As noted, the goal of minimum wage laws was to raise the standard of living, but a consequence was an increase in unemployment. Was the law "effective"? Urban renewal laws were intended to provide decent housing for poor people, but they have also enriched landowners and uprooted many poor persons without providing them with better housing. Were those laws effective?

If "effectiveness" is restricted to the attainment of desired results, it would still be necessary in any discipline concerned with the functions of laws to take account (in an apt vocabulary) of the consequences, some of which were unforseeable when the laws were enacted. It seems strange to say that a well-planned, well-motivated law was effective even though the harm it caused outweighed the good it achieved; and, on the other hand, if it very substantially secured the result aimed at, it would seem equally strange to call it "ineffective" on the above indicated ground. This line of inquiry suggests that "effectiveness" of law, a term borrowed from ordinary speech, may need to be abandoned or given a technical meaning by those who seek the precision of scientific discourse.

There are other complications regarding the meaning of "effectiveness." Does it mean mere conformity, or does it mean compliance in the sense of knowing that the law exists and, also, approving it? Then, as regards the quantitative aspects, does effectiveness mean that, say, 80 percent of the population conform or comply? If only 20 percent conform or comply, but no one would have acted that way had the law not been passed, is the law effective? Anyone can draft a continuum on paper and say at which point he will regard a law as effective or as having a certain degree of effectiveness, but this does not clarify the meaning of that term and may only add an additional subjective use that aggravates its present ambiguity. The difficulties in the way of empirical research go even deeper than has been indicated. One might imagine, e.g., that it would be relatively easy to determine and even measure the effectiveness of *Miranda*.[5] But there is some evidence to indicate that the police sometimes (or often) evade *Miranda* by a quick perfunctory recital of the warnings; and there is the tone of voice, the expression of the face, and other factors that elude not only measurement but even a sound general estimate of merely external conformity with the decision. And the consequences of *Miranda* are so far-ranging and moot that the difficulties noted above infect statements about the effectiveness of the law.

The superficiality of simple, descriptive definitions of "effectiveness" built on a mechanical model is apparent when that term is applied to the related concept of "control." What does it mean for a law to be effective in the sense that policy-makers "control" other persons or their actions? The easiest and quickest way to see that effectiveness in that sense is a very complex matter is to think of one's own actions with regard to laws and policy-makers. Even very simple actions of merely external conformity involve knowledge, motives, estimates of utility, and other facets of personality; thus viewed, "the effectiveness of law" is only a symbol of the whole sweep of theories of individual action and theories of history. In some of those theories, law is only the product of social and economic forces; in others, law is a potent, active instrument of social and economic change. One's view of the effectiveness of law would reflect his position vis-à-vis those wider theories.

In the above discussion, some hints of a preferred normative, or partly normative, meaning were suggested, and it must now be stated that, in the writer's view, there are good reasons for including a normative element in the concept of the "effectiveness of law." Of course, it is easy enough to talk about the effectiveness of law in purely factual terms, and in that view the purpose sought need not be a good one; a sharp knife that is used to cut someone's throat is a good ("effective") knife as regards cutting. Similarly, statutes that kept blacks out of washrooms were also "effective." "Effectiveness" and "law" are sufficiently ambiguous to supply many other examples of purely factual use. The pertinent question, however, is what follows and how that compares with the consequences of normative or normative-factual usage. As was suggested above with reference to the results and consequences of minimum wage and housing laws, it is hardly possible in a social context to use "effectiveness" significantly in a purely descriptive way because relevant values and harms intrude to give meaning to these situations and to statements made about the laws. If, therefore, in the context of dealing with sociolegal problems, "effectiveness" has a partly normative connotation, a law is effective if it maximizes values. So, too, when effectiveness is examined in the context of "social control" where, it was suggested, a significant degree of autonomy must be assumed, we find ourselves concerned largely with self-control, and the "effectiveness of law" again has moral connotations.

It must be emphasized that we are here concerned not with the effectiveness of tools or machines but with the effectiveness of *law*, and, also and of equal importance, that our concern with that question is a theoretical one; hence, the fact that ordinary language may take an opposed direction is irrelevant. The claim that the "effectiveness of law" should be given a normative connotation is part of a larger jurisprudential problem that will be very briefly discussed later. First, it is necessary to discuss less controversial questions about the effectiveness of *law*.

Professor Dolbeare has provided some clues to his theory of law, e.g., in his statement that "obedience to law finds its roots not in any internalized sense of obligation or of the inherent validity of the law, but simply in the prospect of punishment for disobedience." This suggests a positivist concept of law. But there are other theories of law, and "effectiveness" changes in meaning in relation to changes in the meaning of "law" in the different theories of law.

If "law" is viewed in the traditional sense employed by both positivists and natural lawyers, i.e., as comprised of concepts or rules, there is a very difficult problem to be faced, the problem that puzzled Kant and continues to puzzle us, namely, how do rules ("reason") affect action? In this perspective, the "effectiveness of law" concerns the introduction or transmutation of rules into actions. But how is that possible and, if it does happen, what is the process wherein rules influence or become part of actions? In contrast with traditional theories are theories that law consists of more than rules, and this will be discussed shortly.

To pursue the prior question first, we must next consider the problem raised by the legal positivism-natural law polemic, namely, when we ask about the effectiveness of law, are we inquiring about the effectiveness of rules that are recognized as law in legal positivism or are we limiting our inquiry to such of those rules as are recognized as law in natural law philosophy? This latter view of the subject is related to sociological and psychological discussions of internalized norms as opposed to formal or technical norms. But the two are not equivalent, since a norm may be internalized (as, e.g., some southern white mores regarding blacks) but still be not morally valid. Thus, the meaning of "effectiveness of law" changes in relation to formal law, formal and ethically valid law, internalized and not internalized norms, sanctioned and sanctionless rules, combinations of the above criteria, and others to be noted. Plainly, if "law" refers only to certain morally valid norms, the question of their effectiveness is very different from that where "law" also includes archaic, irrational, and immoral norms and even, in Pollock's terms, the commands of an insane dictator. In this latter situation, it is very doubtful that one can discover any empirically significant generalizations about the effectiveness of law, and that is one of the principal reasons for giving "effectiveness of law" a normative meaning; this implies a narrower but uniform substantive field of data than that demarcated in positivist theories. In other words, it is important to ask whether one is concerned with law as a practical matter or whether he confronts law as a social theorist and encounters the limitations imposed by the necessity to delineate a uniform subject matter.

III

Law-as-Action

Most important in any interdisciplinary discussion of law are the factual and factual-normative theories of law that have been prominent since the rise of the German historical school. In this perspective, law has been viewed as a kind of ethos or attitude, as a cultural datum, as official behavior, as decision-making, and as a distinctive type of action, and "effectiveness" differs in meaning in those various contexts. It is the theory of law as a distinctive type of action which not only marks a major departure from the ancient and still prevailing jurisprudence that regards law as comprised only of rules but which also seems to me to be more adequate and suggestive than any other theory of law, and rather obviously so with reference to the effectiveness of law. This theory, unlike behavioral jurisprudence, does not ignore or minimize the importance of rules of law which, instead, are regarded as an essential constituent of law-as-action. Behavior, of course, is included there, and the third constituent is the value of acting to achieve a desirable goal. Consider, e.g., the simple case of a man who has made a contract and proceeds to do the various things required of him. His action toward that goal is an integration of the idea of his promise and of relevant rules of law and other norms, the observable behavior of his performance, and the value of his action—all of these coalesce to comprise a segment of the subject matter of jurisprudence.

For various reasons that cannot be discussed here, I regard the sanction as an additional essential part of law, and one that is obviously important in estimates of the effectiveness of law. This means that the conduct of the corps of officers who enforce the judgments of courts must be included in law-as-action. The inclusion of the sanctions-conduct implies that harm is an essential component of law-as-action, and, finally, the actions of the judges culminating in decision-making and judgment-pronouncing must be included. In sum, law-as-action is "official conduct expressing politically authoritative norms that imply values, deviation from which, implying a judicial process, causes harms that are and must be met by the imposition of and submission to sanctions."[6]

It is impossible to discuss here any of the many questions that would need to be examined in an adequate presentation of this theory of law,[7] but it must be noted that the ascription of value to law-as-action implies that the theory is in that respect in the natural law tradition. As was previously stated, one of the principal reasons for taking that direction rather than that of legal positivism is the fact that the philosophy and science of law consist of generalizations about law which, if they are to be factually and qualitatively significant, must be limited to a uniform field of significant data. High among the factors that are significant in the solution of social problems is the use of valid law. Equally important for relevant theory is the necessity of discovering the conditions in which knowledge of the functions of law can be acquired. To these reasons must be added the fact that unsound or morally invalid rules are merely the contraries of sound or morally valid laws. It is the latter that provide the affirmative subject matter and it is from the vantage point of the knowledge of those laws that we criticize rules that lack the criteria that constitute the sound laws. One can follow the path of the more inclusive definition and bare criteria of legal positivism, in which case he will construct a relatively formal discipline. or he can follow the narrower path of realism, where several other very important substantive criteria become available for the construction of a much more meaningful theory.[8]

Were it not for the deeply rooted tradition that law consists of rules or concepts, it would be superfluous to say that the selection and delineation of law-as-action as the subject matter of a theoretical discipline (jurisprudence) do not challenge the practical use of "law" as rules. Obviously, rules of law "exist" or subsist, as anyone who has paid an income tax or driven an automobile knows very well. But that model of law, however well established in practical needs in complex societies and by the bookishness of academicians, does not suffice for theoretical purposes; it is only after laws have been complied with or disobeyed that we have data that meet the requirements of social theory. The rules distinguish law-as-action from all other actions and thus constitute a unitary field.

The theory of law-as-action not only adds importantly to the meaning of the "effectiveness of law" but it also delineates a subject in ways that suggest the kind of empirical research that may reasonably be expected to add to our knowledge of the effectiveness of law. Instead of speculating about the effectiveness of a set of concepts, we deal with persons and interpersonal actions. Instead of confronting the mystery of how rules or other concepts influence action, we take certain actions as the given data. Instead of railing at "the law," one realizes that what counts is action, not the least of which is our own action in which we use (express) legal rules. In the recent past, e.g., hundreds of young, and also older, lawyers have shown that "the law" can be put to very good use on behalf of poor people, minorities, the consuming public, and others. The rules in the books are inert ideas; what counts not only pragmatically but, also, for significant social theory is law-as-action.

There are two final considerations to be brought very briefly within the range of this discussion. The first is the fact that the strictly negative function of law, associated rather simplistically with 18th-century theories of law, has become inadequate in view of the numerous far-ranging activities which the modern state encourages, supports, and performs. This implies that the Kelsenian construct of harm-sanction, though a necessary part of that of law-as-action, does not suffice and that an equal place must be found for compliance, e.g., as noted above, the conduct of a man performing a contract.

The other fact to be adduced concerns the realm of freedom protected by law. Of course, no legal institution can force or directly induce a Beethoven or a Michelangelo to persevere in a life of sacrifice, and it is obviously no substitute for their creative work. And although law-as-action may influence conscience, there is a realm of individual reflection, experience, and aspiration that that law cannot manipulate. At the same time, however, it is impossible to isolate the actions of businessmen or farmers or clergy or artists from the influence of law-as-action not only because that (the legal institution) protects those activities but also because it provides a climate of opinion and other "conditions of civilization," in which all persons are permitted and encouraged to do their work.

It would unduly expand the length of this paper to discuss the implications for empirical and other research of my effort to elucidate the meaning of "effectiveness of law" and of this theory of law-as-action.[9] It can only be noted that law-as-action is a complex datum and that the character of its constituent parts and their coalescence provide guides to, and set limits on, relevant research.

REFERENCES

[1] The summaries and quotations that follow are based on, or were taken from, the paper kindly supplied by Professor Dolbeare to the participants in the discussion at the annual meeting of the Society in Chicago in December, 1970. [Editors' note: Since the meeting, and since Professor Hall's contribution was written, Professor Dolbeare's paper has been considerably revised.]

[2] Some specification of "elite" is given that is noteworthy for its omission of labor leaders and leaders of associations for the protection and progress of various minorities.

[3] Glendon Schubert, "Behavioral Jurisprudence," *Law and Society Review*, 2 (May 1968), 409, 416.

[4] Georg Henrik von Wright, *The Varieties of Goodness* (New York: Humanities Press, 1963).

[5] In *Miranda* v. *Arizona*, 384 U.S. 436 (1966), the Supreme Court held that the privilege against self-incrimination requires that when an individual is taken into custody, he must be warned prior to any questioning "that he has the right to remain silent, that anything he says can be used against him in a court of law, that he has the right to the presence of an attorney, and that if he cannot afford an attorney one will be appointed for him prior to any questioning if he so desires.

[6] Jerome Hall, *Comparative Law and Social Theory* (Baton Rouge, La: Louisiana State University Press, 1963), p. 78. *Cf.* note 9 for the writer's later analysis of this concept.

[7] *Idem.* See also Carlos Cossio, "Jurisprudence and the Sociology of Law," *Columbia Law Review*, 52 (March and April 1952), 356, 479; Miguel Reale, "La Science du Droit Selon la Théorie Tridimensionnelle," in *Mélanges Jean Dabin* (Brussels, 1963), vol. 1, p. 211; and Jerome Hall, "Integrative Jurisprudence," in *Interpretations of Modern Legal Philosophies*, Paul Sayre, ed. (New York: Oxford University Press, 1947), p. 313, revised and reprinted in Hall, *Studies in Jurisprudence and Criminal Theory* (New York: Oceana Publications Inc., 1958), chap. 2. See note 9 *infra*.

[8] I have worked in some detail in both directions in the field of criminal law where, I believe, the advantages of a realistic theory have been established; the same considerations and the same advantages seem applicable to all fields of law and thus to jurisprudence.

[9] This is discussed in detail in my *Foundations of Jurisprudence* (Indianapolis and New York: The Bobbs-Merrill Co., 1973), especially in chap. 6, which was written after this paper was written.

16

OUR KNOWLEDGE OF THE LAW'S LIMITED EFFECTIVENESS

Hugo Adam Bedau

In his paper "The Limited Effectiveness of the Law," Professor Dolbeare has given us an accoutn of our limited knowledge of the effectiveness of the law and of the all but unlimited ineffectiveness of current empirical research in supplanting this ignorance. As it is not for me to supplement the empirical findings which he reviews for us, or to challenge their reliability, I shall have to dwell exclusively on critical and speculative matters provoked by what he has written. More than once in his paper Dolbeare worriedly shakes his head over the state of the research he reviews. After studying his account, I am rather more inclined to curse the darkness and leave the candle lighting and all higher forms of illumination to others.

These comments on Professor Dolbeare's paper were written on the basis of a version of that paper delivered at the meetings of the Society in December. 1970. They do not, therefore, take into account any alterations Professor Dolbeare may have made in preparing his manuscript for publication.

I

Dolbeare accuses his colleagues of mindless research, of research conducted without leading or heuristic hypotheses, on the question of the effectiveness of the law. It is probably only fair that he should include his own research within the scope of the general indictment. It is not harsh criticism but only becoming candor on his part to say, as he does, that the existing "empirical research" on his topic suffers from being "overparticularized, over-descriptive, and insufficiently linked to larger problems with important (and informative) payoffs." As I have not myself studied all the research findings he cites, I have no independent judgment to bring to bear on the adequacy of his assessment for us of the findings of his colleagues. As for his own research studies, several of which he was kind enough to supply me, I would agree that his general appraisal does apply to them.[1] Which is not, of course, to say that the research they report is worthless, but only that it is not as valuable and as decisive as we would wish in answering certain questions especially relevant to the present topic. Is it true, however, that the chief fault of this research is its insufficient relevance to some "appropriate frame of reference," its remoteness from any "framework in which to understand" its "implications" —two of the ways in which Dolbeare anticipates his chief conclusion, that "contemporary empirical approaches to the effectiveness of law have not employed sufficiently inclusive frames of reference"?

Let us notice, first an obvious and important defect in this research, a criticism not encompassed by Dolbeare's objections to it. (Again, I do not cast doubts on the adequacy with which he has done our collective homework for us in digesting the relevant research for our discussion.) Normally, if one wants to study any given social phenomenon, particularly one (such as the effectiveness of law) which would hardly be assumed to be a constant and thus free from change over time and locale, it is all but impossible to proceed beyond descriptive generalizations of a very low order unless the phenomenon is so analyzed and studied that its presence or absence and, at any rate, its relative frequency (intensity, duration, impact), are themselves under direct scrutiny. But nowhere in the research which Dolbeare reports, or at least nowhere in his report of it, is there any reference to how things were in, say, 1940 or 1900 with regard to the effectiveness of the law under study (or of some comparable law). Yet the thrust of the research cited, and of Dolbeare's criticism, is to allow us to infer that there is not even one law in one community in this country which is applied, utilized, or enforced at the present time with results superior to those achieved in the same community (or a similar one) with the same (or a similar) law in earlier years.

For instance, consider the phenomenon of eviction proceedings in 1970. Are evictions more or less frequently sought, obtained, enforced, and obeyed than in 1920? What about court judgments against divorced husbands in flight from their erstwhile families? Do these men respond more or less promptly and more or less adequately than they used to in, say, 1940 in paying alimony and child support when under court order to do so? How about bankruptcy proceedings? Is this legal device for terminating indebtedness more or less frequently sought and obtained by businessmen during the past decade than from 1900 to 1910? Are injunctions against strikes more or less frequently violated today than in 1930? How about unfair campaign practices in the recent elections, to judge from charges filed against political parties and their candidates? Illegal abortions? Forfeiture of bail bonds? The list of possible areas of inquiry, and possible times and places, is endless. Surely, therefore, the most obvious objection to the research Dolbeare has reviewed is not its failure to fit into some overall scenario, a Big Picture. It is its failure to tell us anything about changes over time and place in the phenomenon under study. The result is that every one of the inferences and generalizations he offers, insofar as they are based on the research he reports for us, is of doubtful significance. Since we are not told how things were for pairs, triplets, or sets of years (decades, generations, what have you), why should we seriously believe that we know anything at all about the effectiveness of law in any of the respects he isolates? We are given no baseline against which to measure the reported findings.

Now, the least plausible baseline is provided by the a priori expectation of perfect and immediate effectiveness of laws upon the conduct of those subject to them. This assumption may be useful in formulating various so-called null hypotheses for the purposes of statistical correlation studies. No doubt it is also the perfection of effective law devoutly to be desired, especially by those imbued with the Hobbesian dichotomy between lawful order and lawless anarchy. But as a prediction of how persons will actually behave, this assumption provides us with a baseline against which to plot deviations that is of no use whatever, as I am sure Dolbeare would agree. If that is so, then the only possible nonarbitrary baseline is to be obtained from our a posteriori knowledge of what happened yesterday, or a decade ago, or what happened concurrently in the next town or the next county.

Is it really true, as Dolbeare's survey invites us to infer, that the entire body of sociologists, criminologists, legal scholars, political scientists, and government bureaus have failed to undertake and to publish any comparative studies of the sort I have indicated? If it is, then our ignorance of the effectiveness of the law—of the relative (in)effectiveness of the law today in our country by contrast to its relative effectiveness in earlier times—must stand as one more monument to the willful indifference of the learned professions toward the pervasive conditions of our most influential social institutions. No doubt there are substantial research difficulties in studying and assessing the relative effectiveness of a given law in a given community over intervals of, say, several decades. But I cannot believe that the difficulties are of a higher order than those encountered in other longitudinal social research. Moreover, I do not believe we are as ignorant as my criticism assumes, though I confess to being myself unskilled at assembling the evidence which I am sure exists and which would serve, at least in some specific areas, as the basis for the cross-temporal and cross-spatial judgments we so plainly need if we are to make progress with our topic. Regrettably, I must leave this large matter for others and other occasions.

II

What chiefly troubles me in Dolbeare's analysis is neither what he says troubles him nor the difficulty I have reviewed above. What I find to be the main weakness is that his account of the limited effectiveness of the law suffers from a failure of analysis. I do not mean by this any fault of exposition or ineptness in the assembled research for our discussion. I mean simply that we really do not know at the end of his remarks much more than we did at the beginning about what is needed to answer our topic questions, and the reason for this is that nowhere does Dolbeare stop and chew over what we are talking about when we are inquiring into empirical measures of "the limited effectiveness of the law." Since not only other philosophers are bound to want to give close scrutiny to this phrase, let me begin here what must be done in greater detail elsewhere if we are ever to understand what we are talking about and what Dolbeare has been trying to tell us about.

The phrase "the limited effectiveness of law" requires preliminary analysis at each of three troubling points.

1. When we ask after the "effectiveness" of the law, what is the tacit goal or purpose we have in mind in terms of which its effectiveness is to be assessed? Do we mean nothing more than the effectiveness with which the law is applied, enforced, utilized? Sometimes this is what the research Dolbeare cites endeavors to report. At other times, however, the effectiveness of the law is measured by some external goal. Here, unfortunately, we have two incompatible alternatives, both of which can be found in the research studies Dolbeare cites. In some studies it appears that the measure of the law's effectiveness is the degree to which it protects the existing social and economic arrangements. In others it is rather the management of social change which is at issue. But it is logically impossible that one and the same law should be equally effective for a given population in protecting the status quo and in managing social change. (We may ignore the degenerate case in which the law is equally effective, by its utter failure to do either.) So the question naturally arises, which laws or legal institutions are more/less effective in preserving the existing social arrangements, which are more/less effective in obtaining their change, and under what conditions and with what rates of change and at what social and economic costs? The entire question of effectiveness (apart from the cases where we mean by "effective law" nothing more than "enforced law") seems to turn on whether what we are trying to obtain is an obstacle to social change or whether we are trying to secure some hitherto untried and novel social behavior. I do not think Dolbeare's appraisal of his evidence is clearly enough sorted out for us by reference to this distinction.

And stasis versus change is not the only distinction of relevance here. We also may want to contrast the effectiveness of the law in achieving goals for some persons (we can ignore whether the goals are to resist or to promote social change) and simultaneously frustrating the goals of others. Thus, the effectiveness of the legal arrangements which have made feasible federally financed urban renewal projects is to be assessed not only by reference to how much change has taken place but also by how much the changes satisfied banks and real estate speculators, in contrast to how much they have satisfied the home-renting and home-owning clientele. Therefore, it seems to me highly likely that one and the same law may be measured as effective in some respects for some populations and ineffective in other respects for perhaps other populations. Only a multidimensional analysis of "effectiveness" can possibly do justice to the complexities of the phenomenon under study.

2. The less than perfect, or "limited," effectiveness of the law in accomplishing its intended purposes has been the complaint of every court, every legislature, every administration in history. What we want empirical research to reveal is not only the nature of the forces which constitute these limits but also their relative strengths and their casual interaction. Pre-experimental analysis itself is sufficient to reveal the likely variety of these forces, and there is plenty of reason in advance to suppose that these limits are of several sorts and do not remain invariant over long periods of time or under radically different (urban, rural, pastoral, pretechnological, etc.) social conditions. Dolbeare's research does not adequately present to us the variety of these limits, even though it does suffice to show that the limits are quite different in origin, function, and strength. Although Dolbeare cites official lawlessness, for instance, I do not think he accords it the importance it deserves as a factor limiting the effectiveness of some laws (e.g., against gambling, prostitution, and drug abuse). His research also isolates a very different limit, the varying desirability which laws may have for those who are subject to them or who might avail themselves of their facilities. But there are many other limiting factors as well. For instance, how important a limit on the law's effectiveness is a low level of bureaucratic morale in the several different institutions involved in creating, interpreting, and enforcing the law? How much of the limited effectiveness of the law can be attributed to the structural weakness of our adversary system of jurisprudence, to cite another favorite whipping boy? Is it true that the courts have "handcuffed" the police and contributed to an ineffectiveness of criminal law enforcement, as every "law and order" candidate for political office has argued in recent years? I know these questions are humdrum ones by comparison to the "crisis of legitimacy" thesis which so interests Professor Dolbeare and others, but it would be more than nice to know what his evidence can tell us about the answers to these and other questions. It is essential for us to have in mind from the start the underlying questions which I cannot

see that Dolbeare has anywhere really asked himself, namely, granted that the effectiveness of the law is imperfect, what are the causes or limits of its effectiveness—extralegal obstacles in other social practices, inherent weaknesses in the control mechanisms at the disposal of the law and its agencies, theoretical boundaries which set up a counterenforcement tendency within the law itself, etc.? I should think it highly unlikely that exactly the same sorts of forces prove to limit the effectiveness of every sort of law in every situation to the same degree.

3. The concept of the "law" itself I have saved for the last, because it is obviously the most troublesome of the lot. Is it not likely, for instance, that some kinds of law, "the law on the books," as they say, meaning statute law and municipal ordinances in particular, are less widely obeyed than particular judgments by particular courts against particular litigants? But which of these—the ineffectiveness of the law on the books, or the effectiveness of the law from the judges—is the more relevant to the central issue? Dolbeare does not help us to answer the question. Do those changes in fundamental law which are achieved by constitutional interpretation obtain less administrative enforcement and less public compliance than those changes which are obtained by public referendum, constitutional convention, or other nonjudicial constitution-modifying devices? I do not know the answer, but the complexity of law as it intersects with society suggests to me, in advance of any empirical data, that it is highly unlikely there are no differences of the sort implied. Again, is not federal law likely to be less effective in certain areas of community life than, say, state or municipal law, whereas the converse would be true in other areas of conduct? Is there in general any significant difference in the effectiveness of those laws which, in Professor H. L. A. Hart's language,[2] are "secondary" in that they prescribe enforceable practices for facilitating public and private wishes (as in giving effect to testamentary declarations), in contrast to those laws which are "primary" in the sense that they impose duties of compliance (as in the criminal law generally)? Again, *ignoramus* but not necessarily *ignorabimus*.

Most of all, I think we need to give further thought to how we are to isolate law as a variable relevant to social constancy and social change from among the complete set of change-relevant variables. This is a theoretical problem of enormous practical significance in any serious attempt to grapple with our topic. Perhaps I can illustrate the problem with two examples. Whose behavior in federal court in Chicago during 1970 illustrates the limited effectiveness of the law—Julius Hoffman's. Bobby Seale's, or William Kunstler's? Is it the judge, the defendant, or the attorney whose conduct offered the chief obstacle to the effective rule of law in that instance? Which of these three persons embodied the law, and which the limits to its effectiveness? Or was the conduct of all three dependent upon hidden or remote variables outside the courtroom and outside the law? As a different example, consider this: does the growth of the American Civil Liberties Union since the 1920s and the NAACP Legal Defense Fund since the 1950s show the increasing effectiveness of the law, or is the history of their efforts in various legal forums irrelevant to our subject? Such simple questions as these are not easy to answer partly because we do not fully understand what it is we want isolated under the rubric of "the law," "the rule of law," "legal institutions." It is hardly any wonder that we are ignorant of the casual consequences over time and space of variables we have not adequately isolated from each other in advance by conceptual analysis. I am reasonably confident that once we analyze our concept of law so as to yield hypotheses which admit of genuine confirmation or disconfirmation, we will find that there is such an enormous variety of relevant phenomena that we will repudiate all current large-scale generalizations about the law's effectiveness.

III

Let us turn now to "the crisis of legitimacy" thesis. If we assume that this thesis is true, what explains the crisis? Does the trouble lie in the very idea of the rule of law? Or only in some particular laws or legal institutions which we, alas, have the misfortune to live under at present? Or is the central explanatory factor of this crisis to be found quite outside the law and current legal institutions, in a growing (or never quite abandoned) populism, anarchism, ludditism? The problem with "the crisis of legitimacy" thesis, unless we can answer these questions, is that it has far less explanatory value for the limited effectiveness of the law than at first it seems. Surely, there is some danger of falling into implicit tautology when we say that the law is less effective than it might be *because* of "a failure of institutions, values and practices to maintain a moral claim, and by the associated rejection of such values, institutions and practices by large segments of the population." The "because" here does little if any work by way of explanation, or at least of causal explanation, as some modest reflection will reveal.

But, surely, an equally plausible tack is to post doubts as to whether "the crisis of legitimacy" thesis is even true at all. I find much less reason (admittedly, perhaps through indifference to or ignorance of some relevant evidence, although I really do not believe this) than Dolbeare does for accepting this thesis as that much-desired overarching "framework" for all the empirical results he has surveyed. I am skeptical because the thesis seems flatly contradicted by the manifest growing use of the law by whole classes of persons hitherto uninterested in the law or even brutally denied its resources, as history would amply show. I refer to the obvious examples—blacks, the poor, conservationists, women, prisoners, consumers—their variety and numbers are legion, and in recent years they have begun to seek protection, redress, nullification, indemnity, and vindication through the very courts, administrative tribunals, and other legal institutions (and of course through state and federal statutory changes) which Dolbeare and others would have us believe are undergoing an unprecedented "crisis." As we have seen, we have little basis if any for distress over our current situation because the available research fails to enable us to compare it with precedent conditions of our society. Current events no doubt provoke the judgment that "The law . . . is surely less relevant to more people than at any other time in recent history."[3] But evidence as to the status quo *ante* is missing, and so the despair is premature. It is true, there may be at present a crisis in all our legal institutions, a challenge to the legitimacy of every legal rule, a growing ineffectiveness of the entire rule of law in our society. But Dolbeare has scant evidence to point to as justification for such hypotheses. Whether our legal institutions will prove adequate to the heavy challenges they face in the closing decades of this century, no one can say. It is also possible that the solutions to struggles earlier in this century between labor and management, the president and the Supreme Court, and Wall Street and the investing public prefigure solutions of current crises by the rule of law and our legal institutions.

There is a well-known danger (and I mention it because I think that Dolbeare's whole approach tends to suffer from it) in the chronic overemphasis upon the *criminal* law when the state of the law is under discussion, as though the rule of law had reference solely to law-breakers, law enforcement, and the whole repressive-custodial pattern so much in the foreground of the daily news. Instead, we need a countervailing emphasis in ordinary thought as well as in empirical research upon the past horrors (or glories, as you wish), the current status, and the future prospects of *legalism* in our society.[4] To what degree do persons, as individuals, corporations, and classes, avail themselves of legal institutions, either the existing ones or new ones they create to accomplish their special purposes? Surely, the most general thing we can say about the law, as Professor Lon Fuller has urged, is that it is "the enterprise of subjecting human conduct to the governance of rules,"[5] not merely moral rules, but those rules which a society through its government authorizes, interprets, and supervises and on behalf of which various instrumentalities, such as the courts, are enlisted. We are, as Tocqueville long ago noted, a litigious people. My own hunch is that more and more of our life is becoming subject to the rule of law, just as more and more classes of persons are resorting to the law in order to protect their interests. This is, of course, not an unmixed blessing, but until we have more evidence on precisely the growth (if I am right) of legalism, we have insufficient reason to cast into doubt the superior (even if far from optimal) effectiveness of the law at the present time.

REFERENCES

[1] I am reluctant, however, to leave it at this and thereby convey a misleading impression of my high regard in every respect for the research and findings Professor Dolbeare has published, particularly in *Little Groups of Neighbors,* his study (co-authored with J. S. Davis, Jr.) of the Selective Service System (Chicago: Markham Publishing Co., 1968). Unfortunately, this volume is not particularly relevant to the present subject, as it does not discuss either the lawless administration of the Selective Service System or the lawless response to the System by draft-age American men. I have dealt with these topics in an as yet unpublished paper, "Selective Service Crimes," delivered before the annual meeting of the American Society of Criminology, October, 1970.

[2] *The Concept of Law* (Oxford: Clarendon Press, 1961), pp. 78-79. Certain difficulties in this distinction I have discussed in "Law, Legal Systems, and Types of Legal Rules," *Memorias del XIII Congreso Internacional de Filosofia,* VII (1964), 17-27.

[3] Alan Dershowitz, in *New York Times Book Review,* October 31, 1971, p. 45, in review of a book somewhat morbidly titled, *Is Law Dead?*

[4] See Judith Shklar, *Legalism* (Cambridge, Mass.: Harvard University Press, 1964). The burden of her book is to attack legalism, partly on empirical but also on moral and conceptual grounds; for criticism, see my review in *The Philosophical Review*, LXXVI (1967), 129-130.

[5] *The Morality of Law* (New Haven, Conn.: Yale University Press, 1969), pp. 53, 74, 91.

17

OF BENEFICIARIES
AND COMPLIANCE

Victor G. Rosenblum

American society would be vastly closer than it is to a governmental ecology of law, order, and justice if it could be said that those who have been the beneficiaries of the legal system comply with its rulings. Such a statement connotes a noblesse oblige in which the traditional victors, on occasions of going down to defeat, gracefully proceed to implement the courts' newly declared norms. After all, only one side can win a law suit, and you can't expect your opponents to obey when they lose if you don't accept the decision when you are defeated.

Such reasoning is impeccable, but the key question is of practice rather than of reason. Simply to assume that the assertion is borne out in practice may blind lawyers and social scientists to the need to investigate alternative hypotheses. One such hypothesis would be that the more accustomed one is to winning in court the more likely the resort to legal and political maneuvers that can alter an adverse ruling's impact, or the resort to noncompliance in the hope that enforcement will be delayed or abandoned. A component of this hypothesis would be the subsidiary contention that traditional losers in court are more likely than steady winners to comply with decisions against them as a result of habit, as well as because of the nonexistence of viable alternatives or the lack of awareness of their existence.

I do not suggest by posing these hypotheses that obligation to obey the law hinges on receipt of quid pro quo's, nor do I contend that one must obey regardless of how unjust law may be. Anticipation of reciprocal responses by others and blind reverence for authority are as unsuited as fear of reprisal to be the foundation for conformity to law in a democratic society. Rather, as T. H. Green said, "a habit of subjection . . . should represent an idea of common good which each member of the society can make his own so far as he is rational."[1]

I have assumed that the norms declared by the courts in the segregation, reapportionment, and welfare cases that form the locus of this essay were not inconsistent with democratic conceptions of justice and common good. My interest lies in disparities in compliance with them by losers who had been consistent victors in the past, and, more particularly, in the light these disparities can throw on understanding law's limits.

The legal odyssey of racial segregation in the public schools to the rocky shores of compliance charts with pain and frustration a prime case in point. Until the late 1930s the Supreme Court's decisions in racial segregation cases required no massive changes of behavior, for they merely validated legally the social status quo of discrimination. The rulings approving segregation were not met with movements to impeach the Chief Justice or threats of organized disobedience since those who might have wished to contest lacked the power legally, economically, and politically to do anything other than acquiesce. When the Court declared that laws requiring segregation are within the competence of state legislatures, the illustration it cited as the most common instance was "the establishment of separate schools for white and colored children, which has been held to be a valid exercise of the legislative power even by courts of states where the political rights of the colored race have been longest and most earnestly enforced."[2]

The impact of the decision in *Plessy* v. *Ferguson* was precisely as Justice Harlan, the lone dissenter, predicted: "to permit the seeds of race hate to be planted under the sanction of law" and thereby to "defeat the beneficent purposes which the people of the United

States had in view when they adopted the recent amendments of the Constitution."[3] The Supreme Court's attacks on the Civil War amendments through its decisions in the *Civil Rights Cases*[4] in 1883 and *Plessy* in 1896 were recognized as *faits accomplis* virtually from the day the decisions were announced.

The judicial foundations for, and citizen compliance with, mandatory racial segregation continued firm for the next forty years. Beginning, however, with the decision in *Missouri* v. *Canada* in 1938,[5] the Supreme Court chipped away at the separate but equal doctrine. The Court ruled in the *Missouri* case that the state's practice of denying Negroes admission to its law schools, though offering to pay for their education at out-of-state schools, was a denial of equal protection of the laws.

Before the decision in *Brown* v. *Board of Education* in 1954,[6] other major cases invalidating racial segregation in higher education killed any remaining rationale for the separate but equal doctrine. *Sweatt* v. *Painter* in 1950 ruled that Texas' separate law schools for Negroes were not equal to the University of Texas, then reserved for whites, in such factors as prestige of the faculty, position and influence of the alumni, and opportunity for interplay of ideas.[7] *McLaurin* v. *Oklahoma*, decided the same year, ruled that admission of Negroes to the same school of education afforded whites, but restricting Negroes' seating, eating, and studying to designated areas, was a deprivation of equal protection.[8] The *Brown* decision simply put the stone on the grave of the separate but equal doctrine.

To anyone who listened when the Court spoke in the major segregation cases between 1937 and 1954, the ruling in *Brown* could have come as no surprise. The tirades, threats, and blatant resistance that greeted the Court's formal invalidation of segregation in the public schools indicated that few indeed had listened. On hearing this decision, many of the previous beneficiaries of judicial construction from the post Civil War period to World War II counseled resistance.

Robert J. Harris chronicled the virulent response to the Court during the five years following the decision in *Brown*:

> Many of the states in the south, in addition to noncompliance with the Court's decision pursued policies of aggressive defiance. Official resistance took such forms as public school closing and leasing laws, pupil placement laws, interposition resolutions, closing of school by executive proclama-

tion, and executive maintenance of segregated education by force in the name of law and order, as examplified by the employment of state police by Governor Allan Shivers to maintain segregated education in Mansfield, Texas and employment of the National Guard by Governor Orval Faubus in Little Rock to prevent nine children from entering Central High School. . . .[9]

In place of moral and political leadership, President Eisenhower "gave verbal aid and comfort to the leaders of resistance."[10] The President repeatedly stressed the inefficacy of law as a means of social advance in race relations, and with neither the President nor Congress charting a policy for meeting the Constitutional crisis, "one of the most important policies of social change in the twentieth century was committed to the tedious and fortuitous process of private litigation."[11] Although active resistance to the law was fading by the mid-sixties, the *New York Times* could still report in May, 1969: "Fifteen years after the Supreme Court held public school segregation to be unconstitutional, nation-wide controversy rages over how—and in some areas whether—the decision should be carried out."[12] Replacing the blatant calls for massive resistance of the fifties and early sixties, however, have been admonitions—some by respected scholars—to abandon the integration ruling in the name of realism. Some advocates, led by Professor Alexander Bickel of Yale, say that whites do flee from integration; hence "it is feckless to ask whether this should happen." Since in Bickel's view the gains from pressing integration do not outweigh the losses, some alternative to enforcement should be sought.[13]

Gary Orfield, replying to Bickel, expressed shock at his justification of abandonment of desegregation as accommodation to white resistance. Orfield concluded, "This is no time for exhaustion. The need is for leadership with the courage and honesty to tell the people that we must face and solve the problem of segregated schools across the nation. A single society cannot be constructed on a base of separate and unequal schools."[14]

In October, 1969,[15] and in April, 1971,[16] the Supreme Court struck down the most recent challenges to its desegregation rulings. Unique in the 1969 action was the fact that for the first time in recent history challenge to a desegregation order was hurled in conjunction with the attorney general of the United States. The Supreme Court summarily reversed the Department of Justice stance and ordered the government to proceed "at once" with desegregation. In the April, 1971, case, the Court stressed that the power of federal district courts to eliminate all vestiges of state-imposed school segregation includes altering attendance zones, requiring necessary busing, and insuring that future school construction and abandonment is not used to establish dual systems. Eighteen years after the *Brown* decision, compliance has become a partial reality, but the journey is far from over. President Nixon's overt rejection of court-ordered busing plans and the burning of school buses in Pontiac, Michigan, as the 1971 school year opened make bleak auguries for the immediate future.

More startling than *Brown* by contrast with the antecedent cases of its genre was the Supreme Court's decision in *Baker* v. *Carr* in 1962.[17] Earlier efforts to involve the courts in redressing the inequities of malapportionment of electoral districts had failed because they posed "political questions," such as whether a state has the constitutionally requisite "republican form of government," for whose resolution the courts traditionally deemed themselves inappropriate if not incompetent. *Baker* v. *Carr* again sought to challenge through the courts a mapping of electoral districts that had become antediluvian with the growth and shifts of population, but the invocation of judicial power was geared this time to the Fourteenth Amendment's equal protection clause.

Justice Frankfurter had written an opinion two years before in *Gomillion* v. *Lightfoot*, applying the Fifteenth Amendment to Alabama's redrawing of electoral boundaries in Tuskegee for the purpose of diluting and negating Negro voting rights.[18] Although his colleagues found the facts in *Gomillion* and *Baker* analogous, Justice Frankfurter, in his eloquent dissent in *Baker*, maintained that there is a world of difference between deliberate misuse of electoral machinery to deprive blacks of the vote and a passive failure to reapportion over a substantial period of time. He warned that the Court, by taking jurisdiction over the latter type of case, was entering a political thicket that would strip it of public esteem and generate both animosity and noncompliance.[19]

Justice Frankfurter was certainly correct in his prediction of animosity. Within months of the Court's decision, the General Assembly of the Council of State Governments called for a Constitutional amendment to limit the power of the Supreme Court to restrict any state in the apportionment of representation in its legislature. A Court of the Union, composed of the Chief Justices of the highest courts of the fifty states, was proposed to review "any judgment of the Supreme Court relating to the rights reserved to the states or to the people."[20] Decisions by the Court of the Union would be final.

Senator Dirksen proposed a Constitutional amendment less blatantly hostile to the Supreme Court. His amendment proposed no new judiciary and made no reference to the Supreme Court at all. It simply provided that bicameral state legislatures could apportion one house on the basis of population, geography, and political subdivisions. Unicameral legislatures would be apportioned on the basis of substantial equality of population "with such weight given to geography and political subdivisions as will insure effective representation of the various groups and interests making up the electorate." Before becoming effective, any apportionment plan under Dirksen's amendment would need approval by a majority of the state's voters.[21]

The Council on State Governments' resolution for a Court of the Union lost momentum when the American Bar Association's House of Delegates voted at its 1963 convention expressly to "disapprove and oppose" the proposal.[22] Senator Dirksen's proposal that a Constitutional convention be called to consider the Dirksen amendment came within one state vote of success. But antipathy to and noncompliance with the Supreme Court's decision did not go hand in hand in this instance.

Robert McCloskey, writing in the *Harvard Law Review*, noted that many legislatures throughout the country set going their laborious machinery of conflict and compromise immediately after the Supreme Court's decision in *Baker* v. *Carr*.[23] By 1968, Dean Robert McKay of New York University reported that "it is not easy to think of any other major Supreme Court decisions to which significant adjustment was so swiftly accomplished." Although there was some footdragging, "the astonishing fact is that by the spring of 1968 the task of revision was essentially completed."[24]

Why was compliance the rule in the case of reapportionment and the exception for more than a decade after the decision in *Brown* in the case of racial desegregation? Part of the explanation could be that people favored reapportionment whereas they opposed desegregation. McCloskey speculated in his 1962 article that "it may be that most Americans have come to think of some version of the majority principle as at least the presumptive democratic standard."

If so, the Reapportionment Cases may have struck them as "the common sense of the subject" and commanded their assent.

Part of the explanation for compliance must also have been the forthrightness with which President Kennedy expressed support of the Court's decision. Unlike Eisenhower in the case of *Brown*, Kennedy used his press conference after the decision was announced to reiterate his administration's endorsement of the decision and to call on "all of us who hold office in the states and national government to take every action that we can to have this matter settled by the responsible political groups."[25] As noted earlier, the American Bar Association behaved responsibly by opposing vigorously and forthrightly the drastic proposal of the Council of State Governments to deprive the Supreme Court of authority in reapportionment cases.

In short, Justice Frankfurter was proven egregiously wrong as a forecaster of noncompliance. In *Baker* v. *Carr* the Court did not ally itself, as in effect it did in *Brown*, with a politically weak minority which could not even bring the president to endorse compliance with the Court's rule. Some powerful political organizations were losers in the reapportionment cases, but others with considerable influence, especially in suburban areas, were winners. There was greater balance of power between winners and losers in *Baker* than in *Brown*. By this I mean not *numerical* balance but rather a greater balance of *intensity* of feelings on the part of national leaders, professional associations, and other individuals and groups with access to the political system. The actions of the ABA and the president threw both moral and political support to the Court, which helped to convince opponents otherwise of a mind to engage in massive disobedience that the consequences would be too costly.

The central point I want to make through these illustrations is that compliance is more a matter of practical politics than of morality or ideology per se. Of course morality and ideology are component variables of any political system, but they alone do not account for the system's allocations of values. Not only Justice Holmes' classic bad man but most good men as well are likely to want to know the costs and benefits of noncompliance before determining their own behavior. Recognizing this fact, Professors Albert Reiss and Donald Black of Yale have proposed a salutary reconceptualization of theory on deviant behavior to take into account the organized processes by which deviance is detected and the patterns by which it is sanctioned or ignored. In essence they have defined deviance in terms of the probability of a control response. They say: "Individual or group behavior is deviant if it falls within a class of behavior for which there is a probability of negative sanctions subsequent to its detection."[26] Sanctioning, they find, acknowledging their intellectual debt to Max Weber's work, is usually contingent upon a configuration of situational properties, of which rule-violative behavior is only one. Hence, a critical aspect of the social scientist's work is to discover the social organization of deviance and control.

The task of developing theories of deviance, sanction, and compliance is complex; yet failure to undertake it would leave us victims either of the myth that sanction and compliance follow automatically from findings of rule-violative behavior or the myth, echoing Frankfurter's dissents in the reapportionment cases, that they do not and cannot follow at all when Court findings are made in "political thickets." Research that can spawn workable theories of deviance, control, and compliance is typified by James P. Levine's article on compliance with Supreme Court decisions.[27] Levine starts with the premise that dissensus about the efficacy of Supreme Court decisions is often the product of differences in the range of consequences investigated. The relationship between any Supreme Court decision and its outcome is probabilistic, sequential, and contingent rather than deterministic, concomitant, and inevitable. The further one moves from the locus of Supreme Court orders and the more other social or political processes intervene, the more attenuation of effects should be anticipated. "It is much easier for the Supreme Court to curb a few cantankerous federal judges than to reallocate fundamental values of the society."[28]

Levine lists three categories of factors as necessary conditions for Supreme Court efficacy: internal processes or attributes of decisions such as clarity of announced policy, consensus, and craftsmanship of opinions; external governmental conditions such as accurate communication to elites, fiscal costs of compliance, and positive reactions by public attorneys; and environment conditions, such as favorable commentary by opinion leaders and a high ratio between resources of beneficiaries and resources of victims of decisions.

What is important about these categorizations is not their exhaustiveness but rather their establishment of a systemic, analytical framework. The framework depicts the multifaceted, interrelated factors that should be measured, tested, and compared if adequate causal hypotheses about decisions and compliance are to be derived.

Utilization of this framework enables Levine to chart sequentially the major steps toward compliance with the *Brown* decisions from 1954 to 1969. He sees the decade following the decision as one of political controversy with little, if any, implementing action. Legislative action by Congress prohibiting the funding of segregated public schools, beginning in 1965, led in turn to administrative action by the Department of Health, Education, and Welfare, which withheld funds from segregated schools from 1966 to 1968. The beginning of substantial integration in the deep South came in 1969.

The Supreme Court's action in *Brown* can be viewed as the cause of a major social transformation as long as the premise is accepted that but for the 1954 decision the subsequent legislative and administrative events leading toward compliance would not have occurred. Of course, as Mayhew points out in his study *Law and Equal Opportunity*, "the bare fact of change is not enough to demonstrate that any particular proposition is attributable to legal causes."[29] A complete solution to the problem of how much compliance law produces, how much opportunity it creates, or how much discrimination it eliminates requires comparative study of a large number of communities over extended time periods. Nonetheless, comparison of the compliance record in *Brown* with that in *Baker* warrants the hypothesis that compliance begins in earnest with court decisions when resources of politics, administration, and legal counsel support the judicial norms. This raises in turn the likelihood that the very opposite of Frankfurter's fears about judicial intervention into political questions may be true. Frankfurter had argued in *Baker* that the people would not comply with the Court's decision. Since the Court's authority ultimately rests on sustained public confidence in its moral sanction, "such feeling must be nourished by the Court's complete detachment . . . from political entanglements and by abstention from injecting itself into the clash of political forces in political settlements."[30] On the contrary, since clashes of political forces precede and accompany all significant change, compliance with judicial norms that call for change is likely to come faster when legal, administrative, and economic resources generated by the political forces are available (*Baker*) than when such resources must be elicited for the first time by the Court's appeals to morality (*Brown*).

The correlation between compliance and the availability of resources to implement judicial norms has led both opponents and proponents of change through the courts to focus in recent years on means of access to the legal system. The achievements of legal services lawyers in providing access to the courts for the poor and in producing compliance with norms that received only lip service in the past are sometimes bypassed or ignored by social scientists in probing the compliance problem. Legal services programs are still flourishing aspects of the war on poverty, and legal services attorneys are still pursuing their clients' causes with zeal and success.[31]

Important gains have been achieved in such areas as landlord-tenant relationships, administration of public welfare benefits, and consumer rights, and much activity is under way to bring the poor to full and equal access to quality health care. In the category of health care cases, one of the most significant in obliging a state to comply with its own laws was the victory of legal services attorneys in enjoining California from cutting back its Medi-Cal program.[32]

Governor Reagan had urged cutbacks by the state's welfare agency in view of budgetary limitations placed on Medi-Cal expenditures in the 1967-1968 fiscal year. The cutback was ordered through administrative regulations reducing minimum coverage for recipients of public welfare. Coverage eliminated for public assistance recipients by the order included nonemergency surgery, outpatient psychiatric care, eye refractions, and hearing examinations. Harvey Morris, a recipient of welfare assistance and otherwise eligible under California law for the state's Medi-Cal benefits, sought a permanent injunction and declaratory judgment that the cutbacks violated existing state law.

The California Supreme Court agreed with Mr. Morris. Applying accepted principles of administrative law, the judges ruled that the administrator of the Health and Welfare agency exceeded the statutory mandate in ordering the cutback. Small wonder that Governor Reagan has sought consistently, but thus far without success, to eliminate California Rural Legal Assistance, the legal services agency responsible for this and other successful challenges to his administration.

Other welfare cases initiated by legal services offices which have produced rapid compliance have been the invalidation of state action terminating needy children from Aid For Dependent Children benefits because of the mother's sexual relationship with a man,[33] the invalidation of residency requirements for welfare eligibility under federal assistance programs,[34] and the invalidation of termination or suspension of benefits prior to an administrative hearing.[35]

That legal services lawyers are not likely to be as successful in the Burger Supreme Court as they were in the Warren Court in winning support for their substantive arguments has already been well established. The Burger Court's position on access to the courts, however—for example in its decision upholding the right of the indigent to obtain divorces without having to pay customary court fees—should encourage these creative and dedicated lawyers to carry on.[36]

The Court upheld the argument of Professor La France of Arizona State University, who began working on *Boddie* when he was counsel for the New Haven Legal Assistance Association, that the due process clause of the Fourteenth Amendment prohibits the state from denying access to its courts to indigents who seek dissolution of their marriages. The Court was careful to add that it was not saying that access for all individuals to the courts is "in all circumstances guaranteed by the due process clause of the Fourteenth Amendment," but the basic principle espoused by the Court was that "absent a countervailing state interest of overriding significance, persons forced to settle their claims of right and duty through the judicial process must be given a meaningful opportunity to be heard."[37] A cost requirement, even though valid on its face, may offend due process because it forecloses a particular party's opportunity to be heard. Thus, the Burger Court in the *Boddie* case remained consistent with the Warren Court's emphasis on the judicial obligation to provide equal justice under law to rich and poor alike.

The judiciary's doctrinal commitment to equal justice under law, plus the fact that legal services agencies funded by the federal government employ more than two thousand lawyers in more than nine hundred offices throughout the United States, involving expenditures in excess of fifty million dollars a year, increases the probability of compliance, if only because the legal resources of beneficiaries and losers are being equalized. In addition to the substantial increment in legal resources to ensure compliance, there has been occurring in some measure what Mayhew termed the mobilization of lip service values and "the effective organization of the symbols of value consensus."[38]

We are at a point in the development of the social sciences where we know enough about the factors that heighten or reduce compliance with court decisions that it becomes intellectually inexcusable any longer to accept meretricious homilies as truths. We know that prior victors in court actions *do not* comply automatically with rulings in which they lose, but experience also shows that legal rules can be institutionalized effectively even though significant percentages of powerful sectors of the people are intensely opposed to them. The judiciary doesn't exist for the purpose of courting popularity. Of course, certain judge-made norms require the measurement of public opinion and belief, such as the contemporary community standard utilized in obscenity cases. But the overriding responsibility of the courts is to provide equal justice under law, and predictions by judges about the public's compliance with their decisions are as irrelevant as they are beyond the professional capacity of judges to make.

The judiciary can and should provide help for people with grievances but without power. The alternative would be to ignore legitimate grievances, and, by denying access to redress through the system, to bolster the rhetoric of revolutionaries in the quest for the loyalties of the alienated. The activist function for the judiciary is inherent in a constitutional system of separation of powers that facilitates the pluralism of leadership and control. It enables change to come about in any particular era not only when the three branches act in concert but also when one takes the initiative while the others are passive out of disinterest or acquiescence.

Former Attorney-General Mitchell's attack on the judiciary for being "preoccupied in the exhilarating venture of making new public policy from the bench" indicates that my conception of judicial obligation is not universally shared. Whatever one's view of judicial activism, it should be clear that understanding the factors involved in compliance and their interrelationships is within our analytical grasp. The sooner we probe the realities of compliance the sooner we will be able to strengthen the courts as instruments of public policy and as essential spurs to and supports for the public's sense of justice.

REFERENCES

[1] T. H. Green, *Lectures on the Principles of Political Obligation* (Ann Arbor, Mich.: University of Michigan Press, 1967), p. 126.

[2] *Plessy v. Ferguson,* 163 U.S. 537 (1896), p. 544.

[3] *Id.,* p. 560.

[4] *Civil Rights Cases,* 109 U.S. 3 (1883).

[5] *Missouri ex rel. Gaines v. Canada,* 305 U.S. 337 (1938).

[6] *Brown* v. *Board of Education*, 347 U.S. 483 (1954).

[7] *Sweatt* v. *Painter*, 339 U.S. 629 (1950).

[8] *McLaurin* v. *Oklahoma State Regents*, 339 U.S. 637 (1950).

[9] Robert Harris, *The Quest for Equality* (Baton Rouge, La.: Louisiana State University Press, 1960).

[10] *Id.*, pp. 154-155.

[11] *Id.*, p. 156.

[12] *New York Times*, May 17, 1969, pp. 1, 40.

[13] Alexander Bickel, "Desegregation: Where Do We Go From Here?" *New Republic*, February 7, 1970, pp. 20-22; cited in Joel Grossman and Mary Grossman, eds., *Law and Change in Modern America* (Pacific Palisades, Calif.: Goodyear Publishers, Inc., 1971), pp. 298-303.

[14] Gary Orfield, "The Debate over School Desegregation," *New Republic*, March 7, 1970, pp. 32-35.

[15] *Alexander* v. *Holmes County Board of Education*, 396 U.S. 19 (1969).

[16] *Swann* v. *Charlotte-Mecklenburg Board of Education*, 402 U.S. 1 (1971).

[17] *Baker* v. *Carr*, 369 U.S. 186 (1962).

[18] *Gomillion* v. *Lightfoot*, 364 U.S. 339 (1960).

[19] *Baker* v. *Carr*, 369 U.S. 186 (1962), pp. 266-270.

[20] The text of the Council of State Governments' proposal and a summary of the discussion at the 1962 Biennial of the General Assembly of the States leading to its formulation by a vote of 21 to 20 may be found in *State Government*, XXXVI (winter 1963), 10-15.

[21] For a concise discussion of the chronology and fate of the Dirksen amendment, see *Congress and the Nation* (Washington, D.C.: Congressional Quarterly, 1969), vol. II, pp. 431-435.

[22] *American Bar Association Journal*, 49 (October 1963), 986-987.

[23] Robert G. McCloskey, "The Reapportionment Cases," *Harvard Law Review*, 76 (1962), 54-59.

[24] Robert B. McKay, "Reapportionment: Success Story of the Warren Court," *Michigan Law Review*, 67 (1968), 223-236, at p. 229. For an examination of Congressional attempts to upset the *Baker* decision, see McKay, *Reapportionment* (New York: 20th Century Fund, 1965), pp. 203-218.

[25] *Public Papers of the President of the U.S., 1962* (Washington: U.S. Government Printing Office, 1963), p. 274.

[26] Albert Reiss and Donald Black, "Police Control of Juveniles," *American Sociological Review*, 35:1 (February 1970), 63.

[27] James P. Levine, "Methodological Concerns in Studying Supreme Court Efficacy," *Law and Society Review*, 4 (May 1970), pp. 583-613.

[28] *Id.*, p. 584.

[29] Leon Mayhew, *Law and Equal Opportunity* (Cambridge, Mass.: Harvard University Press, 1968), p. 4.

[30] *Baker* v. *Carr*, 369 U.S. 186 (1962), p. 267.

[31] The Director of the National Legal Program on Health Problems for the Poor stressed the continuity, enthusiasm, and efficacy of legal services lawyers in a recent symposium. See Laurens H. Silver, "Medical Care Delivery Systems and the Poor: New Challenges for Poverty Lawyers," *Wisconsin Law Review* (1970), pp. 644-681.

[32] *Morris* v. *Williams*, 67 Cal. 2d 733 (1967).

[33] *King* v. *Smith*, 392 U.S. 309 (1968).

[34] *Shapiro* v. *Thompson*, 394 U.S. 618 (1969).

[35] *Goldberg* v. *Kelly*, 397 U.S. 254 (1970).

[36] *Boddie* v. *Connecticut*, 401 U.S. 371 (1971).

[37] *Id.*, pp. 380, 383.

[38] Mayhew, *op. cit.*, p. 260.

INDEX